SHOES THAT FIT
OUR FEET

SHOES THAT FIT
OUR FEET

Sources for a Constructive
Black Theology

Dwight N. Hopkins

ORBIS BOOKS

Maryknoll, New York 10545

The Catholic Foreign Mission Society of America (Maryknoll) recruits and trains people for overseas missionary service. Through Orbis Books, Maryknoll aims to foster the international dialogue that is essential to mission. The books published, however, reflect the opinions of their authors and are not meant to represent the official position of the society.

Library of Congress Cataloging-in-Publication Data

Hopkins, Dwight N.
   Shoes that fit our feet : sources for a constructive Black
theology / Dwight N. Hopkins.
     p. cm.
   Includes bibliographical references and index.
   ISBN 0-88344-848-3 (pbk.)
   1. Black theology. 2. Afro-Americans—Religion. I. Title.
BT82.7.H667 1993
230'.089'96073—dc20   92-38713
                                           CIP

To My Sisters
Shirley H. Langley
&
Brenda H. Jones

Shoes was the worstest trouble. We weared rough russets when it got cold, and it seem powerful strange they'd never git them to fit. . . . We prays for the end of tribulation and the end of beatings and for shoes that fit our feet.

Mary Reynolds, ex-slave

Contents

Acknowledgments

I am deeply grateful to people who have helped make this book a reality.

I received a Ford Foundation Postdoctoral Fellowship. I also received the Thomas Terry Research Award and the Irvine Foundation Research Grant from Santa Clara University. All three awards aided my time and research activities.

Several people helped in various other ways. James H. Cone read the entire manuscript and posed insightful questions regarding the task of systematic theology and black theology. In conversations, Will Coleman offered commentary on slave narratives and the nature of interpretation of African American folk culture. In our talks, Charles H. Long posed issues to me concerning black theology's relation to diverse religious thinking of black folk. Vincent Harding and Manning Marable, early in my research stages, suggested several research sites and encouraged this project. Robert Ellsberg (Orbis Books) gave timely editorial assistance. And George Cummings and James Noel supported this effort from its inception.

Parts of this book were also presented in public forums where I gained valuable feedback — particularly at two conferences in France (in Tours and Paris), the Graduate Theological Union (Berkeley, Cal.), the national American Academy of Religion annual meeting, the Harvard Divinity School, and the Allen Temple Baptist Church (Oakland, Cal., J. Alfred Smith, senior pastor). Likewise, the challenging questions and opinions of students in my classes at Santa Clara University reflect a younger generation's thirst to link faith and life.

Staffs at the Martin Luther King, Jr., Library and Archives in Atlanta, the Library of Congress, Graduate Theological Union, the National Archives, Boston University Mugar Memorial Library, and the W. E. B. Du Bois Memorial Centre for Pan African Culture (Accra, Ghana) were all helpful. While in Accra, (the late) Kofe Appiah-Kubi and family were gracious in hosting me; and Gershon Tefe-Addo (coordinator at the Du Bois Centre) offered invaluable assistance.

I'll always be grateful for conversations and interviews with my father, Robert R. Hopkins, Sr., who passed on tales of his parents and slavery, the historical importance of black faith, as well as rich stories from slave and post-slavery black folk culture. Born in 1907, he remains a sharp and humorous working-class intellectual.

Final thanks go to my wife, Nancy, for her continued support, editorial help, and theological challenges.

SHOES THAT FIT
OUR FEET

Introduction

Keeping Faith on the Road to Freedom

African Americans are a religious people on the road to freedom. It has always been that way. In fact, the one thing that Africans and African Americans possessed and owned in the New World was the history, memory, and practice of faith. For black folk since slavery, the church and other freedom faith gatherings have served many different functions; the African American God never left the poor alone at any time along the way. The church and religion pervaded and acted as the context for total black life. Clubs, burial societies, and hospitals originated from the church; individuals, rich and poor— politicans, professionals, actors, and musicians—were influenced by it. Moreover, the only liberated place that enslaved black folk controlled was the Invisible Institution (for example, secret religious meetings), the foundation for the black Christian church.

However, this religious institution bore more the marks of a holistic community—a political free space and a cultural affirmation of identity—than the white Western notion separating "sacred" from "secular." From the time white Christian profit-seekers used violence to steal Africans from the Continent until this very day, the African American church remains the most organized, visible, and nurturing institution for the overall life of black North Americans.

And so to discover what black people think about God, we travel a road where African Americans live a faith of freedom. This journey actually becomes a walk through the stories of the folk. In their unedited tales of life, the black poor yearn for the freedom to name themselves and determine the space around them. As they press on toward this mark, they seek a spirituality of full humanity. Their final quest is both a belief in and a search for a God as the ultimate power of total justice and radical equality for all of creation. For God's compassion toward the poor is to labor along with them in life's vineyards to attain their unrestricted potentiality. Thus, as sung in the black church, God "walks with you and talks with you and tells you you are his own." But likewise in African American folk wisdom, God also helps those who help themselves. To keep step with this walking and talking of the folk, we need to move with them through the twists and turns of their tales—stories about their belief expressed in culture, politics, and spirituality. We need to share the "shoes" of faith that fit their feet on the way forward.

Indeed, *Shoes That Fit Our Feet* seeks to penetrate the core of poor African Americans' religious convictions in order to gather up lessons and sources for a constructive black theology today. It calls on black theology to set its compass for the avenues African American folk are traveling. Black theology, then, must develop itself from justice beliefs deeply embedded in the very blood and bones of an African American reality. Black resources are the heart of black theology.

Of course, the most institutionalized historical and contemporary movement for our theological discoveries is the black church. It has been both progressively faithful and reactionarily unfaithful to its commission. Still it laid the cornerstone. Transplanted from an African religious backdrop into a so-called New World, black poor folk have always traveled the "rough side of the mountain," sought a land of milk and honey, but too often felt like strangers in a strange land. Yet their sticking to a faith in freedom has remained unshaken as witnessed by the black church's persistence along with other religious experiences in a freedom belief.

It is no wonder, then, that a faith permeates, consciously and unconsciously, the total "sacred" and "secular," joy and sorrow, love making and love breaking, success and failure, and serious and playful dimensions of black life. Even after Emancipation (1865), African Americans found both refuge and creativity within black church walls. On the one hand, the folk had to develop most of their initiatives and make the majority of their contributions to themselves and the broader society out of the African American church. This occurred because both the immediate post-slavery and, even more so, the post–Hayes-Tilden Compromise (1877) periods unleashed a reign of terror on African American access to avenues and resources in the larger society. Given this white terrorism and lynching practices against an entire people, blacks fell back on the soothing balm of the black church. It was truly their rock in a weary land, a shelter in a time of storm, and a haven in a godless (white) country.

On the other hand, regardless of external racial repression, black people recognized on their own that African American creativity could best flourish in an institution and lifestyle that had seen them through their own "Egypt land" slavery. Thus reliance on the African American church was not only dictated by white fear and hatred, but it was also determined by an ebony people wanting to control positively their own organizational and innovative resources.

As the road to freedom turned into the twentieth century, more "secular," professional, and club organizations began to spring up in the African American community. This could have suggested a displacing of the church from the center of black folk unity. However, the majority of the personalities that enjoyed such secular professions, jobs, and organizations came out of church or church-related formations and the church's freedom faith ethos. Even those who claimed no direct sprouting from black church seeds would have to give recognition to African American religious influences to a certain degree.

So with blacks seeping out into previously restricted areas in the broader society either through jobs, professions, mass political movements (for example, Garveyites), cultural renaissance developments (such as the New Negro movement), or intellectual ability (for instance, W. E. B. Du Bois), it would seem that the ground was broken for a split into two distinct realms—the holy and the profane. Yet black churches maintained their direct links to the so-called secular realm through organizational ties, interchange of leadership, or more important, through the fact that black culture was saturated with habits and instincts imbued with the African American religious worldview. Faith always intertwined with black life and history.

Especially during the late 1940s and early 1950s Civil Rights movements, we see the southern church in particular raising up the historical leadership role of black faith communities into the so-called privileged public sphere. And from that time until the present we would be remiss, if not blind, if we did not and do not see steps toward justice. Electoral campaigns, Black Power movements,[1] international solidarity initiatives, community organizing, an individual's public credibility, sports-movie-entertainment figures, coalition attempts, and a host of other activities have some relation to or have been influenced one way or another by the presence or lack of presence of the African American church.

This faith in freedom—most recognized in the black church tradition—has also blanketed other walks of African American life. Thus we can truly say that black belief in liberation is holistic life for an oppressed people. It transcends denominations, institutions, personalities, and movements and empowers them on the road to freedom.

Faith in Freedom

A faith in freedom originated in Africa. Though black North American slaves did not retain the identical faith structure of their African ancestors, they did maintain the belief in freedom bequeathed by their African forebears.[2] Thus from slavery until today, the liberation impulse has penetrated and infused and energized black life in different ways. The most dominant current has been, and remains, African American Christianity. Yet a faith in freedom as the ultimate concern in the black American experience has also revealed itself in non-Christian sources.[3] Why does such a faith show us a religious dimension in non-Christian sections of the African American community? God liberates where God chooses to liberate. Therefore, non-Christian instances and movements for black freedom testify to God's own freedom to empower whomever God wishes to empower. Through faith, it is our calling to discern the signs of the times. Moreover, in black folk living, in line with an African way of life, the sacred and secular realms are less separated and torn than they are in the white Western religious worldview. So even in seemingly non-religious situations, one discovers the power of God. Finally, because black liberation has been an ultimate goal, it has motivated African American life just as other quests of faith have possessed their believers. Religion is something a community holds close to its heart. At the same time, this justice journey grips the faith community and further propels it toward the final achievement of free humanity.

Shoes That Fit Our Feet looks at fresh examples of how a gripping and compelling faith of freedom within the African American experience itself lays the foundation for constructing a black theology of liberation today. Indeed, the keeping of faith along the rocky road to freedom requires black theology to put on shoes "made" in the crucible of black people's belief in their full humanity. If black theology remains accountable to the Good News for oppressed people and recognizable to the African American folk, then it must be indigenous to the folk's faith. *Shoes* builds a black theology from the steppingstones of African American history, women, culture, politics, and religion.

What important sources of faith in the African American community can foster the construction of a contemporary black theology of liberation? Simply put, what is the connection between black theology and black sources? A black theology of liberation today is woven together from at least the following political and cultural strands found in the fabric of black North American life: the African American church, black women, African American cultural folklore, major black political representatives, and an analysis and vision coming out of the African American legacy of struggle. Furthermore, an authentic account of the God of freedom, whom black people have worshiped and continue to worship in its sources, dictates that a contemporary black theology of liberation must start from the perspective of achieving justice for the "least of these" — God's poor.

As we develop a systematic black theology today from stories and histories indigenous to the black community, each source is examined for its contributions to three commitments: theology (God), Christology (Jesus Christ) or appropriate intermediaries, and theological anthropology (human purpose). Furthermore, each source's assistance to the freedom of the black poor and, at the same time, the poor in general, is elaborated. And finally, each source of faith is explored to discover how political and cultural traditions and practices can complement one another.

Systematic Black Theology

A systematic black theology of liberation helps the African American poor on their faith road to justice. First, theology refers to a critical investigation of a community's belief in the divine. This conviction in an ultimate, life-and-death concern is usually instinctive and unrefined. A systematic theology, therefore, makes a believing community more self-conscious and deliberate about the sounds, feel, nuances, and requirements of an instinctive theology. When such a theology gravitates toward a liberating faith, then the theologian can make it even more intentional. Theology makes the group accountable to what its faith tells it to do. Thus theology continually questions the identity and purpose of a specific people in new situations and for new generations. Because today's African American community and church have the unique experience of God both in their *political* resistance against white racism and in their positive assertions of black *culture*, there is a need to understand and present clearly the particular witness of this black-God union.

More specifically, theology affirms and challenges how we act at the intersection between God's liberating practice and humanity's faithful practice with God. It arises from life or human activity. Circumstances of life encourage people to ask ultimate questions about themselves and their connection to what they consider the divine. Theology is more than a Christian church discipline. It includes all segments of the black community (Christian, non-Christian, religious, non-religious) of which the black church is the dominant part. Thus, in order to adequately construct an indigenous theology of a particular people, one has to research carefully major developments within a specific community. To construct a black theology, one has to highlight important trends within the black setting and, from these trends, draw out their theological significance for the African American community's justice concern and, indeed, for all of humanity. The black theologian stands at the crossroads, the spot where the power of liberation beckons the African American poor to walk this way toward freedom.

Along this way, political and cultural trends are two major influences indigenous to the black North American community. Politics refers to those individuals or movements who focus their efforts primarily on fighting the system of racial discrimination. Their goal is to restructure the power relations between blacks and whites. Furthermore, they spend their energies on attacking perceived restrictions caused and imposed by a "white power structure." Oftentimes one identifies the political trend with black self-determination for political power, claiming one's space.

In contrast (but not necessarily in contradiction) to targeting racial discrimination as the primary problem, people within the cultural trend focus more on using and consciously developing black resources such as art, language, literature, and so forth. Their main emphasis is building black institutions and movements. Oftentimes one associates this trend with the cultural beauty of black self-identity. Of course, the political and cultural traditions overlap in the same black institutions, people, and movements. Therefore, we can expect to find these two shades of difference united on the same path of a liberation journey. For example, as a theological source, the African American church shows its faith both politically and culturally.

In addition to the political-cultural, space-identity relationship, a liberation belief has always been with the folk in their travels throughout life and in the African American church's interpretation of the Christian Bible. In fact, the religion of the black community and black church has been and remains a faith in freedom. For the *black community*, diverse political and cultural spokespersons and movements express the drive toward liberation. Sometimes, however, the community lacks a conscious awareness of its faith claims. Here the challenge to theology is comprehensively to measure the words and deeds of the community against its faith in freedom. For the *black church*, since its birth in the antebellum South, the Bible has revealed a movement of Old Testament Hebrews on an exodus toward freedom. Likewise, the New Testament Jesus has come to walk and talk with the poor and the victims, to comfort and deliver them, and to tell them they are his own. For this journey, then, the overall black experience and the black church's biblical understanding necessitate a black theology of liberation. There has always existed a faith in freedom among the poor within the African American community. Otherwise, they could not have gotten over.

Belief in liberation of the poor is also the centerpiece for black liberation theology today. This assertion flows from an actual textual examination of the indigenous sources for black theology as well as a specific interpretation of the Bible. There exists a connection and agreement between the lived experiences of the African American community and the core message of the Christian Bible; both use the lens of the poor and express faith in the ultimate freedom of the poor. Both make up the engine that moves African American resources toward a constructive black theology.

Sources for Today's Black Theology

With each chapter exploring the theological lessons of an indigenous black source, *Shoes That Fit Our Feet* pursues the path of the following five faith expressions.

Chapter 1 focuses on slave religion as the plumb line for black church theology, because today's African American beliefs and practices have their starting point there. Specifically, the black Christian church has been the most stable institution in its persistent effort toward political and cultural liberation in the African American community.[4] Because of its central role and its explicit attention to religious matters, the black church has to be a primary source for a constructive black theology. Consequently, a look at the antebellum black church, as an Invisible Institution, is in order.[5] In defiance of banned worship gatherings or church services mandated by white slave masters, slaves illegally and surreptitiously assembled (for example, in the Invisible Institution) to praise God and pray for freedom as both a political protest against racism and as a positive assertion of (quasi-African) religious culture.

Chapter 1 investigates black theology in the slave narratives, spirituals, and autobiographies, and the slaves' understanding of God's being, nature, and attributes. It also explores the offices and work of Jesus Christ. And finally, it examines how slaves interpreted and lived their theological understanding of human purpose.[6] The theological source for African American women, chapter 2, draws from the fictional writings of Toni Morrison, especially focusing on black women's spirituality. Although Morrison's writings cover different twists and turns in black folk's trek in the United States, she emphasizes the particular pain, joy, weakness, and strength of African American women. Out of these stories, one can sense the unique female encounters with and allegiance to spiritual values and traditions. Here we get a taste of poor black women pursuing their religious callings in diverse ways. In particular, their "spirituality of funk" comes through their values of connectedness and traditions of embodiment.

Chapter 3 touches on theology in black folk culture through the prism of the Way Maker or Way Made, the Trickster, and a Get Over human witness. It is in these basic and raw expressions of the "folk" that we also get at the foundational planks for contemporary black theological development. In poor people's acts of cultural self-identity, we are halted and enriched by the diverse expressions in the African American community's religious worldview and capacity to survive and create. Here we'll confront challenges from the liberation faiths of such notorious characters as Stackolee, Shine, and Brer Rabbit.

Chapter 4 presents W. E. B. Du Bois as one signifier of black people's theological reality illustrated politically. Though Du Bois is usually and correctly acclaimed as a brilliant social critic and historian, he also had a political theological viewpoint, which has not been readily perceived by scholars of black history.[7] Du Bois's political theology included positions on God or a Force, Jesus Christ, and human purpose. What does Du Bois's religious thought teach black theology about that sector of African American life which pursues primarily the politics of direct confrontation against systemic white power? Du Bois's religious thought stands for a part of the African American journey symbolized in a freedom through political struggle.

Chapter 5 argues that a constructive black theology has to examine the adequacy of the theological social analyses and social visions of Minister Malcolm X and Rev. Martin Luther King, Jr., representatives of two contrasting trends within a unified African American religious venture. In the contemporary era King and Malcolm symbolize the two most dominant schools of thought in the black community. Their beliefs and actions were linked to and reflect the larger African American experience. Therefore, it is no accident that two such decisive figures were religious leaders with explicit theological positions. In addition to their insights on the black church, race, women, and the international situation, both figures, at the end of their lives, appear to have been exploring various forms of democratic socialism. The larger current of black faith and their own personal growth were moving them to similar analyses and visions for a full humanity for the African American poor.

The concluding chapter outlines a theological methodology, that is, foundational principles for constructing black theology. Briefly, the conclusion suggests guidelines, relationships, and types of disciplines in constructing black theology today. It is here that we find out how to get the right "shoes" to fit.

Moreover, as we walk toward a constructive black theology of liberation, the first five chapters are directly interrelated on several levels. Chapters 1, 2, and 3 (the slave church, women's stories, and folk culture) signify the untapped and basic faith tales of poor black folk. Here the attempt is to hear and learn (theologically) from the unlettered in the black community as they speak their voices. Together they make up part 1—folk religion. Chapters 4 and 5 (Du Bois and King-Malcolm) represent the recognized theological positions of pioneering crusaders who rose to prominence out of the struggles of the folk and who, in turn, have their liberation faiths fueled by the folk. They make up part 2—the faith of social movement leaders. In this sense chapters 1, 2, and 3 lay the theological basis and must precede chapters 4 and 5.

On a second level, chapters 1 through 5 complement and correct one another. Chapter 1 (slave church theology) tells the non-church institutions (reflected in cultural and political movements in chapters 3 and 4 respectively) in the African American community that the foundation of black church theology is a fight for justice on earth. Therefore larger political and cultural phenomena are reminded about the well where their water springs. In addition, chapter 1 is a message to the contemporary black church insofar as it serves to prick today's church's historical amnesia regarding its own liberation legacy. Black women's spirituality (chapter 2) immediately follows after slave church foundations in order to tell the institutional black church that regardless of what it thinks about African American women's vocation, black women are called by God and not by black male church leaders. God, not males, commands and nurtures female ministerial leadership.

Likewise, chapters 2 through 4 inform the African American church that God is involved in emancipatory works in non-church institutions and movements in the community, some of which claim God's grace for freedom shining through non-Christian windows. Thus a freedom faith resides in the so-called secular realm, further meaning that the church and the non-church and the Christian and non-Christian African American realities need to forge bonds wherever the common norm of divine-poor co-agency for liberation dwells. Chapter 5 speaks to the previous four chapters and says all are lacking unless one deals with theology vis-à-vis social analyses and social visions. It urges black theology to use radical (that is, getting at the root of systems) tools of interpretation and witness through social change.

Finally, having drawn out theological insights and indicators in the first five chapters the conclusion lays out the framework for synthesizing black church foundations, African American women's spirituality, culture, politics, and social analyses and social visions into a future systematic black theology of liberation.

Unity through a Justice Faith

The present work seeks to contribute the following to today's discussions on black theology and theology in general. It shows that an analysis of both politics and culture (for example, emphasis on poor folk's self-determining their own space and identity) is important for understanding the theology and religion of African Americans. Thus, the above-mentioned five sources are brought together for their politico-cultural importance for theology. Black theology requires a fresh initiative based on indigenous sources.

Furthermore, this book pursues several other goals in the wider theological conversation. I hope to enhance a closer working relationship between the black church and non-church segments of the African American community; both are united by a common faith in justice. In addition, the role of black women's stories is crucial in the development and survival of a contemporary theology. *Shoes That Fit Our Feet* also attempts to strengthen black and non–African American relations by pointing out the necessity for non-blacks to grasp the importance of the belief in justice that permeates the diverse segments of black politics, culture, and spirituality. This theological liberation impulse in the African American reality resonates with the essential doctrine of Christianity, that is, the yearning for final freedom. Ultimately, therefore, the authenticity of white dominating theology and its church hangs on its repentance and dialogue with a black theology of liberation, one form of third world liberation theologies.

Moreover, this study informs the black church and the entire African American community of the need for a black theology for today. We need to delve into the divine freeing power revealed in sources of black life, thought, and tradition in order to uncover the unique theological lessons of the African American reality. God "moves" in black sources. Consequently, black folk make a decisive contribution to theology, church, and the broader society. To manifest that contribution, however, we need "shoes that fit our feet." Again, what we are attempting to do is discover how African American religious faith, language, and practice display liberating theological convictions about the divine's relation to the African American church and community's own self-identity and self-determination. Systematic black theology can make this liberating journey of discovery much more self-conscious in the black church and black life.

Finally, *Shoes That Fit Our Feet* travels toward a systematic and constructive black theology of liberation and embraces the global poor and, through them, all humanity. Though black folk have been distinct and often segregated, they have always been connected to the larger world around them. African American shoes are also humanity's shoes.

PART ONE

FOLK RELIGIOUS EXPERIENCES

1

Religious Meetings in de Bushes

My uncle, Ben, he could read de Bible, and he allus tell us some day us be free. And Massa Henry laugh, "Haw, haw, haw." And he say, "Hell, no, yous never be free. Yous ain't got sense 'nuf to make de livin', if yous was free." Den, he takes de Bible 'way from Uncle Ben and say it put de bad ideas in he head, but Uncle gits 'nother Bible and hides it, and Massa never finds out.

John Bates, ex-slave

The African American church begins in slavery; so, slave religion provides the first source for a constructive statement on a black theology of liberation. The black church's unique tradition springs from the emerging theology of African American chattel. Enslaved African Americans creatively forged their own understanding of God, Jesus Christ, and the purpose of humanity. Through scriptural insights, theological imagination, and direct contact with God, black bondsmen and bondswomen combined faith instincts from their African traditional religions with the justice message of the Christian gospel and planted the seeds for a black theology expressed through politics and culture. This practical and sacred worldview evolved into an institutional worship setting under bondage.

While white masters attempted to force their Christianity onto their black property, slaves secretly worshiped God. These illegal and hidden religious practices formed the Invisible Institution, out of which black Christianity and black theology arose. Though chained and illiterate, African American people dared to *think* theologically by testifying to what the God of Moses had done for them. For example, recording the Christian substance of the spirituals (the novel religious songs created by blacks under slavery), Colonel Thomas Wentworth Higginson, a white officer in the Civil War, observed:

[The slaves'] memories are a vast bewildered chaos of Jewish history and biography; and most of the great events of the past, down to the period of the American Revolution, they instinctively attribute to Moses.[1]

Unfortunately, Higginson described these penetrating theological insights of the unlettered black bondsmen as "bewildered chaos." He failed to appreciate the hermeneutical insights and the interpretive cunning of the poor. For the slaves, Moses acted as a human instrument of divine liberation, because Yahweh had utilized him to emancipate the slaves. If Yahweh could do this against Pharaoh, then surely Yahweh had brought about all "the great events" of liberation movements, including the American Revolution against the British oppressors. Furthermore, because black slaves identified themselves with the biblical Hebrew slaves, and because Yahweh had continued to act in human history, black American bondsmen and bondswomen maintained hope and certainty for their own deliverance from the cauldron of white American chattel. This "bewildered chaos," in fact, marked the slaves' developing theological critique from the Bible's powerless voices.

An examination of slaves' lives and thought about God conveys several important factors in the religious lineage of the black church. For instance, slave theology consistently experienced God dwelling with those in bondage, personal and systemic. The black religious experience prevented any separation between the sacred and the secular, the church and the community. On the contrary, in the Invisible Institution black theology grew out of the community and the "church." As a result, *God* ruled with unquestioned omnipotence and realized release from total captivity. And *Jesus* assumed an intimate and kingly relation with the poor black chattel. Slaves emphasized both the suffering human Jesus as well as Jesus' warrior ability to set the downtrodden free. Moreover, the slaves distinguished their *humanity* from the white slavemaster. For blacks, God and Jesus called them to use all means possible to pursue religiously a human status of equality.

Furthermore, in radical distinction to white Christianity, religious encounters in ex-slave narratives, autobiographies, and the spirituals suggest an alternative theological interpretation with at least two aspects. First, African American slaves pictured a political dimension in their theology. They saw a direct political power struggle between serving their God and serving the white slavemaster's god. In certain situations whites claimed to be God on earth and mandated black submissiveness to a white idolatry, which contradicted the slaves' loyalty to the ultimacy of God. Second, slaves' religious thought accented an original cultural expression. Not only did they wage a political battle for the supremacy of their liberator God, they also chose to worship this God in their own language and idiom, and in the extraordinary clandestineness of their own black religious community. Thus God's self-revelation took place in the specific textures of an African American slave story. Today's black theology, church, and community need to be thankful that God spared a few formerly enslaved African Americans to pass on this black theological tradition. In the words of ex-slave John Brown, who gave praise to God for the opportunity to tell it as it actually was, we read:

> Lord! have mercy! have um mercy! Lord you done spared a few un us to tell de tale um, um, um, bout how hit was um, um wid us poor folks in dem days um, um, um. We done pray for dis day to come of freedom.[2]

Before we look at specific examples of how slaves told their story about the coming of freedom (through the slaves' black theology expressed in their experiences with God, Jesus, and human purpose), we investigate and define the contours of the Invisible Institution, the secret religious organization that served as the backdrop for the slaves' black theology.

THE CONTOURS OF THE INVISIBLE INSTITUTION

From the Slaves' Perspective

To tell the slaves' religious story as the first source for today's black theology, one has to acknowledge the convergence of a reinterpreted white Christianity with the remains of African religions under slavery. Precisely in the Invisible Institution, black chattel synthesized these two foundational God-encounters to form slave theology.

Though slaves did not have direct access to the specifics of their former African religious practices and beliefs, they did maintain some theological remnants — religious Africanisms. Unfortunately, the European slave trade, the practice of mixing Africans from different villages, white people's prohibition of the use of African languages, and the fading memories of succeeding slave progeny[3] all served to dampen the vibrancy of a systematic African theology in slave thought. Nevertheless, enslaved Africans brought religious ideas and forces of theological habit with them to the so-called New World.

These Africans in bondage were not ignorant theologically. On the contrary, it was their structural religious worldview of God, Jesus, and human purpose that sustained them against the racist assaults of European slavers and their descendants in the New World. Yet despite the existence of the slaves' black theology, white people continued to brand enslaved Africans as biologically subhuman, culturally uncivilized, and religiously heathen. Note the following emphasis of a prominent white missionary to Africa:

> I arrived at Bende to attempt anew the dredging and purifying of that ugly jungle pool of heathenism, with its ooze-life of shocking cruelty, reptilian passions and sprouting evil, spreading itself broad in the

shadows amidst the most fruitful land on earth. . . . Thus Christianity views her domain-to-be, lifting herself high above the secret springs of paganism's turgid streams below.[4]

Whites viewed Africans as possessing reptilian qualities of passion and an inherent theological anthropology of evil. Conversely, white theology and white Christianity were normative and by definition superior ("lifting herself high above"), hence by nature dominating ("Christianity views her domain-to-be"). For white missionaries who accompanied European slave traders to Africa, African communities offered no points of convergences between Christianity and African traditional religions. Instead of seeking points of theological contact with African indigenous religions, white theology served as the religious justification for Christian colonialism and racist plundering of black lands ("the most fruitful land on earth").

But Africans, even as they were bound as booty for the "New World," survived and resisted by remembering and relying on their traditional religions. It is this primordial religious reflex that was bequeathed to the future black slaves in the Invisible Institution.

The African Contribution to Slave Theology

In spite of the horrors of the slave trade, enslaved Africans, the majority coming from the African West Coast, brought a distinct perception of God to North America. The Ghanaian religious scholar Kofi Asare Opoku describes their indigenous worldview:

> To West Africans, God is essentially a spirit, a being without concrete form or body. He is therefore never represented in the form of images or worshipped through them. God is also thought of as different from all the other spirits and divinities. His powers transcend theirs and He has the unique attribute of immanence. God is present everywhere and is involved in the affairs of men. He rules and sustains the universe, which He created, with love, compassion and justice.[5]

African traditional religions described their ultimate divinity as the High God. "God has nowhere or nowhen" speaks to the omnipresence and non-derivative status of the divinity.[6] Some even called God "the Almighty," denoting divine omnipotence. The unbounded power of God allows God to do all things in heaven and on earth. This power is also what enables human beings to achieve their goals. God is both transcendent and immanent in African traditional religions. And God's authority entails all of creation. As the first and last cause, God created all things and thus holds the ultimate and final power over the visible and invisible creations. Humanity is contingent, but God is absolute authority.[7]

Furthermore, African indigenous religions believe in a God who cares;

some call God "the Compassionate One"; others see "the God of pity," who rescues victims in need. Even more, God is kind and "looks after the case of the poor man." In fact, God is the main hope of the poor in society. As Guardian and Keeper, God is named "the Protector of the poor" by some African traditional religions. They further specify that "there is a Saviour and only he can keep our lives."[8] As judge, God metes out justice, punishment, and retribution. Similarly, God displays protectiveness by avenging injustice. God is a divinity of partiality to the victim; God sides with the political powerlessness of society's injured.

In addition to these definite attributes of God, the theological framework shared by enslaved Africans in the New World also included a belief in theological anthropology—what it means to be God's created humanity.

African traditional religions shared a belief in a dynamic and interdependent relation between the individual and the community. The latter defined the former. Individualism proved anathema. To be human meant to stand in connection with the larger community of the invisible ancestors and God and, of course, the visible community and family.

> Africans recognize life as life-in-community. We can truly know ourselves if we remain true to our community, past and present. The concept of individual success or failure is secondary. . . . Our nature as beings-in-relation is a two-way relation: with God and with our fellow human-beings.[9]

African religions gave rise to a dynamic interplay between community and individual. Whatever happened to the communal gathering affected the individual; whatever happened to the individual had an impact on the community. Such a theological view of humanity cuts across bourgeois notions of white Christianity's individualism and "me-first-isms." It seeks to forge a group solidarity and identity, beginning with God, proceeding through the ancestors to the community and immediate family, and continuing even to the unborn. One cannot be a human being unless one becomes a part of, feels a responsibility to, and serves the community. To preserve the community's well-being (through liberation) in African religions is to preserve the individual's well-being (through salvation). Thus salvation and liberation become a holistic individual-collective and personal-systemic ultimate concern.

In this theological anthropology African traditional religions also accent the role and importance of the ancestors. The ancestors are connections to past religious traditions and practices. They are the glue to the sacredness of culture or way of life. Oftentimes one would have to placate the ancestors in order to reach the High God. So lack of connectedness or connectedness to those who hold religio-cultural deposits have grave implications regarding one's relation to the divine. Here, the cultural significance of the ancestors' role is the most relevant because the memory and presence of the ancestors help preserve and teach the cultural heritage of the community. Thus to be human-in-community necessitated a cultural dimension in African traditional religions.

Furthermore, enslaved Africans brought with them a sense of wholeness in the High God's relation to creation. Because God created all things, there was no separation between the sacred and secular, the church and the community.

> A sense of wholeness of the person is manifested in the African attitude to life. Just as there is no separation between the sacred and the secular in communal life, neither is there a separation between the soul and the body in a person. Spiritual needs are as important for the body as bodily needs are for the soul.[10]

One did not dichotomize God's sovereignty in any sphere. African traditional religions did not see the possibility of saving the spirit or the soul while the freedom of the body went unattended.[11]

Bush Arbor Theology

Enslaved Africans took the remnants of their traditional religious structures and meshed them together with their interpretation of the Bible. All this occurred in the Invisible Institution, far away from the watchful eyes of white people. Only in their own cultural idiom and political space could black slaves truly worship God. Ex-slave Becky Ilsey describes the hidden nature of the Invisible Institution pre-Civil War: " 'Fo de war when we'd have a meetin' at night, wuz mos' always 'way in de woods or de bushes some whar so de white folks couldn't hear."[12] Slaves would sneak off "twixt eight an' twelve at night"[13] to hold church. At times, slaves sought whatever shelter they could find for their sanctuary in order "to talk wid Jesus." They "used to go 'cross de fields nights to a old tobacco barn on de side of a hill."[14] If they found no standing shelter, they would construct a bush arbor for their illegal prayer meetings. Ex-slave Arthur Greene remembers:

> Well-er talkin' 'bout de church in dem days, we po' colored people ain' had none lak you have now. We jes made er bush arbor by cuttin' bushes dat was full of green leaves an' puttin' em on top of four poles reachin' from pole to pole. Den sometimes we'd have dem bushes put roun' to kiver de sides an' back from der bottom to der top. All us get together in dis arbor fer de meetin'.[15]

Other times slaves secretly gathered in an appointed cabin in the slave quarters. "Niggers have benches in dey house dat dey use when dey have prayer-meetin's."[16] Some ingeniously set up worship spots in the fields ("Dey hab big holes out in de fiel's dey git down in and pray"). Some developed regular praying grounds. "Us niggers used to have a prayin' ground down in the hollow," remembers Richard Carruthers. And Andrew Moss echoes: "Us colored folks had prayer grounds. My mammy's was a old twisted thick-rooted muscadine bush." And still others would simply "slip down the hill" to worship.[17]

In the Invisible Institution the slaves displayed a remarkable clarity concerning the cultural dimension of their theology. They knew that God spoke to them in their own medium. In fact, African American chattel could not worship God truthfully unless they "talked" with God through their black culture. Ex-slave Emily Dixon makes it plain:

> Us could go to de white folk's church [in a segregated section], but us wanted ter go whar us could sing all de way through, an' hum 'long, an' shout—yo' all know, jist turn loose lack.

In slave religious culture, the liberating Spirit made one "jist turn loose lack." The Spirit fed the people and instructed them how to communicate with God using their own indigenous resources. "We used to steal off to de woods and have church, like de spirit moved us—sing and pray to our own liking and soul satisfaction," states Susan Rhodes. Her testimony exemplifies the slaves' need to be filled with the Spirit to *their* liking and soul's satisfaction. When they claimed their relation to God through the Spirit's pouring into their unique expressions, Rhodes resumes, "we sure did have good meetings, honey . . . like God said."[18]

Like their self-expression in the cultural sphere, slaves acknowledged that their religious worship and theological development meant a political fight to preserve the Invisible Institution. White folks not only passed laws to prevent African American bondsmen and bondswomen from receiving unsupervised religious instructions, they sought to whip and kill slaves if the latter met secretly to praise God. Thus the Invisible Institution symbolized both a cultural statement of slave theology as well as a liberated space in which slaves controlled the political power to develop their theology.

To fight white folks politically—to claim and worship in their own space of sacred power—blacks devised various stratagems to conceal the Invisible Institution. Minnie Folkes remembers: "So to keep de soun' from goin' out, slaves would put a gra' big iron pot at de do'." Katie Blackwess Johnson concurs: "I would see them turn down the pots to keep the folks at the big-house from hearin' them singin' and prayin'."[19] Yet the whites proved relentless in imposing their theology on the slaves and attempting to squash the bondsmen and bondswomen's political struggle to "hold church." Whites sent out "patrollers" to make bed checks in the slave shacks and to comb the woods to stifle the Invisible Institution. Consequently, slaves responded with "lookouts" as decoys to confuse the patrollers. West Turner testifies, "Well, dey made me de lookout boy, an' when de paddyrollers [the patrollers] come down de lane past de church . . . well, sir, dey tell me to step out f'm de woods an' let 'em see me." The patrollers chased after Turner, who led them into a booby trap. Turner continues:

> Dem ole paddyrollers done rid plumb into a great line of grape vines dat de slaves had stretched 'cross de path. An' dese vines tripped up de horses an' throwed de ole paddyrollers off in de bushes.[20]

Turner's eyewitness account of the slaves' illegal church gatherings indicates a virtual political guerrilla warfare. Similarly, the picturesque story of former slave Rev. Ishrael Massie attests to the expression of slave religion in the Invisible Institution as hand-to-hand combat over who would have power to control the theology of the oppressed African Americans. Rev. Massie underscores this point:

> Lemme tell ya dis happenin' at a meetin'. Ole preacher would come in bringing . . . a long knot of lightwood. . . . When de paterrolers knock at de dow . . . dis preacher would run to de fiah place, git him a light an' take dat torch an' wave hit back an' fo'th so dat de pitch an' fiah would be flyin' every which a way in dese paterrolers faces— you know dat burnt 'em.[21]

Clearly part of the black preacher's pastoral duties included waging a physical war against white "principalities and powers" on earth.

In the development of the political and cultural dimensions of the Invisible Institution, the preacher and his or her following had no choice but to steal away and "call on the name of the Lord" without fear of white power's lethal presence. Two factors brought this about—the proscriptions of white theology and the slaves' faith in God's partiality to the poor.

White Theology's Proscriptions

White theology forced its domination upon black life by maintaining ruthless control and rendering slaves subservient to white humanity. First, the *practice* of white slavemasters' Christianity restricted African Americans' access to an independent encounter with religion. For instance, in those cases where whites allowed blacks to attend church, slaves experienced segregation in seating. Samuel Walter Chilton recalls: "Colored folks had to set in de gallery. Dey [white Christians] didn' 'low dem to take part in service." Similarly, Caroline Hunter's former slavemaster would not permit slaves to enter even the church sanctuary. A white man would preach to them in the basement of the church building. Mr. Beverly Jones confirms: " 'Couse they wouldn' let us have no services lessen a white man was present. Most times the white preacher preached. . . . That was the law at that time."[22]

In addition to legal restrictions in worship, the everyday practice of white Christianity displayed no ethical difference between "Christian" whites and non-Christian whites. The white master of ex-slave Jack White was a "Mef'dis preacher" who whipped his blacks just as often and as cruelly as other white people did. To intensify the pain and heinousness of the lashing, this preacher would "drap pitch an' tuppentine on dem [the slaves' welts] from a bu'nin' to'ch." Another white preacher would intentionally put out any fires built by his slaves during the winter. As a result, his bondsmen and bondswomen "et frozen meat and bread many times in cold weather." Maintaining the tradition of white Christianity's practical barbarity, this particular preacher would soak the raw whipping wounds of his slaves in a "salt bath."[23]

Summarizing the slaves' perspective of white Christianity's daily brutalities, former bondswoman Mrs. Joseph Smith offers this succinct and insightful conclusion:

Those who were Christians [and] held slaves were the hardest masters. A card-player and drunkard wouldn't flog you half to death. Well, it is something like this—the Christians will oppress you more.[24]

Besides the practice of white slavemasters' Christianity, white theology sought to control and make black people slaves in its doctrinal propositions. The uncivilized witness and ethics of whites were not simply aberrations from their faith claims about God. On the contrary, white folks literally practiced what they preached. Their theology itself propagated white control and black subservience as the normative expression of the Christian gospel. As ex-slave Oliver Wendell Jackson remembers:

Every Sunday all us niggers went to Sunday School. They [the white church and its theology] had two kinds of doctrine, one for the white folks, and one for the niggers. The white preacher he told us that a nigger had no more business in heaven than a hog had to be a preacher.[25]

The slave narratives overflow with white theological justifications for the "peculiar institution." First, the worship leader "always took his text from Ephesians, the white preacher did, the part what said, 'Obey your masters, be good servant.'" Hence whites employed the authority of the Bible in a self-serving and racist interpretation. Having adopted this Pauline epistle to Ephesus as the standard homily, slavemasters further construed a catechism for their black human property. "We had a catechism to learn," narrates old Sister Robinson. "This wuz it: 'Be nice to massa an' missus, don't tell lies, don't be mean, be obedient an' wuk hard.'" Coupling this religious instruction with the following white man's sermon renders more clearly the intricacies of slavemaster theology. Quoting a white preacher, former slave Jenny Proctor restates:

> Now I takes my text, which is, Nigger obey your master and your mistress, 'cause what you git from them here in this world am all you ever going to git, 'cause you just like the hogs and the other animals—when you dies you ain't no more, after you been throwed in that hole.[26]

What does this tell us about white theological convictions regarding black religious humanity? Whites viewed slaves like other livestock ("hogs and the other animals"). Therefore, God had created and intended for them to work for their white masters with a cheerful and loyal countenance. Further, lacking any ultimate future of heavenly reward, slaves needed to rest content with the earthly constraints of bondage.

Finally, even if slavemasters granted any possibility of slaves attaining the blessed repose of heaven, they had to beseech the white man as their savior. For example, a slavemaster caught his slave praying and demanded that the slave explain to whom he offered supplications. The slave replied: "Oh Marster, I'se just prayin' to Jesus 'cause I wants to go to Heaven when I dies." Belligerently and arrogantly, the Marster replied, "You's my Negro. I get ye to Heaven."[27] Here we touch the heart of white Christianity and its theology. The white man believed he replaced the mediating and liberating role of Jesus Christ. As the anointed Jesus, the white man possessed omnipotent and salvific capabilities. For black chattel to reach God, then, whites forced African Americans to accept the intermediary and divine status of the white race.

However, black folks rejected these scurrilous and heretical faith claims.[28] Though physically bound, slaves nevertheless directly encountered the biblical God in their own theological creativity.

THE SLAVES' BLACK THEOLOGY

White theological proscriptions served as a negative incentive for slaves to pursue their independent religious thinking. On the positive side, blacks felt the powerful living presence of divinity in the midst of their daily burdens and concentrated in the Invisible Institution. These radical religious experiences colored their biblical interpretation; and, thus, they produced a theology of liberation. Given the contours of the Invisible Institution as backdrop, the slaves' liberation faith in the divine burst through in their own theological perspectives on God, Jesus Christ, and human purpose.

GOD

Exodus: God Heard Our Cries

African American bondsmen and bondswomen discovered their own predicament and deliverance in the story of the Old Testament Israelites who fled into the wilderness to escape bondage in Egypt.

> All us had was church meetin's in arbors out in de woods. De preachers would exhort us dat us was de chillen o' Israel in de wilderness an' de Lord done sent us to take dis land o' milk and honey.[29]

And so they reached back into biblical times and appropriated Yahweh's promises and accomplishments for their contemporary dilemma. Paralleling the faith of the Israelites, ex-slave Henry Bibb wrote in his autobiography: "I never omitted to pray for deliverance. I had faith to believe that the Lord could see our wrongs and hear our cries."[30] Pursuing a theological journey from the Old Testament Yahweh to their current religious life with God, slaves directly experienced for themselves the mighty words of Yahweh: "I have surely seen the affliction of my people which are in Egypt and I have heard their cry. . . . And I am come down to deliver them" (Exodus 3:1-8a). In this biblical passage American slaves discovered the *nature* of God as the One who sees the afflictions of the oppressed, hears their cries, and delivers them to freedom.

Despite white folks' prohibitions against learning to read the Bible and despite the apparent immortality of the slave system, black chattel persisted in a faith in the God of freedom. They combined aspects of African traditional religions with the liberation message in the Bible and simply refused to accept white theology. John Bates fondly recalls: "My uncle, Ben, he could read de Bible, and he allus tell us some day us be free." Bates's statement signifies the slaves' unshakeable intellectual analysis and heartfelt belief that the *being* and *work* of God was liberation. Consequently, they repeatedly prayed for deliverance.[31]

Indeed, God heard their cries.[32] God did not turn a deaf ear to such soul-wrenching supplications; neither did God ignore God's "little ones" in distress. God displayed the *compassion* of a loving and caring parent with the inherent attribute of *agape* — an unflinching divine love for the poor. This knowledge of Yahweh-God's steadfast love empowered illiterate slave preachers to risk the pain of death in order to proclaim the Word of God to a bush arbor "congregation." An unidentified slave preacher remembers how he first began preaching by regurgitating the prescribed words of the slavemaster ("obeys the master"). Though lacking in literacy, this preacher nonetheless felt filled with God's spirit, which moved him to contradict his previous sermon on subservience obliged by white theological doctrine ("I knowed there's something better for [the slaves]"). As a result, he felt compelled to proclaim the word of God "but daren't tell [the slaves] 'cept on the sly. That I done lots." Perhaps surreptitiously crowded deep in a damp ravine under the bright blackness of a midnight moon, this preacher in chains brought forth the Good News to his brothers and sisters: "I tells 'em iffen they keeps praying, the Lord will set 'em free."[33] God hears and God frees.

More specifically, God freed the slaves in one decisive divine action—the Civil War. Various slave stories, accordingly, attribute the success of the Yankee forces over the Confederates to God's will. Charles Grandy typifies this sentiment.

> Den a gra' big star over in de east come right down almos' to de earth. I seed it myself. 'Twas sign o' war alright. Niggers got glad. All dem what could pray 'gin to pray more 'n ever. So glad God sendin' de war.[34]

Like the Old Testament Yahweh, who sent natural signs of plagues before freeing the Israelites, God disrupted the normal course of nature with a "gra' big star" coming from the east as a sign of war. And the poor became "so glad God sendin' de war." Clearly, for African American chattel, God's compassion and *agape* did not exclude a belligerent deed against the enemies of God's people. Consistent with the biblical narrative and reflecting out of their own story, slaves knew that divine pathos brought God to the defense of victims of injustice. Because of love, the divinity resorted to a warlike nature. As J. W. Lindsay stated: "I think that perhaps God means to bring good out of this great war [Civil War]. God is a man of war, and Jehovah is his name."[35] The slaves, then, conjured up theological images of Jehovah with arms outstretched leading the victorious advance on the battlefield against the evil system of slavery.

Yet the slaves did not restrict the image of God as warrior to the Civil War. They also linked this war notion against evil and bondage to a holistic concept of God's mercy as a balm for individual tribulations. In other words, God served the reliable role of black people's total deliverer, both in the systemic and personal realms. For instance, Ole Aunt Sissy had suffered from paralysis for numerous years. But when she heard of the war's conclusion and the abolition of slavery, she "hobbled on out de do', an stood dere prayin' to Gawd fo' his Mercy." Theologically, bondsmen and bondswomen coupled corporate freedom with personal healing. Note how the Good News of victory through battle yields a cure for paralysis. "God is a momentary God" whose mercy can answer one's prayers in a mere moment.[36]

We Have a Just God

The slaves' prayerful beseeching of God for deliverance indicates that they believed God's nature was just and liberating. In fact, such a faith kept hope alive for these poor chattel, who groaned under the heel of a stultifying existence. All around them stood white Christians taunting them with a supposedly biblically based and inherent superiority of white skin over black. Moreover, whites apparently had the military and intellectual power to implement this heretical claim of theological racism. But divine justice radically subverted the priority of white-skinned privileges in the slaves' sacred worldview. More specifically, with solemn certainty and joyful delight blacks sang:

> We have a just God to plead-a our cause
> We have a just God to plead-a our cause
> We are the people of God.
> He sits in Heaven and he answers prayer.[37]

A just God brought righteousness in situations of conflict between the weak and the strong. For human property, righteousness corrected unjust relations and placed divinity squarely and unapologetically on the side of the oppressed. How could it be otherwise? Surely, since Yahweh heard their anguished cries and saw their cruel plight, Yahweh would "make things right." By bearing the innocent victims' burden, God stood with them and, furthermore, burst asunder systemic tentacles that literally choked the very lives of African American bondsmen and bondswomen. In an interview former slave James L. Bradley boldly declared: "God will help those who take part with the oppressed. Yes, blessed be His holy name! He will surely do it."[38] God sided with the downtrodden.

Conversely, God punished the wicked. Understandably, the slaves believed in a theological formula of divine justice and righteousness in which the oppressor reaped the deserved reward of condemnation. Black chattel underwent sadistic and savage treatment at the hands of fiendish white folks. Whites often gave slaves fifty to five hundred lashes and then poured salt, turpentine, or ground bricks into the fresh wounds. White males entered slave cabins and raped black women in the presence of their husbands. White males consistently "broke in" young black girls just arriving into puberty. Quite often slaves had their thumbs cut off for attempting to learn reading and writing. Slavetraders purchased black women, snatched their children from their nursing breasts, and then threw these babies on the side of the road to die. Death stalked the slaves like a bounty hunter dogging a fugitive. The slightest whim could set off the vicious nature of whites. In one instance a slave woman accidentally spilled gravy on the white dress of a slavemistress. The master took the black woman outdoors and cut her head off.[39]

Hence, for the enslaved, the justice and righteousness of God could only bring retribution for tormentors. Referring to her slavemaster, Julia Brown concurs: "When he died we all said God got tired of Mister Jim being so mean and kilt him." But divine establishment of right relations entailed even more chastisement for the offender. "God has whipped some of 'em worse dan dey beat us."[40] Similarly, satisfaction for sinful and vicious acts against society's weak did not cease with the slavemasters. It resumed with and haunted their descendants. Drawing on all of his theological knowledge and religious experience, former slave Rev. Ishrael Massie asserted: "God's gwine punish deir chillun's chillun, yas sur!"[41]

Slaves linked this divine justice with the Kingdom of God. In fact, they perceived institutional slavery as a struggle between two kingdoms—that of God and that of Satan. Not surprisingly, the white master proxied for Satan and belonged to the latter's domain. The fruits of the master's earthly labor, then, yielded a permanent dwelling in hell. "I ain' plannin' on meetin' him in heaven," recollects a slave about her master. And the fact that "Marse was an' ole Methodist preacher" did not prevent his arrival in the flames of hell. Others claimed that their masters were so mean that their white owners "went past heaven."[42]

Not only did a biblical interpretation of divine sovereignty inform bondsmen and bondswomen about the masters' demonic kingdom, white theology gave justification for such a belief. When white patrollers happened upon the secret worship services of the Invisible Institution, they inevitably commenced with violently whipping slaves fresh from prayer. As white hands ferociously gripped bullwhips and broke the exposed skin of bent black backs, the patrollers mocked God and claimed: "Ef I ketch you heah agin servin' God, I'll beat you. You havn' time to serve God. We bought you to serve us." Based on black folks' reading of Christian scriptures, all who opposed God served Satan. And when one master arrogantly self-proclaimed, "The Lord rule Heaven, but Jim Smith rule the earth," slaves knew to which kingdom they belonged.[43]

To belong to God's realm of rule meant African American chattel professed themselves children of God; they reasoned that they, the meek, should inherit the earth. Like Israel, if God owned them in God's sacred domain, they held the deed to a land of milk and honey, for the God of deliverance would fulfill the divine promise to God's possessions. Under slavery, the children of God secretly hoped for the day of Jubilee, the inbreaking of heaven's Kingdom on earth. In fact, when "the walls came tumbling down" with God's Civil War, former chattel could "jist turn loose lack" and speak the truth. If previously they practiced stealth and ambiguity in theological imagery, now they plainly proclaimed. While former white masters slithered into hiding at the sound of advancing cannon fire, former slaves joyously jumped for Jubilee. They cried out with a renewed spirit and an open, defiant chorus:

> Old massa run away
> And us darkies stay at home.
> It must be now dat Kingdom's comin'
> And de year of Jubilee.[44]

Finally, the issue of the black slaves' perception of God (that is, King-dom-coming talk) in contrast to the white masters' faith is in the most fundamental and profound sense a theological debate about the nature of God. One ex-slave tells a story about a white minister sent to preach, no doubt, the standard "slaves obey your master" sermon to the blacks on the plantation. Uncle Silas, a 100-year-old slave, hobbled up to the front row and challenged the white preacher with a pointed inquiry: "Is us slaves gonna be free in Heaven?" The preacher abruptly halted his religious instructions and eyed Uncle Silas with vile contempt and a desire to kill him for questioning the normalcy of white theological doctrine. However, Uncle Silas did not budge and this time resumed the debate with a yell: "Is God gonna free us slaves when we git to Heaven?" The white preacher withdrew a handkerchief, mopped the sweat from his pale white brow and replied, "Jesus says come unto Me ye who are free fum sin an' I will give you salvation." Undaunted Uncle Silas rebutted: "Gonna give us freedom 'long wid salvation?" The preacher resumed his homily and Uncle Silas remained standing up front during the rest of the service.[45] Uncle Silas epitomizes the millions of blacks under slavery who refused to accept white people's notion of God, that is, that blacks were to serve whites and receive some amorphous reward after death. On the one hand stood a white male, symbolizing theological degrees, recognized Christian ordination, patriar-chy, racial privilege, economic power, and Satan. On the other stood Uncle Silas, poor, black, unlettered, and a child of God.

For Uncle Silas and the slaves, the debate revolved around the nature of God's liberation, the nature of the inbreaking of God's Kingdom. Above all, Yahweh brought freedom; without it personal salvation proved an opi-ate of the oppressed. Note that Uncle Silas does not deny the fruit of individual salvific power. What he wants to know and what he demands to know is whether individual release from sin intersected with the radical overthrow of a racist system of injustice. What does God have to say about that? From the vantage point of chattel, we have seen how God embodies the Exodus, realizes justice for the marginalized, and brings God's children into the Kingdom.

JESUS

Jesus Won't Die No More

In the above story, the white preacher attempted to undermine the press-ing theological queries of Uncle Silas by bastardizing Jesus' promise of salvation. Still Uncle Silas remained undeterred and vigorously pressed the question of Jesus' salvation in relation to liberation. This raises the slaves' interpretation of Jesus' role in their overall theological worldview.

Deeply rooted in the Old Testament scripture, black people linked Jesus to Israel's fate and, consequently, pinpointed the ultimate and decisive dimension of divine presence. The following spiritual confirms this assertion:

> Jesus said He wouldn't die no mo',
> Said He wouldn't die no mo',
> So my dear chillens don' yer fear,
> Said He wouldn't die no mo'.

> De Lord tole Moses what ter do,
> Said He wouldn't die no mo',
> Lead de chillen ob Isr'el froo',
> Said He wouldn' die no mo'.[46]

Immediately one recognizes slaves' positioning Jesus in the time of Moses. "De Lord tole Moses what ter do" indicates that Jesus becomes a contemporary within the Old Testament narrative. Again, bondsmen and bondswomen anchor themselves in the great deliverance achievements of Yahweh and the story of the oppressed Israelites. Therefore, the black slaves' sense of divine time did not restrict itself to a linear progression of God's interaction in human affairs. In fact, contrary to a whimsical interpretation of the Bible, black folks' retro-projection of Jesus to Moses' days reflects an authentic and faithful reading of scripture. The slaves correctly follow instructions from the prologue of John's New Testament gospel, which teaches us that in the beginning was the Word and the Word was with God. If the Word, who is Jesus, existed in the beginning of time, then surely Jesus had the ability and the power to exhort Moses during the latter's time.

However, the appearance of Jesus during Moses' time speaks about more than human time. In addition to and more fundamental than human conceptions, the above quoted spiritual focuses on the divine time of *kairos* — the sacred importance of Jesus' earthly mission of liberation. The constant refrain of Jesus never dying anymore underlines the momentous significance of Jesus' death and resurrection for humankind, particularly the prototype, oppressed Israel. Why the heavy emphasis on "die no mo'"? Because Jesus defeated the kingdom of Satan and all the political forces of evil representative of the demonic in all realms. "Today this Scripture is fulfilled in your hearing" (Luke 4:21). Therefore Jesus won't "die no mo'" because there does not exist a need for a future divine intermediary to conquer the political demons of evil powers. For black chattel, then, the liberating nature of Jesus dying meant a radical alteration witnessed by Jesus initiating the Kingdom.

At the same time that we stress the importance of Jesus' final death, we must be careful not to miss the slaves' conscious interplay between the liberation motif of poor oppressed Israel of the Old Testament and the liberation motif of Jesus in the New Testament. Positioning Jesus back with

Moses in the Old Testament does not mean black folks made relative or negated the earth-shattering divide between the political power of Satan and that of Jesus, realized by the latter's earthly appearance (in the New Testament). On the contrary, by stationing Jesus back with Moses, the entire Exodus event becomes a paradigmatic foreshadowing of the liberation consequences of Jesus' death and resurrection—the universal poor's grand exodus from poverty to freedom. The slaves were radically centered on Jesus.

In a sense, Israel's rough wilderness journey and ultimate victory in Canaan mirrored Jesus' cross and resurrection experience. The interweaving of the Israel story with Jesus not dying anymore points to the slaves' claim of such a theological parallel. The one Jesus, noted for a sacrificial emptying-suffering and resurrection-glorification, acted as the freedom Word in Israel's suffering and eventual "glorification." Thus placing Jesus during the time when Moses led the first cross-resurrection journey recounted in the Old Testament or first covenant prepares the slave for and confirms the omnipotent, liberating, and irresistible grace of the cross-resurrection event of the New Testament or final and ultimate covenant. Jesus had a hand in the movement of Israel. And when Jesus died, Jesus would never "die no mo' " because his cross-resurrection event symbolized the finality of satanic powers' absolute rout. Moreover, the constant emphasis on "die no mo' " sounds a note of confidence, courage, and hope for the blacks in bondage—"So my dear chillens don' yer fear." There is no need to fear the earthly white power structure. Since Jesus, through Moses, led the exploited Israelite people to victory and finished off Satan with the cross and resurrection, no human advocates for the devil could defeat Jesus' just cause of black people's struggle for liberation.

The ultimate goal of Jesus' liberation movement by necessity must lead to freedom because the very being of Jesus is freedom. The following famous slave spiritual defines this ontological character.

> Steal away, steal away,
> Steal away to Jesus,
> Steal away, steal away home,
> I hain't got long to stay here.

In this instance slaves employed a double meaning as a communication code to deceive paranoid whites ever on the lookout for religiously inspired slave rebellions. Such disguised slave songs heralded a distinct slave language. Thus bondsmen and bondswomen spoke of Jesus in their own black tongues. African Americans related to one another in a religious cultural medium that befuddled the normative white English and circumvented standard (white) speech patterns.

Accordingly in certain instances, "Steal Away" utilized Jesus to represent a secret prayer meeting of the Invisible Institution. In other cases Jesus stood for passage on Harriet Tubman's Underground Railroad to Canada or up North. For the Rev. Nat Turner, a black Baptist preacher, "Steal Away to Jesus" symbolized the gathering of his prophetic band of Christian witnesses in preparation for armed struggle and guerrilla warfare against slavery.[47] Regardless of the usage of "Jesus" in black slave English, whether a free space or a meeting to plan strategy for freedom or freedom in heaven (the land of milk and honey in the cultural language of African American chattel), the essential being of Jesus is freedom.

Jesus' Offices and Attributes

In addition to ascribing an ultimate significance and a liberation reality to Jesus, slaves also experienced specific offices in Jesus, in particular, the kingly and priestly offices.[48] King Jesus presented the image of a conquering hero, a valiant warrior defiantly and triumphantly situated upon his majestic stallion. Given the slaves' lowly and persecuted existence, nothing could better picture the kingly office than a mighty warrior of royalty. Slaves, therefore, sang from the depths of hearts that yearned for the King to come upon his steed as the Liberator. "Ride on, King Jesus," cry out the lyrics of one spiritual. "Ride on, conquering King."[49] Another verse states that "King Jesus ride a milk-white horse," whereas "Satan ride an iron-gray horse." The slaves made their Jesus theology explicit; the Warrior King fought Satan, the king of another kingdom. Because Jesus brought the Good News of ultimate deliverance and revealed a being of liberation, then King Satan stood for all that prevented freedom. For black chattel, King Satan's earthly domain was the slavery system, which would inevitably succumb to the Conquering King.

The kingly office linked directly to the priestly office of Jesus in another slave spiritual.

> King Jesus lit de candle by de waterside,
> To see de little chillun when dey truly baptize.
> Honor! Honor unto de dying lamb.
>
> Oh, run along chillun, an be baptize
> Might pretty meetin' by de waterside.
> Honor! Honor! unto de dying Lamb.[50]

Here the Conquering King serves as the pastor over the Invisible Institution—"pretty meetin' by de waterside." In the office of priest, Jesus officiates at the baptismal rituals, initiating the religious service by lighting the candles. Secretly gathered at a stream or brook around midnight, black chattel called on the Lord to preside over their ceremony of dying and rising again through the process of full immersion, that is, "when dey truly baptize." Quite fittingly, just as Jesus had died and risen again and thus become a new person, the slaves wanted to experience that same manifestation of new life in the presence of the One who was born again so that they too might be free in the new being of Jesus. Coupled with this fundamental alteration from an old to a unique creation, baptism in the presence of the priestly Jesus signified deliverance from the earthly snares of sin and oppression. Therefore, to become new a slave died and buried the old self of subservience and attachment to sin-slavery and raised up the new self from the baptismal waters into salvation-liberation before the Priest. To be in Jesus is to be in freedom.

Also one has to grasp the significance of the "dying lamb" metaphor in the spiritual. Jesus offered himself as the exemplary sacrifice on the altar for the welfare of all humankind by spilling blood and dying. Quite conscious of this theological and cosmological priestly function, slaves accordingly gave "Honor! unto de dying lamb," and they ran along to partake of the effects of the lamb's death by plunging themselves in the baptismal waters. One honors the lamb through imitation and by service. Hence, under the loving eye of the priestly Jesus, slave baptism marked both a religious ceremonial and theological rite of passage. Reflecting their correct grasp of the New Testament, bondsmen and bondswomen knew that the blood of the Lamb washes one clean of all sin through the ritual of baptism and, at the same time, the dying lamb shifts the new person forever into the domain of Jesus — a theological transformation.

Besides the kingly and priestly offices, slaves acknowledged certain personal attributes of Jesus in the role of friend, converter in conversion, and mother. Slaves deeply cherished friendship; under their circumstances, a friend was one with whom you literally trusted your life. For example, the religious rebellions led by Denmark Vesey and Gabriel Prosser against slavery were both imperiled and betrayed by obedient slaves subservient to white theological idolatry. Such denial of friendship resulted in black men and women losing their lives in these aborted religious uprisings.[51] So friendship did not hold a status of casual acquaintance; quite the opposite, it literally brought either life or death. Understandably, slaves attributed the supreme title of Friend to Jesus, the One who never would forsake you in trials and tribulations. Black folk sang with confidence:

> Old Satan is one busy ole man;
> He rolls dem blocks all in my way;
> But Jesus is my bosom friend;
> He rolls dem blocks away.[52]

Jesus the Friend fights your battles and rolls away all of Satan's blocks. There is some ambiguity about the nature of Satan's blocks in this particular spiritual. But one can understand that slaves laboring in the cotton fields and singing these lines in the presence of the white master wanted to create enough confusion in their words to keep Ole Massa from detecting the full

meaning of Satan and his blocks. Out of necessity slaves developed a deceptive linguistic culture of survival to subvert white theological discovery of
genuine slave thought. But when this spiritual burst forth from the prayerful
lips of black folk in the Invisible Institution, their own sacred political and
cultural space, Satan distinctly and most definitely defined slavery and the
evils of white people. For the slaves, Jesus the "bosom friend" ceaselessly
and consistently destroyed the "blocks" of the devilish slave system and
thereby thwarted death and preserved black life.

In the second personal attribute Jesus plays the central role of converter
and dynamically holds together individual and communal, sacred and secular salvation-liberation. When Jesus entered their lives for the first time,
slaves sensed a profound turning away from sin and evil and a turning
toward Jesus. Black folks named this process conversion, the movement
toward the divineness in Jesus. To share in salvation one underwent a
conversion experience. Fannie Moore relates this testimony of her mother
immediately after the elder's conversion engagement with Jesus:

> "I'se saved. De Lord done tell me I'se saved. Now I know de Lord
> will show me de way, I ain't gwine to grieve no more. No matter how
> much you all done beat me and my chillen de Lord will show me de
> way. And some day we never be slaves."[53]

When Jesus converts a person, he or she no longer can live and see in
the old manner. Jesus communicates directly and instructs the convert that
past sins have been washed away and he or she has been set on a new path.
This new direction of salvation, this new journey or way, provides certainty
about future liberation and a radically new vision about upcoming events
in both individual and collective life. The above conversion witness has
such a definite faith in the new life that, with the word of Jesus, even
whippings and severe punishment cannot deter the proclamation of the
hope of Good News to come.

Certainly the conversion process first frees Fannie Moore's mother from
grievance and heavy burdens. Indeed, her personal transformation gives
her nothing but joy and hope in those things not yet seen but promised;
Jesus frees her personally. But glad tidings do not restrict themselves to
one individual. Moore's mother rejoices not only because Jesus has given
her strength to bear torment and distress, but also because, now having
met Jesus, she knows that "trouble won't last always"; that is, slavery will
soon perish and all things will be made new in the Lord's time. She joins
personal salvation with the future redemption of the entire black community; she links her own existential sacred release with the total deliverance
fulfillment of the complete secular communal predicament. Harking back
to her African cosmological connection between sacred and secular as well
as accurately building off the biblical intertwining of religious and "non-
religious," a converted slave cannot shout for joy unless that joy encom-

passes the deliverance for her co-oppressed humankind.

Resuming the story, Fannie Moore describes her mother in this manner: "My mammy just grin all over her black wrinkled face." Though her face is jet black, with all the consequent negative and harmful implications conjured up under slavery, "Mammy" nonetheless experienced the future vision of earthly liberation granted to her by Jesus' grace in conversion. Not even the whip of the slavemaster prevented Mammy from rejoicing in the Lord always for what the Lord had done for her. Jesus set her on the straight and narrow way. And even when the cowhide lashes had just freshly ripped the skin off of her back, she "just go back to de field a singin.' " Neither the bullwhip nor the backbreaking labor could stop her melodious voice rising to heaven. No doubt she sang with a renewed theological clarity and energy such sentiments as: "I don't feel weary and noways tired" and "Good news, member, good news, And I hearde from heav'n today."[54]

The image of Jesus as mother, the third and last personal attribute, evolves in the following spiritual:

> I heard the voice of Jesus callin'
> Come unto me and live.
> Lie, lie down, weepin' one,
> Rest thy head on my breast
> I come to Jesus as I was,
> Weary and lone and tired and sad,
> I finds in him a restin' place,
> And he has made me glad.[55]

Weighed down with aches and pains caused by forced labor (which yielded absolute profit for whites), black human property struggled to maintain some sense of physical relief and spiritual nourishment. No earthly force could provide an adequate "restin' place" as Jesus could. Slaves needed suckling and nurturing; Jesus bestowed both. Jesus, exhibiting maternal qualities, beckoned them to "rest thy head on my breast," a secure place where those in bondage could relax in the warmth and renewing milk of divine comfort. A mother's sustenance supplies all the physical, intellectual, and spiritual support required to fend off the "troubles of de world" so that Jesus' little children could survive the deadly snares of Satan on their journey down the straight and narrow path. Yes, conversion enabled one to turn away from the vicious entrapments of the sinful slavery system — that is, not succumb to the false omnipotence of white folks — and pursue the righteousness of a new way. But conversion did not completely remove one from the brutal realities of the white man's rawhide whip. Rather, to maintain a faithful and liberated mind, spirit, and body, converted from Satan's path, one needed to lean on the Lord even more.

Thus Jesus extended outstretched arms and offered the manna of life: "Come unto me and live." A child of the Lord needed only to come to

Jesus as any son or daughter would approach a loving parent for restoration and life-giving renewal. For the poor, all the world says No! But Jesus calls the earth's downtrodden to lie down in the cradle of divine arms. Jesus offers soothing solace for and acceptance of one's weary, tired, and sad predicament in life. Summoned from the cotton, sugar cane, or tobacco fields after eighteen hours of work, whipped with one hundred stripes from a cat-o-nine tails, soul crushed when one's babies were sold to the highest slavetrading bidder, raped repeatedly by white slavemasters and their sons,[56] assaulted intellectually by laws forbidding teaching reading and writing to slaves, and kicked into the "nigger box" for several weeks because white people wanted to break a person down, black chattel needed and craved the loving and life-giving breast of Jesus the Mother who "made me glad."

Jesus' offices and attributes brought joy because slaves rightly perceived an incarnational divine purpose that not only favored poor blacks in their lowly social location but also marshalled all of creation for their ultimate deliverance. Rev. Bentley, a black baptist preacher, recounts a sermon he once gave to his co-bondsmen and bondswomen pre-emancipation:

> I remember on one occasion, when the President of the United States came to Georgia. . . . The president came in a grand, beautiful carriage and drove to the best house in the whole town. . . . But a cord was drawn around the house to keep us negroes and other poor folks from coming too near. . . . But the great gentlemen and the rich folks went freely up the steps and in through the door and shook hands with him.

Rev. Bentley draws from the depths of his slave theological knowledge and convictions in order to paint an accurate picture of Jesus' sole incarnational intent. On the one side, he distinguishes the president decked out in all the etiquette of luxury and royal privilege. The president of the United States, the supreme political figurehead, holds the reins of the white power structure. The president assumes his commander-in-chief status as the servant of the nation's economically wealthy. Boasting the best of white, slavemaster Christianity, he struts about under the mantle of absolute prestige with a sense of authoritative wisdom like a king before his subjects. He epitomizes the sacred bearer of white culture and language; he depicts the pinnacle of male dominance in society. Consequently, the president surrounds himself with wealth and with elites like himself; he has a grand, beautiful carriage, the best white house, and the company of the rich white folks.

On the other hand, Rev. Bentley indicates a theological divide symbolized by the "cord." The cord images slavery, a rope used to whip and hang blacks, a barrier forcefully to lock out the poor African Americans from the earth's riches, which they have labored to create. Unlike the rich white folks, blacks huddle at the bottom of the steps to the wealthy white house; they cannot "freely" enter anywhere. They have no grand carriage or fine horses, and they never shake the president's hand. They lack decent clothing, adequate food, and sufficient shelter. No. The cord serves to rope them in and press them to the plow like the harness around a mule's neck. The cord wraps around their mind and spirit to stunt their theological and emotional development. The cord hides and ghettoizes them in the dinginess of the slave quarters. They cannot be seen or heard or plead their cases before earthly "royalty." White people have given them the gift of slavery and a rope, not liberation.

Then Rev. Bentley resumes his sermon:

> Now, did Christ come in that way? Did he come only to the rich? . . .
> No! Blessed be the Lord! He came to the poor! He came to us, and
> for our sakes![57]

Indeed, from the viewpoint of those at the bottom of the steps, Jesus Christ was incarnated in poverty. Was not Jesus born in a manger amid cow dung because the powerful "capitalist" owner of the inn refused admission to wealthless strangers like Mary and Joseph? Did not Jesus become homeless and have to wander in the trash cans of this world—"no place to lay his head"? Jesus too had been hunted like a criminal and outcast by the bloodhounds and rulers of his day. Had not the official and established theologians and religious leaders mocked and scorned Jesus' scriptural interpretations? And finally, did Jesus not endure stoning, whippings, and a bloodied body pierced by nails to a wooden cross like the black ones lynched from a sagging tree on white folks' plantations?

Rev. Bentley preached a theology that resonated with his slave congregation. With rustic but sophisticated clarity, he understood the divine self-emptying into the human Jesus among squalor ("He came to the poor!") and he knew that Jesus with all of God's creation came "for our sakes." Jesus Christ materialized for the poor and intended liberation for the poor. Hence Jesus delivers the Good News of incarnational divine purpose for human freedom.

HUMANITY

Created in Freedom

Perceptions of God and Jesus paved the way for the slaves' notion of a God-given humanity; African American chattel were created in freedom. White theology and white Christian ethical practices notwithstanding, black folk maintained that they were not livestock but sculptured by divine hands and made in a human image of God. Former slave Charlie Moses sums up this belief in theological anthropology: "God Almighty never meant for human beings to be like animals. Us niggers has a soul an' a heart an' a mine. We ain't like a dog or horse."[58] The omnipotence of divine creation cursed white heretical faith claims and produced African American people as God's possessions, fully equipped with necessary and sufficient qualities and resources to function in a liberated manner. Black folk knew who they were and "whose" they were. Though enslaved, bondsmen and bondswomen believed God brought them into this world with a soul, which allowed them to express their spirituality and religious experience. Likewise, God gave them a heart to beat with the feelings and emotions that characterize human capabilities in situations of pathos and exhilaration. They were not uncaring labor items. And God provided them with "a mine" to think independently and rationally about theological phenomena in relation to their full hearts and spirit-filled souls.

A soul signified a space for the Spirit to enter and transform black chattels' servile pariah status. A heart offered a receptacle for the divine compassion for liberation. And a mind provided a vital asset in systematizing the black-God encounter so that the slaves' struggle for liberation was not simply a spontaneous and random assault against the heights of white power, but a deliberate and cohesive sacred worldview marching with the Spirit's warmth and God's passion for justice. So to know in one's mind the freedom of God's liberation movement brought a feeling of the spiritual warmth in one's conversion process from the grip of sinful racism toward the straight and narrow path of righteousness. Moreover, to have this knowledge meant that one possessed the emotional capability and intellectual gift to contrast the former non-converted, enslaved self with a renewed self full of deliverance.

In fact, black folk felt so deeply about their God-given humanity that none yearned to be a "dog or horse," but rather a liberated person. Once planted on free soil, James L. Bradley speaks the truth about his former slave colleagues: "How strange it is that anybody should believe any human being could be a slave, and yet be contented!" Bradley strikes at the heart of white theological anthropology. Whites believe that blacks want to be and enjoy being subservient to white power. This basic fallacy lies in white people interpreting their original God-createdness as normative for black human self-definition. This view defines, at worst, an inherent lowly status to black possibilities for handling major theological issues of the heart, soul, and mind. At best, it showers empty, false praises on black theological endeavors that attempt to imitate and, thereby, hopefully become white. Contrary to white folks' self-created notions of black humanity, Bradley responds with the true image of African American humanity endowed with divine virtues when he proclaims: "I was never acquainted with a slave, however well he was treated, who did not long to be free."[59]

Black people longed for liberation because they possessed not an ingrained lowliness or desire for a white mindset but an inherent and natural gravitation toward freedom. An irrepressible longing to be free engulfed black humanity. In his autobiography, Henry Bibb describes this irresistible divine impulse: "It kindled a fire of liberty within my breast which has never yet been quenched." Thus in the very definition of black humanity, the yearning for liberation burned like a prairie fire, swift and wide. Nothing, neither white supremacy nor theological heresy, could put out this flame sparking slaves to achieve their God-intended full creativity. Bibb believed that the flames of resistance are part of his nature. They were like fire shut up in his bones.

Furthermore, he finds proofs of divine liberation for humankind in what he terms "the inevitable laws of nature's God." He concludes the necessity for black liberation from two divinely created sources. First, from the natural disposition of slaves, in contrast to their existential disposition, the heat of deliverance never wanes or subsides, even after attaining freedom. Second, the tug of liberation is manifest in God's creation of nature, whose laws display the foundational beauty of inevitable liberty unrestricted by human constraints. Echoing the slaves' heart-soul-mind human quest, which whites named treasonous, Bibb concludes: "I could see that the All-wise Creator, had made man a free, moral, intelligent and accountable being."[60]

This subversiveness in black chattels' belief in theological anthropology grew out of their use of the intellect from the perspective of the poor. They knew that humanity spells liberty. Hence slaves constantly had to struggle with unraveling the false theological consciousness existentially imposed by white definition (the slaves' temporary predicament) and the natural basic gift from God (the slaves' created humanity). One can observe the slaves' struggle with these two contradictory states of being in the theological testimony of ex-slave Thomas Likers.

> But as soon as I came to the age of maturity, and could think for myself, I came to the conclusion that God never meant me for a slave, [and] that I should be a fool if I didn't take my liberty if I got the chance.[61]

Once reaching that religious intellectual maturity and thinking for himself without the forbidding noose of white religious catechism, homily, or doctrine, Likers discovered a whole new world of liberation, no doubt in the Bible, nature, and in himself. Like his fellow slaves post-conversion, he perceived a three-part movement of human transformation. In part one the divine had originally molded him out of nothing into freedom; in the second part, the white man had refashioned and skewed his given nature into the warped satanic system of slavery. But, upon reaching theological adulthood, Likers felt beckoned to participate with God through Jesus Christ in the re-creation of himself along the natural intent of unchained humanity. To act as God's co-partner in the third phase of divinely inspired re-created humanity, Likers had to take his liberty through the resistance of politics and the culture of resistance.

Resistance of Politics

Through the grace of the ultimate new humanity of Jesus Christ, attaining the fully re-created African American self required political resistance. In this regard slaves were not lacking in ingenuity, courage, or creativity. God called them in their natural createdness to pursue a human life in opposition to unbridled white power. Accordingly, they devised means and mechanisms for combating slave forces of evil; they resisted individually and collectively for their free humanity.

Individually slaves ran away from plantation labor and the overseers' lashes. Such acts of defiance represented in microcosm slave insurrection by way of sporadic strikes, for African American chattel stood at the core of slavery's successful economic production. Likewise, uncompensated slave work built the infrastructure of the southern territory. Thus individual runaways launched continual sorties against the very underpinnings of white societal well-being when they refused to remain chattel — an instrument of production for white profit. Numerous slave interviews testify to black folks' assertion of humanity by speaking with their feet. Former slave Arthur Greene confirms these illegal departures from white plantations: "Lord, Lord! Yes indeed, plenty of slaves uster run away. Why dem woods was full o' 'em chile." Greene continues to describe a particular acquaintance of his who lived in the wilderness to avoid reintroduction into slavery.

I knowd one man dat took an' run away 'cause his master was so mean an' cruel. He lived in a cave in de groun' fer fifteen yeahs 'fo' Lee's surrender. He made himself a den under de groun'; he an' his wife, an' raised fifteen chillun down dar.[62]

In the wilderness one immersed oneself in God's manifestation of the divine laws of natural freedom. Above we discovered that Henry Bibb's attestation of human freedom was revealed to him in "inevitable laws of nature's God." So the wilderness setting and nature tradition provided both a haven from white imposition of political power over black humanity and a surrendering to and reaffirmation of God's word of deliverance. Black people knew that Yahweh had brought the oppressed Israelite laborers out of Egypt into the wilderness on their way toward Canaan land. God had led them. In this temporary sojourn of the "Hebrew children," Yahweh had provided manna from heaven. Apparently the biblical God also maintained and nourished this same slave who dwelled in a cave for fifteen years. Not only did he survive off of the fruits of the wilderness, but God blessed him and his wife with their own lives and the lives of fifteen children. For them, the wilderness experience supplied protection from ever-present white eyes and assisted their free humanity with sustenance. Truly God could make a way out of no way for those who dared to claim their genuine humanity.

Dwelling in the woods, in a cave in the wilderness, individual contraband slaves, no doubt, sent their voices up to Jesus. One of their spirituals indicates this:

1. I sought . . . my Lord in de wilderness,
   [I seek my Lord] in de wilderness, in de wilderness;
   I sought . . . my Lord in de wilderness,
   For I'm a-going home.

2. I found . . . grace in the wilderness . . .[63]

Why were the woods so full of runaways, slaves who defined their humanity as more than white folks' private property and no less than as free children of God? Because the One who offered freedom to oppressed humanity tarried there on the boundaries of society in opposition to the whitewashed columns of the slavemasters' residence. Therefore, African American bondsmen and bondswomen sought the Lord Jesus in "de wilderness" in order to exist with Jesus, who had conquered Satan's evil hold on all humanity. This momentous victory empowered those who dared to reach out to receive the divine offer of liberation. That is, slaves sought to bring to fruition the full potential of their humanness by making themselves available in the wilderness to Jesus' power to break burdensome yokes and secure deliverance. No wonder they shouted, "I found free grace in the wilderness." Wilderness grace freely offered by Jesus conveyed a calling and commission to realize African American freedom; free grace for human freedom.

Individual political resistance to the desecration of God's black humanity also showed in the slaves' tenacious acts of self-defense. Because God created them, slaves had faith that their very being contained deposits of divine presence; this faith compelled them to use the act of self-defense to preserve these life-giving deposits from the finger of God. In one example, an overseer severely lashed an old black woman for what he perceived as her slow plowing in the fields. In response, the slave woman took her work implement and defended herself. "The woman became sore [from the whipping] and took her hoe and chopped him right across his head, and, child, you should have seen how she chopped this man to a bloody death."

To attack slaves, then, equaled a demonic attack on God within them. One could not allow Satan's earthly devils to prevail over that which belonged to the Kingdom of God. On the contrary, once converted to the path of God through Jesus, black chattel believed they were obligated to wage a battle against the evil forces who relentlessly and untiringly struggled to pull African Americans back to the dominion of Satan's white representatives.

In a similar situation, another overseer expressed his anger toward Aunt Susie Ann and "beat her till the blood run off her on the ground." Aunt

Susie faked unconsciousness, fell to the aggressor's feet, and after the white overseer had put away his whip, Aunt Susie grabbed his weapon and "whips him till he couldn't stand up."[64] God did not intend for God's children to suffer despoiling of their bodies—temples of God's creation—in order for them to clothe themselves again with the idolatrous raiments of sin. Therefore, black chattel had to draw an unyielding line of demarcation between their humanity, crafted by divinity, and a subservient self slaving beneath Satan's rule.

But single acts of resistance were not isolated attempts of black loners who fought politically in an individualistic manner. Neither could one black slave succeed against the monstrosity of the slavery institution from a practical standpoint. Nor was the African American definition of humanity limited to an individual's singular rebellious nature. In fact, the resistance of politics connected individual opposition to communal insurrectionary support; for one person succeeded in achieving full humanity only when the community aided in the deliverance process. The individual black humanity was manifested fully in relation to and in the context of a larger African American communal humanity. "Runaways use to come to our house all de time," relates former slave Mollie Booker, "to git somepin to eat." No one person, no matter how self-reliant, could sustain himself or herself in an absolute condition of isolation from the protective eyes and ears of fellow slaves if he or she wished to succeed in political resistance.

In certain cases the shrewd "antennas" of one group of slaves detected trouble for another group prior to the arrival of imminent danger. For example, Susan Broaddus worked in the white folks' Big House where she overheard the slavemaster exclaim, "Gonna sell 'em, I swear fo' Christ, I gonna sell 'em." But Broaddus could not read or write. Knowing his house servant's illiteracy, the master spelled the names of the two slaves he intended to sell further south into a harder and more cruel life in slavery. Susan Broaddus made "believe I didn't even hear" as the master spoke the letters of the chattel to be sold. But she "was packin' dem letters up in my haid all de time" and the first opportunity she got, she hurried out to the slave quarters and unpacked those letters to her own father "an' say 'em to him jus' like Marsa say 'em." Immediately her father, who could read and spell, notified the two slaves in question. The next day the two "had run away . . . dey never could fin' dose two slaves. Was gone to free land!"[65]

Clearly, to get to free land individual slaves relied upon various schemes of communal ingenuity. However, in the individual-collective definition of African American humanity, the most organized and efficient black political resistance—short of the slaves' victory in the Civil War—was the Underground Railroad with Moses, known more familiarly as Harriet Tubman, leading the way. Harriet Tubman one day set out for freedom by walking off of her white master's plantation in Maryland. Yet God spoke with her in such a way that she believed her own liberated existence, after successfully reaching "up north," contained a void as long as the remainder of her former slave community languished under the whimsical whips of wicked whites "down south." Though she tasted the fruit of freedom, the plight of her fellow oppressed humankind and the weight of their chains under the institution of slavery moved her to return to the land of "Egypt" under God's instruction to set God's people free.

Slaves throughout the South recognized the name of Moses, the captain of the Underground Railroad. For instance, former slave Robert Ellett describes the success of Moses in her elusive moving of slaves from bondage to freedom, from deformed life to full humanity, from Satan's domain to God's kingdom. " 'Moses' would come around ... [and] she would run [slaves] away and get them over near the border line ... the next night on what you call the 'Underground Railroad.' "[66] In sum, slaves employed both individual and collective courage to pursue their God-given free humanity through the resistance of politics against the wickedness of the slavemasters.

The Culture of Resistance

The human resistance expressed politically went hand-in-hand with African American theological notions of a culture of resistance. Since slaves understood their created being through the lens of liberation, they defined, affirmed and carved out an appropriate way of life — a culture of resistance — that provided them with an ethic of survival in the grip of white supremacy. Three instances of this cultural ethic, this lifestyle of black human resistance, will suffice: (a) a taking-not-stealing practice, (b) a duality of survival, and (c) a discourse of solidarity.

Taking-not-stealing. Slavemasters and their paid Christian ministers constantly exhorted slaves against stealing their masters' livestock and, of course, stealing away to freedom. White theologians condemningly preached against such survival activities on the slaves' part as the work of the Anti-Christ and, hence, as anti-Christian beliefs. Instead of obeying their earthly owner, African American chattel rebuffed such doctrinal maxims and differentiated between stealing and taking. Accordingly, they attributed "stealing" to the illegal removal of a fellow bondsman or bondswoman's private property and labeled "taking" the reclaiming of that which they believed the master had wrongfully stolen from the slaves. One former slave sums up the consensus: "Chile, nigger had to steal, an' I know ma mommer didn't tell no lie."

What compelled enslaved African Americans to disobey one of the cardinal rules of white law and risk certain brutal punishment if not death? The necessity of sheer survival mandated that they had to preserve their life, that is, their humanity, by removing the basic provisions of life from their masters' storehouses. "See ole Mars and Missus give us such little rations," comments Marrinda Jane Singleton, "[that it] led her slaves to stealin'." For slaves, authentic religion and a Christian way of life did not mechanically flow from an abstract white set of ethical commands. A perspective from below, a perspective of black human survival, determined right and wrong in contrast to white folks, who held privilege and power in society and could, thus, pontificate, legislate, and propagate the moral axioms of an oppressor class.

Furthermore, while white people ate well and wrote sermons and theology about how their black human property should do good and not succumb to ethical impurities, African American chattel suffered emaciated bodies. The slaves "didn't get nothing but fat meat and corn bread and molasses. And they got tired of that same old thing," comments one ex-slave. Consequently, they had to enter the henhouse "illegally" to get chickens or the smokehouse to get hams or the vegetable patches to procure adequate nourishment. In a word, they had to carve out a way of life and develop a culture of resistance in order to survive slavery's onslaught on their humanity. Posing a rhetorical question, one former slave asks: "That ain't stealin', is it."[67]

Blacks claimed they learned their stealing or taking from the biggest rogue of all, the white master. Another ex-bondsman offers his theological anthropological insight:

All you hear now is 'bout de nigger stealin' from dese here po' white devils. De whole cause of stealin' an' crime is 'cause dey fo'ced the nigger to do hit in dem back days. ... White folks certainly taught niggers to steal. If they had given them enough to eat dey wouldn' have no cause to steal.[68]

This former slave underscores the insidious ethical nature of whites by classifying them with Satan ("po' white devils"). Hence evil human beings, that is white humanity, utilized coercion against the children of God; this resulted in the latter's devising a new survival ethic. Whites did not give blacks enough to eat. On the contrary, they intentionally starved African Americans, consequently giving their slaves a "cause to steal."

Also because slaves were forbidden normal sustenance, black chattel maintained a historical perspective and connection to their native origins. This attachment to their roots led them to a new ethical interpretation. They did not suffer historical amnesia about how whites emerged as the dominating social class in North America. Rather, they rebelled against white practices due to the blatant hypocrisy of white theological instructions about the ethics of black humanity.

"Dey allus done tell us it am wrong to lie and steal," explained Josephine Howard of Texas, "but why did de white folks steal my mammy and her mammy? Dey lives clost to some water, somewhere over in Africy. ... Dat de sinfulles' stealin' dey is."[69]

White folks did the first stealing, "de sinfulles' stealin' dey is." How could slavemasters discourse about the right and wrong of human ethics when they had forcefully taken Africans from their motherland and from the protective and watchful eyes of their parents? In Africa, blacks had lived in their own political kingdoms with indigenous cultural expressions and theological worldviews. Thus white folks, in the slaves' opinion, had committed a grave anthropological sin by stealing a race of people from their God-given space on earth and would forever reap the whirlwind of their own original sin. Specifically, their black property would never submit to white theology as long as African Americans retained their own historical theological consciousness.

The white slavemaster class was not unaware of the theological foundation to black differentiation between stealing and taking. Indeed, a white slavemistress unwittingly surmised the biblical basis for the slaves' "robbing our [whites'] store room, meat house, etc." when she commented that slaves "think it right to steal from us, to spoil us, as the Israelites did the Egyptians."[70] Even in their theological anthropology, black bondsmen and bondswomen upheld a scriptural stance. Just as the Israelites struggled in a land of bondage and formulated their own ethical norms as Yahweh's possessions, black folk perceived their plight similarly. To take from a white pharaoh, then, resulted naturally from what Yahweh-God required of God's created offspring. To fall short of what divinity required would upset the slaves' theological grasp of their original intended purpose — to be free. Hence they developed their culture of resistance with their taking-not-stealing practice. Sarah Fitzpatrick succinctly summarizes:

> Niggers didn't think dat stealin' wuz so bad in dem times. Fak' is dey didn't call it stealin', dey called it takin'. Dey sa, "I ain't takin' fo'm nobody but ma' mistrus an' Marster, an' I'm doin' dat 'cause I'se hongry!"[71]

Duality of survival. Black chattel practiced a way of life that separated a conscious false display of the slave self (in the company of the white master) from an authentic expression of the true African American self (in the presence of fellow enslaved blacks), in order to preserve further their humanity in their culture of survival. Again, slaves viewed their dire straits from the marginalized vantage of ill-equipped underdogs waging a religious and theological war against evil earthly powers. To engage successfully a well-fortified enemy and prove victorious in the long run, then, necessitated the shrewdest possible techniques in one's total way of life. Therefore, on a daily basis slaves cultivated an uncanny astuteness to show one carefully sculptured facade to the white folks in order to live another day.

For example, generally blacks regurgitated all the theological catechisms taught by white theologians and preachers. Blacks did their jobs in the fields and in the Big House just as white folks instructed them. Likewise, blacks carried out a host of other orders forced upon them by slavemasters and mistresses. On the surface, however, this acceptance of the institution of slavery was the "slave" face performed to keep the white folks off balance so that black chattel could survive and plan further the next move in a long-range strategy to be free, to assume full humanity. In his autobiography ex-slave Henry Bibb testifies to this duality of survival: "The only weapon of self defence that I could use successfully, was that of deception."[72] Not only did one defend oneself by politically resisting with physical force, one also preserved one's God-given humanity by culturally, in one's lifestyle, utilizing an ethic of deception.

But such a culture of resistance does not necessarily indicate African American fear of whites. Rather, it suggests a sober assessment that the enemy of slave humanity was a formidable opponent, one who had to be taken very seriously. To avoid becoming "uppity" or "obnoxious" to white folks, blacks faked an acceptance of white anthropological normalcy. Former slave Lunsford Lane wrote the following in his narrative:

> Ever after I entertained the first idea of being free, I had endeavered so to conduct myself as not to become obnoxious to the white inhabitants, knowing as I did their power, and their hostility to the colored people.[73]

Once attaining knowledge of their original liberated humanity created by divinity ("the first idea of being free"), they consciously conducted themselves in such a manner as to keep slavemasters off balance in the black-white relationship on the plantation. So they gave whites the absolute appearance of submissiveness and good-natured cooperation. For the more whites believed they had total control of blacks — minds, souls, and bodies — the more blacks received breathing space to chart their next secret move of resistance for freedom.

This duality of survival also contained an "African American" face in addition to the "slave" face, the former signifying the true humanity of the bondsmen and bondswomen. One gained privileged access into this real face in situations controlled by blacks. For instance, the Invisible Institution represents the premier example. Here, the African American life or humanity forged its unadulterated self with the attendance of God's Spirit. Here the full process of conversion positioned the slave forever along the path of deliverance. The Invisible Institution, in a word, exemplified the raw African African human life. Assembled deep in the woods with only an overturned pot for protection, African Americans found worship space in which to thrive: maintaining morale and thus avoiding demoralization in situations that seemed hopeless; preserving mental sanity and thus avoiding neuroses in the irrational white world; holding on to a sense of definiteness in contrast to a world where slaves lacked control over their present and future; refueling their energy in order to face the next day in a white world full of sorrow; synthesizing memories of African religious structures and practices with reinterpreted Christian beliefs to build a unique black theology under slavery; organizing and plotting slave political and cultural resistance; and praising God for the divine intent of liberation against a world where the Marsa branded them with hot irons as white people's animals. It was this African American face that slaves forever withheld from slavemasters.

During an American Freedmen's Inquiry Commision interview in 1863, former slave Robert Smalls gives the interviewer a hint of this duality of survival:

Q. Do the masters know anything of the secret life of the colored people?

A. No, sir; one life they show their masters and another life they don't show.[74]

Discourse of solidarity. After emancipation, ex-slave Rev. Ishrael Massie informs us about a cave that a runaway had built in the woods during slavery time. Despite the fact that all the bondsmen and bondswomen, including Rev. Massie, "knew whar he [the fugitive] wuz," no one turned him in to his Massa. The good Rev. explains why: "In dem days, ya kno', nigger didn't tell on each other."[75] Indeed, not to tell on each other proved a vital ethical discourse of solidarity and survival for African American humanity. To betray this slave's cave in the southern backwoods was tantamount to desecrating a place where God had revealed the inherent gift of freedom through the inevitable laws of nature. Fellow slaves, then, could not surrender the space in which a co-chattel had liberated himself or herself and, consequently, responded to the free grace of deliverance offered by Jesus in the wilderness. Moreover, an escaped slave graphically symbolized the efficient success of blacks' resistance through politics and culture of resistance. The longer the escapee survived, the more he or she gave fellow sufferers hope for ultimate freedom.

No adherent to a liberation theology, a religious experience constructed out of the poor's biblical interpretation, would break the religious individual-collective connection ("all us slaves knew whar he wuz"). Everyone was aware of the fugitive's whereabouts. But they were likewise knowledgeable of their own African American and (perhaps more unconsciously) African tradition, which correctly perceived the freedom of the individual immensely benefiting the potential or realized emancipation of the collective and vice versa. Also, breaking the discourse of solidarity ("didn't tell on each other") would be the slaves' self-admission of submission to white folks' religious and theological instructions concerning "slaves obey your masters."

Similarly, surrender to white theology would confirm blacks' actual allegiance to the kingdom of Satan—the peculiar institution of slavery. All that the Invisible Institution stood for would amount to nought. Contrary to surrendering, those words "don't tell on each other" articulated slaves' dogged refusal and life-and-death determination not to commit suicide, that is, not to mimic white theology. On another plantation former slave Mrs. Jennie Patterson echoes the sacred vow: "You see we never tole on each other."[76] Though legally private property belonging to whites, slaves defiantly refused to tell on each other in order to uphold their natural African American humanity. God had created them and, to keep the faith in God's grace, they used all possible political and cultural resistance.

CONCLUSION

After successfully defeating the Confederates in the Civil War, four million African Americans claimed their freedom. We saw how they attributed that historic accomplishment to God sending "de war" and to Jesus as warrior and liberator. Between 1619, when the initial group of Africans stolen from their homeland arrived in the New World, and 1865, the conclusion of the Civil War, black chattel mixed together the memory of their African traditional religions with biblical Christianity. In particular, they illegally and secretly met and worshiped in the Invisible Institution. Their hidden religious gatherings allowed them to create a coherent and dynamic theology, which, if today's African American church is to take itself seriously, cannot be ignored. How can contemporary black faith gatherings continue to drift on and be tossed to and fro by the battering and harmful waves of white theology without an authentic Christian rudder? How can the black church call itself church if it refuses to study systematically and learn from the profound experience of its slave forebears with the divine? Truly, over two hundred years of African American "God-talk" provide an abundant source for the development of a contemporary black theology.

This chapter has only scratched the surface. Still we have discovered the beginnings of some of the key elements needed in the constructive task for today's black theology. For instance, we saw how slave theology verified the intimate link between the church and the community, a connection that does not pit the sacred against the secular as certain elements in European-American theology do. Because God rules all of creation, slaves understood that the political and the cultural dimensions of life carried theological implications. Moreover, to make religion private and leave the secular to the secularist is, in fact, to surrender black humanity to heretical faith assertions perpetrated by the demonic dimensions of white theology.

We discovered, also, the emphasis on the communal ethic in the Invisible Institution. Drawing on their African traditional religions and the Bible, especially the Old Testament, slaves could only comprehend total deliverance as including both the individual and the community. Thus they did not fall prey to the white capitalist theological precept that glorifies individualism and a capitalist, private-property democracy. Today's black theology has to promote individuality and communalism, and not individualism and selfish motivations.

Furthermore, the black theology of the Invisible Institution tells us about the importance of perseverance through cross-bearing. For over two centuries African Americans endured and resisted white Christian assaults on black humanity. Through prayer and proper supplication to God, with Jesus as the captain of their old ship of Zion, and through the Spirit's empowerment, black folks made it to emancipation. Paraphrasing old slave wisdom, "God may not come when you call him, but he's right on time!"

Thus the slaves' religious story verifies a contemporary black theological emphasis on doing theology from the perspective of the black poor. To deny this theological privilege—to speak of God from below—is to betray the African American church's Christian tradition. We only hear God's word of liberation and salvation from the position of God's hearing and freeing a marginalized community as that chosen community moves toward justice. Moreover, since God freely gives deliverance to those who have nothing to lose in this world (that is, God's grace of freedom operates and reveals itself in the total life of an oppressed communal people), then black theology today must discern the signs of the times in the political and cultural life of the black church and community. And so, God's self-revelation shows in attempts to alter unjust power relations and in the linguistics, thought forms, and way of life of the have-nots.

Christian slaves encountered divine *agape*, which demanded that God's love be made real and true through unyielding partiality to the poor. God's love was not an abstract dogma or a two-faced lie. God's love for humanity frees all only by removing oppressive structures and systemic exploitation. Then and only then will the abolition of poverty take place and the attendant universal pain disappear.

Also, for the slaves, Jesus was the decisive intermediary of God's loving liberation for oppressed humanity. Therefore, as the slave spiritual claims, Jesus won't "die no mo'." Slave theology employed metaphors for both Jesus' kingly and priestly offices and Jesus' attributes of friend and mother. Black theology in slave religious experiences required such descriptions because slaves needed hope in their warfare against evil visible principalities and powers; they had to have the nurturing of friendship and wisdom.

Enslaved Africans realized that God had created them originally with a free soul, heart, and mind. Yet white American Christians had re-created them in the demonic image of a distorted Christianity. Hence, for the slave, the purpose of humanity was to show fully the spark of God's created equality implanted deep within black breasts. To return to original creation, then, African American slaves pursued a resistance of politics and a culture of resistance.

Finally, slave religious experience based itself on the Bible. As one slave graphically confessed:

I am no mathematician, no biologist, neither grammarian, but when it comes to handling the Bible I knocks down verbs, break up prepositions and jumps over adjectives. Now I tell you something—I am a God-sent man.[77]

Consequently, in their knocking down, breaking up, and jumping over, African Americans under slavery glued themselves to a theology filled with the let-my-people-go witness of Yahweh in the Old Testament and Jesus, the liberator of the poor in the New Testament. It is this faith, this black theology, that powered them through over two centuries of white theological heresy and white supremacy. Therefore, when their judgment (freedom) day arrived, we can appreciate the following account of a former slave regarding the Civil War's end:

[When freedom came] we was dancin' an' prancin' an' yellin' wid a big barn fir jus' ablazin' an' de white folks not darin' to come outside de big house. Guess dey [the slaves] made 'em up [spirituals], 'cause purty soon ev'ybody fo' miles around was singin' freedom songs. One went like dis:

I's free, I's free, I's free at las'!
Thank God A'mighty, I's free at las'![78]

African Americans in bondage were the first to position freedom practically at the core of Christianity in the New World and, at the same time, liberation at the heart of theology in North America. Starting with the Invisible Institution, the foundation of the African American community's heartbeat for emancipation comes from the black church. Therefore, any constructive black theology of liberation must center on the black church. Though God moves in diverse ways within the African Americans' freedom journey, the black church is the oldest, most organized, and most influential gathering of justice-loving folk among black people.

We have begun the search for appropriate "shoes" with a look at faith commitments suggested in slave religious experiences. A liberative African American church legacy and its theology are derived from slavery times.

This belief in justice reminds all non-Christians and nonreligious movements that conceptually and historically the black church has had a struggling tradition on this side of Jordan. And it challenges the so-called secular black community representatives to dig within and rely on the same African American freedom impulse.

2

Black Women's Spirituality of Funk

I have to trust the uncontrolled, wild parts of myself, it's really danger-
ous. . . .
   What was valued was [Nel and Sula's] friendship . . . it was spiritual,
of first order priority; the 'other I.'

Toni Morrison[1]

From slavery to today, African American women have contributed their unique spirituality to black survival and liberation. In the face of white and black male and white female discrimination, African American women have simply claimed their right to be God's children on earth. Often they acted out their leadership roles in traditional church structures. In other situations they crafted new models of religious witness however and whenever they felt called to say and do God's word of freedom. Black women expressed emancipating spiritual power on the divine, not "man's" agenda.

Today African American women religious scholars name their survival and liberation God-encounters as "womanist theology." Womanist theologians acknowledge a belief connection to all humanity, whether male or female, black or white. Yet there is a difference, and it is this disturbing and freeing uniqueness black women celebrate. It is disturbing because for too long others have attempted to stifle God's winds of spiritual life in African American women. It is freeing because no human denials can forever keep hidden the persistent presence of a spirit-filled black woman.

In fact, Jacquelyn Grant raised this challenge in the first womanist article in the contemporary period. She accused black theology of maintaining the invisibility of African American women. How could a male black theology hoist the banner of liberation when black women suffer from pains of gender discrimination?[2] Womanists since have asserted an irrevocable presence in all theology. In the words of womanist Katie G. Cannon:

> Black women live out a moral wisdom in their real-lived context that
> does not appeal to the fixed rules or absolute principles of the white-

oriented, male-structured society. Black women's analysis and appraisal of what is right or wrong and good or bad develop out of the various coping mechanisms related to the conditions of their own cultural circumstances.[3]

Womanists bring fresh air to the discussion. They are less inhibited by the constraints of "orthodox" (that is, Euro-American and male) doctrines. Such freshness breathes a newness more akin to what God would have us do to free our people.

For instance, Delores S. Williams has delved into literary fiction and named "a language of the spirit." It is this spirit talking that has taken women beyond traditional boundaries, out to the margins, into the mainstream, wherever they want to go in the church, society, the Bible, and educational institutions for discovering (and declaring) their own voices.[4]

Clearly a constructive black theology of liberation requires African American women's spirituality as a resource. And the "uncontrolled" and "dangerous" dimensions of Toni Morrison's fictional female communities offer a fertile starting point for constructive work. The theological imagination in Morrison's characters helps us to understand poor black women's spirituality as a cornerstone of theological development.

In Morrision's novels, poor black women's spirituality is a manifestation of *God's spirit of liberation incarnated in their values and traditions*. Such a spirit permeates particular women while, simultaneously, transcending the limitations of a single individual. In fact, the potency of poor black women's values and traditions lies in their ability to deliver and sustain each succeeding generation, their mark of immortality. Spirituality is embodied in concrete people, which alerts us to the fact that we only know the work of the spirit by locating the dynamic interplay between specific values and traditions. Real embodiment testifies to material reality. Yet, though the spirit hovers in identifiable groups of women, it goes beyond them, beyond the material. God, therefore, is a spiritual presence who is greater than (transcends) the Christian and non-Christian representations in any one person or community depicted in Toni Morrison's stories.

To pursue a deeper understanding of poor black women's spirituality and its challenges and holistic contributions to black theology, then, this chapter will first assess Morrison's own use of the terms "The Thing" and "The Funk" in their connection to African American women's spiritual practices and, second, develop an extended treatment of the actual *values* and *traditions* that are the heart of that same spirituality.

The poor black women in these stories act out their faith in God's spirit of liberation through their values and traditions. God's spirit of liberation and poor black women's faith in this spirit coalesce in values and traditions permeating the entire lives of these women. These women do not do theology with proclamations of systematic dogma. Poor African American women do not have the privilege to write. However, it is the theologian's task (1) to make apparent the spiritual movement of God's freedom in the midst of these women's practical activity, and (2) to systematize their practical activity of faith in God's spirit of justice. Thus a spirituality arising out of black women's faith experiences pushes black theology to an encounter with God's holistic liberation.

THE THING AND THE FUNK

The Thing is a demonic, sterile, and life-denying spirituality that oppresses poor black women. Consequently, one cannot grasp their spirituality without noting the context in which these women find themselves. In contrast to the Thing, the Funk comprises women's spirit of liberation. It is found in values and traditions used by poor black women in order to survive and free themselves from the evil grip of the Thing.

The Thing

In *The Bluest Eye* Claudia, a very poor African American girl who narrates Morrison's first novel, pinpoints the all-encompassing presence of the Thing when she comments: "The Thing to fear was the Thing that made her beautiful, and not us."[5] The "her" refers to a new girl in school, a half-white "high-yellow dream child" with "sloe green eyes."[6] The "us" refers to poor black females such as Claudia. The Thing symbolizes the totality of black women's oppression. Fundamentally, it suggests a sinister spirituality that weaves throughout all forms of oppression faced by these women. It is a political attack, in the sense that it subverts black women's power to control the space they occupy on earth, and it is a cultural attack, in the sense that it negatively defines the identity of African American women. Briefly, the Thing represents an attempt to negate God's spirit of liberation expressed through poor black women. Thus a war unfolds between suffering brought about by the demonic, on the one hand, and grace freely given by God's spirit, on the other.

More specifically, Claudia fleshes out the face of the Thing's spirit in the following observation:

> Everybody in the world was in a position to give [poor black women] orders. White women said, "Do this." White children said, "Give me that." White men said, "Come here." Black men said, "Lay down." They had carried a world on their heads.[7]

Here, in Toni Morrison's writings, poor black women face triple expressions of the spirit of the Thing. These women share the unique spiritual pain of three facets of injustice in North American society—sexism (as victims of white and black male dominance); racism (as victims of white male and female supremacy); and poverty (as victims of economic exploitation). The convergence of these three realities exists only for poor African American women. They indeed carry "a world on their heads." As women, they are victimized by the desires of both white and black males ("come here" and "lay down"). As African Americans, they experience racism from both white men and women ("come here" and "do this"). And as mere labor commodities, they are subjected to the foreman-like commands signified by little white children ("give me that"). In sum, the politics and culture of the Thing reveal themselves in the totality of poor black women's lives through a complex web of gender, race and poverty that strangles the spirit of these women.

Gender. As women, the characters in Toni Morrison's novels experience the spirituality of the Thing defining both their cultural identity, as objects satisfying the sexual appetite of men, and their political identity, by denying women's right to self-determination and independence from men's power and control. For example, two white males on the Sweet Home plantation in *Beloved*[8] rape the slave woman Sethe. They do not violate in the classic understanding of rape; there is no forced vaginal penetration. However, their violation of her suggests an even more violent rape of Sethe's own definition of her female self. What these spiritually sick whites do instead is knock her to the ground in a barn and suck the milk from her breast. Sethe oozed with milk because she was full of drink for her baby daughter. Though the two rapists see Sethe as a female cow, without a spirit, in fact the taking of her milk signifies the theft of that which represents one of the defining characteristics of her spiritual motherness, part of the suste- nance that defines her culturally as a woman. These white men forcefully take the life-sustaining material and spiritual food meant for her child.

Similarly, Ella, another poor black woman in *Beloved*, accounts for the degree of white male sexual pathology by "the lowest yet." Ella's "puberty was spent in a house where she was shared by father and son, whom she called 'the lowest yet.' " Ella did not have the power to name her spiritual identity as a woman during her teenage and young adult life. On the con- trary, she grew up as a plaything for the morbid sexual taste of a white father-son tag team. Because her womanist spirit suffered such a grave encroachment in so many unspeakable acts and for so many years, Ella measured all attacks on women through her own historical confrontation with the Thing. "A killing, a kidnap, a rape. . . . Nothing compared to 'the lowest yet.' "[9]

The poor black women of Morrison's narratives also endure lack of gender self-definition in several of their relationships with black men. Milk- man, the protagonist in *Song of Solomon*, tires of sexually conquering his cousin Hagar because he no longer feels that she is a challenge to his warped male sexual ego. And, furthermore, given the ratio of black men to women in the novel, he believes he can pick and choose his sexual objects from black or white females.

Now, after more than a dozen years, he was getting tired of her. Her eccentricities were no longer provocative and the stupefying ease with which he had gotten and stayed between her legs had changed from the great good fortune he'd considered it, to annoyance at her refusal to make him hustle for it.

Milkman no longer defines Hagar as a woman but as "the third beer . . . the third, the one you drink because . . . what difference does it make?"[10] He pictures part of her womanist nature as a beer—a thing without a difference, without a spirit.

Likewise, in *The Bluest Eye* Pauline Breedlove, a poor black woman with a disabled foot, suffers from her husband's distorted definition of their marriage. At the beginning of their relationship both saw their sexuality as an equal sharing of their mutual spiritual selves. For her, it used to "be rainbow all inside." Later her husband, Cholly, treats her as a mere receptor of his physical release. Analyzing the latter part of their marriage Pauline says: "But it ain't like that anymore. Most times he's thrashing away inside me before I'm woke, and through when I am."[11]

But some black males' inclination to define black women as pleasure receptors in Morrison's novels does not begin with the later institution of marriage. For some, this naming starts with little black girls. For instance, Nel and Sula, the two main characters in *Sula*, habitually confront catcalls and receive new names whenever they walk past the Time and a Half Pool Hall in order to get to an ice cream store. Old and young black men lustfully watch them. "Nel and Sula walked through this valley of eyes chilled by the wind and heated by the embarrassment of appraising stares. . . . Pig meat. The words were in all [the men's] minds."[12]

However, the spirit of the Thing does not only deny African American women's spirituality by culturally defining women's sexuality in a patriarchal manner, it also takes away women's political right to self-determination. The Thing prevents the free spirit of womanist spirituality and thus determines, controls, and maps out what is woman's space and place. Again in *Sula*, we find Nel and Sula in conversation; this time they are discussing whether a woman has the power to control her own life. In a moment of submission to the power of the Thing, Nel tells Sula:

"You can't have it all, Sula. . . . You can't do it all. You a woman and a colored woman at that. You can't act like a man. You can't be walking around all independent-like, doing whatever you like, taking what you want, leaving what you don't."[13]

Here Nel cannot conceive of a womanist spirituality that lets women make decisions about their own lives independently of men. Note how Nel does not admonish Sula to decide and claim her own space by herself and then raise her own views to a man. No. Nel warns Sula to make all decisions as an absolute appendage to a man, implying that women's alternatives and ideas about place are subordinate to men's.

Race. The Thing's demonic spirituality expresses itself by denying black women the freedom to control the spiritual definition of their own gender. In this sense womanist spirituality connects with white women who suffer from patriarchy. We see this in an encounter between Sethe and Amy, a poor white woman in *Beloved*. Sethe has escaped from slavery but hovers on the verge of death. While Sethe contemplates her mortality out in the woods, Amy comes along and nurses Sethe back to life and sends Sethe to the next stop on her freedom journey. Amy tells Sethe how she (Amy) was an indentured servant fleeing from whippings and the cruelty of male patriarchy. Both women have been objects of male dominance; in this sense they are spiritual mates.

Yet not only does the Thing attack black women's reality in the area of gender, it also separates black women's spirituality from that of white women because of racial discrimination.[14] Although Amy heals Sethe's feet and tends to the bruises on her back, thus exhibiting a common gender solidarity, Amy still calls Sethe a "nigger." Likewise, Sethe still has to call Amy "ma'am."[15] So, the Thing is more insidious for poor black women. Even within black-white sister spirituality, black women suffer more because white culture rules as normative.

The same white-skinned privileges separate black and white female relations in *Tar Baby*. Margaret Street prides herself for her classic white liberal attitude toward her black cook Ondine. Historically, Margaret used to spend hours talking with Ondine and even working in the kitchen with her. But when Ondine begins publicly to expose Margaret because Margaret tortured her own son, Margaret puts Ondine in her place by shouting: "Shut up! You nigger! You nigger bitch!"[16] Here Margaret exemplifies white women's option to exercise their white cultural privileges over poor African American women. Margaret wields her white power to define Ondine's black identity as a female dog.

Indeed, the Thing begins to work against a positive womanist racial spirituality at a very young age. In *Sula*, the little black girl Nel has to hear commands continually from her own mother (Mrs. Wright), who exhorts her to pull her nose with a clothespin and thus make her black nose white.

> When Mrs. Wright reminded Nel to pull her nose, she would do it enthusiastically but without the least hope in the world. "While you sittin' there, honey, go 'head and pull you nose." "It hurts, Mamma." "Don't you want a nice nose when you grow up?"[17]

A nice pair of nostrils is a white woman's nose because the African cultural features of poor black women must be obliterated with a clothespin, even if "It hurts, Mamma."

But the depths of the Thing's white supremacy in the lives of poor black women reveals itself most pointedly in *The Bluest Eye.* "It had begun with Christmas and the gift of dolls. The big, the special, the loving gift was always a big, blue-eyed Baby Doll,"[18] narrates little black girl Claudia. For her, these premium Christmas gifts symbolized the unrelenting attempt by society to eradicate the beauty of her black culture. Society told her that the epitome of beauty was a blond, blue-eyed Shirley Temple doll with pale skin and rosy cheeks. "I knew," continues Claudia, "that the doll represented what they thought was my fondest wish." Summing up the process that denied her own African American cultural identity, Claudia concludes:

> Adults, older girls, shops, magazines, newspapers, window signs—all the world had agreed that a blue-eyed, yellow-haired, pink-skinned doll was what every girl child treasured. "Here," they said, "this is beautiful, and if you are on this day 'worthy' you may have it."[19]

To be "worthy" of the gift of whiteness can drive black women insane. In fact, Pecola, one of Claudia's black playmates, comes to believe that she has finally received the gift of blue eyes. Pecola suffers a mental derailment and goes insane. She "stepped over into madness" and was forever seen "searching the garbage" while both of her arms twitched like chicken wings.[20] The Thing succeeded with Pecola, a beautiful, poor little black girl. It broke her own self-love for her cultural identity. It forced her into a psychological suicide in quest of a sickly female whiteness. And it drove her into the realm of spiritual self-destruction.

Though gender oppression unites black and white women's spirituality (against men, white and black), racial discrimination (perpetrated by whites, male and female) links womanist spirituality with the survival of the entire African American community. When it comes to white supremacy, the Thing knows no gender difference for black folk. For instance, in *Beloved*, Stamp Paid, an old black man who helps slaves escape on the Underground Railroad, capsulizes the Thingness of white oppression. He reflects on the years of lynchings ("human blood cooked in a lynch fire" so much that the "stench stank"), genocide ("whole towns wiped clean of Negroes"), whippings, schools burned, and property stolen. Stamp concludes with a query to the divine: "What are these people? You tell me, Jesus. What are they?"[21] Not *who* are they, but what type of Thing were white folk anyway?

Poverty. Finally, the oppressive spirit of the Thing displays itself by relegating black women to poverty. We have seen poor black women victimized both politically and culturally by male gender chauvinism, and culturally by white racial discrimination. The Thing also extends its kingdom to include economic exploitation—poverty. In this manner black women lack the political right and power to determine the destiny of their own daily sustenance and livelihood.

The majority of Toni Morrison's main characters find themselves trapped in a web of forced economic inequality.[22] These are hardworking black mothers, grandmothers, sisters, daughters, and wives struggling to hold on to a job or fighting to make a way out of no way.

> They ran the houses of white people, and knew it. When white men beat their men, they cleaned up the blood and went home to receive abuse from the victim. They beat their children with one hand and stole for them with the other. The hands that felled trees also cut umbilical cords; the hands that wrung the necks of chickens and butchered hogs also nudged African violets into bloom; the arms that loaded sheaves, bales, and sacks rocked babies into sleep. They patted biscuits into flaky ovals of innocence — and shrouded the dead. They plowed all day and came home to nestle like plums under the limbs of their men.[23]

More specifically, Pauline Breedlove (*The Bluest Eye*) labored as a cook and laundrywoman in the house of middle-class white folks. A slave on the Sweet Home plantation, Baby Suggs (*Beloved*) worked in the Big House. Eva Peace (*Sula*) raised her children on three beets. Some folks rumored that she later left town and cut off her own leg in order to collect insurance money for her children's survival. Pilate Dead (*Song of Solomon*) was a bootlegger. And Therese, the blind woman, held an occasional washer-woman position, while her friend, Alma Estee, cleaned toilets at the airport (*Tar Baby*).

The poverty status of African American women in Morrison's novels also teaches us how the Thing's spirit caused class divisions among black women, thus underscoring the unique assault on *poor* black women's spirituality. For instance, Geraldine, a bourgeois colored woman, taught her son, Junior, the class distinctions within the black community. "She had explained to him the difference between colored people and niggers. They were easily identifiable. Colored people were neat and quiet; niggers were dirty and loud."[24] One day Junior tricks Pecola, a poor little black girl, into his house. When his mother, Geraldine, eventually arrives home, she looks at Pecola.

> Saw the dirty torn dress, the plaits sticking out on her head, hair matted where the plaits had come undone, the muddy shoes with the wad of gum peeping out from between the cheap soles, the soiled socks. . . . She saw the safety pin holding the hem of the dress up.

With hatred, revulsion, and a coldblooded spirituality, colored Geraldine stares at little black Pecola and says: "Get out. . . . You nasty little black bitch. Get out of my house."[25]

But the class cleavages (the Thing's spirituality of poverty) is more than an individual demon in Morrison's narratives. They also reflect a systemic economic evil which squashes poor African American women to mere labor commodities in human relations based on ruthless, uncaring profit. As a result, these women do not control their lives politically or economically.

Perhaps Valerian Street, a white entrepreneur in *Tar Baby*, epitomizes this economic reality most clearly. Valerian inherits a capitalist corporation that makes candy. Not wanting to spend the rest of his life "working" too hard, he purchases an island in the Caribbean and retires there. One Christmas he summarily fires two poor Caribbean servants merely because they take some apples to eat. Son, a mysterious black visitor at Valerian's island home, describes the exploitative spiritual values and traditions of Valerian and the economic system they represent:

[Valerian] had been able to dismiss with a flutter of the fingers the people whose sugar and cocoa had allowed him to grow old in regal comfort; although he had taken the sugar and cocoa and paid for it as though it had no value, as though the cutting of cane and picking of beans was child's play and had no value; but he turned it into candy, the invention of which really was child's play, and sold it to other children and made a fortune.

Linking Valerian and his economic system to the demonic, Son tells how Valerian paid poor people "according to some scale of value that would outrage Satan himself." But these harmful spiritual values and traditions did not surprise the poor because the rich "loved property," so much that "they had killed it soiled it defecated on it."[26]

Thus the Thing's spirit incarnates in the gender, racial, and poverty persecution and repression of poor African American women. Essentially, the spirit of the Thing flows from a larger theological notion held by white males of privilege in the novels. Commenting on Sethe, who has just attempted to "free" her children by killing them and thus avert a return to slavery on the Sweet Home plantation, Schoolteacher (a white overseer on the same plantation) arrogantly remarks: "See what happened when you overbeat creatures God had given you the responsibility of?"[27] Consequently, these white men have faith in a theology in which God's spirit has anointed them to be responsible over poor black women. This is the essence of the Thing.

The Funk

Given the reality of the Thing, who will speak for these poor African American women? Who will defend their unique cultural identities and the right to determine their own political space on this earth? Fundamentally, for a Christian the question is whether or not God has forgotten the cries and predicament of these "little ones" and has left them to the devilish spirit of the Thing. Quite the contrary, God's grace has given these women the liberating spirituality of the Funk.

Below, in discussing values and traditions, we will develop a detailed and systematic treatment of womanist spirituality—or the Funk—as it is revealed specifically in the values and traditions of poor black women. However, in general terms, womanist spirituality can be defined as the Funk—entailing the resources for survival and freedom implanted by the divine spirit's dwelling in the total lives of the women found in Toni Morrison's novels. The Funk is a free spirit constantly warding off the Thing's oppressive attacks.

In *The Bluest Eye* Morrison highlights the intentional designs of the Thing when it grooms and prepares a section of African American women to defeat the Funk. Black women susceptible to the Thing's reign, Morrison writes,

> go to land-grant colleges, normal schools, and learn how to do the white man's work with refinement: home economics to prepare his food; teacher education to instruct black children in obedience; music to soothe the weary master and entertain his blunted soul. . . . In short, how to get rid of the funkiness. The dreadful funkiness of passion, the funkiness of nature, the funkiness of the wide range of human emotions.

The Thing does not want black women to have a humanity or human spirit ("the wide range of human emotions"). Over against the God-given spirituality of these women (that is, the funkiness of their created nature and the funkiness of their passion for a total liberated existence), the Thing seeks to convert these women into a life of dead spirituality, where poor black women no longer have their own identities and power to control their own lives. Referencing the struggle between the Thing and the Funk, Morrison resumes: "Wherever it erupts, this Funk, they wipe it away." The battle between the domain of the Funk (womanist spirituality empowered by the presence of God's spirit of liberation) and the domain of the Thing (the political and cultural spiritual death of gender, racial, and economic oppression) continues "all the way to the grave."[28]

Oftentimes those entrapped by the Thing call the Funk "wild blood." In *Sula*, Helene Sabat's mother was a Creole whore in New Orleans. Both Helene and her grandmother detested the profession of Helene's mother. Overreacting to the mother's immoral activities, the grandmother removed Helene from her mother and also crushed any sense of womanist spirituality in the child.

> The grandmother took Helene away from the soft lights and flowered carpets of the Sundown House and raised her under the dolesome

eyes of a multicolored Virgin Mary, counseling her to be constantly on guard for any sign of her mother's wild blood.[29]

Here we discover how the deadly spirit of the Thing can disguise itself under the mantle of authentic Christianity in order to control the liberating spirit of the Funk by characterizing it as wild blood. Helene grew up worshiping a sorrowful and melancholy Virgin Mary. All her life she believed in a white, gloomy, grief-filled Christianity that taught African American women not to free themselves but rather to maintain the status quo of gender, racial, and economic enslavement.

Yet the Funk persists. It empowers poor black women to confront face to face powerful representatives of the Thing. After sixteen years of slaving for a white male of privilege (a Mr. Sawyer), Sethe (*Beloved*) finally reacts "wildly" to her boss. She boldly states: "Don't talk to me, Mr. Sawyer. Don't say nothing to me this morning." Responding to Sethe's declaration of womanist independence as if she has gone completely insane, Sawyer replies: "What? What? What? You talking back to me?" Sethe tenaciously holds her ground and shouts: "I'm telling you don't say nothing to me."[30] It appears as if God's spirit of liberation had finally enveloped Sethe and moved her to act freely. The fact that she took the risk to defend herself against Sawyer, her employer, was no small matter. Because her income from this job helped to feed and keep her children alive, her move toward the freedom of the Funk could have brought literal starvation and death to her family.

The Funk not only allows poor African American women to stand up against a wicked gender-racial-poverty spirituality, it also gives them confidence to move beyond the boundaries defined by the Thing. Gripped by womanist spirituality, Sula Peace, in *Sula*, one day decides to travel and educate herself. Without announcement, she departs from her small hometown and in the next ten years goes to college and travels to Nashville, Detroit, New Orleans, New York, Philadelphia, Macon, and San Diego. In the 1920s it would have been extremely difficult for a black person, a poor person, or a woman to move independently about the United States without the authority of a white person, a rich person, or a male of privilege. Yet Sula's Funk empowered her to travel beyond the prohibited boundaries of gender, racial, and economic restrictions. Her funky free passion for a holistic life allowed her to define herself culturally as a free black woman. Consequently, she assumed the risk to define politically what to do in life and where to walk on earth. Her self-definition and self-direction beyond the status quo boundaries exhibited the freeing spirit of the Funk.

We have seen how the Funk is womanist spirituality—God's spirit of liberation dwelling and incarnated in poor black women's total reality. This spirit of freedom authorizes them to challenge the rule of the Thing. In opposition, the demonic spirit of the Thing (expressed through gender, racial, and economic inequalities) doggedly hounds poor black women. Culturally, the Thing produces a sterile spirituality and prevents the naming of women's self; no longer are women themselves and connected to themselves. Once the Thing grips them culturally (defines them as something else), they also become political supporters of their own three-pronged oppression.

On the other hand, the Funk undermines the Thing culturally and politically. God's spirit of liberation gives women the power to know themselves and be connected to themselves culturally. The ability to know who they are and thus define themselves aids these women in the transformation of the conditions in which they find themselves politically. The ability to determine and alter the space and conditions around them, in turn, provides these women more freedom further to define themselves. In brief, freedom to be themselves (a cultural act of spiritual liberation) stands in a vibrant relationship with freedom to determine their space (a political act of spiritual liberation). The politics and culture of womanist spirituality interpenetrate.

Now, having established the context of and the need for poor African American women's spirituality in opposition to the Thing and having explored womanist spirituality in general terms with an explanation of the Funk, we can move to a systematic engagement with the heart of womanist spirituality—God's spirit of liberation incarnated in poor black women's values and tradition.

VALUES OF CONNECTEDNESS

Womanist spirituality entails the relationship between a series of four "values of connectedness": to the poor black woman herself; to her immediate community; to her broader community; and to nature. In Toni Morrison's novels these values of connectedness facilitate black women's survival and liberation toward wholeness, a movement to realize a full life granted by God's spirit. Thus values of connectedness instruct black women how to name (culturally) who they are and to claim (politically) this world created by God.

Connectedness to Herself

While still young children, poor black girls realize, somewhat automatically, their connection to themselves. For example, Claudia and her sister Frieda, in *The Bluest Eye*, have a positive self-identity at a very early age. "Guileless and without vanity, we were still in love with ourselves then. We felt comfortable in our skins, enjoyed the news that our senses released to us, admired our dirt, cultivated our scars."[31] Before society (the Thing) socializes them negatively, these two little girls consciously acknowledge their ease with themselves, with their black skins. They were in tune with their senses and how they enabled them both to communicate with and to listen to the world around them. They accepted the material stuff that made up their bodies, even their scars and dirt. During their initial stages of life, poor little black girls naturally accept and connect with the self created by God. Essentially, womanist values of self-connectedness mean loving themselves—"ourselves," "our skins," "our senses," "our dirt," and "our scars."

Indeed, womanist spirituality is anchored in self-connectedness and self-love ("guileless and without vanity"). Consequently, these women cannot relate to their immediate community, broader community, and nature until they appreciate the value of self-connectedness God freely gives them. They may be poor, black, and women; but they are still loved children of God. God's empowering divine love infuses their created nature. The Holy's love for them to be liberated in all spheres of their lives fashioned these women. And so to love themselves is to also love God's spirit of liberating love that dwells in them.

Grasping the potency of this perspective, for instance, Nel (in *Sula*) one day discovers herself through her *own* eyes and loves herself. Consequently, she begins to fight the manifestation of the Thing that engendered her self-hate. "There [in a mirror] was her face, plain brown eyes, three braids and the nose her mother hated." All of society condemned her because of her African American features—her face, her hair, eye color, and her nose. All of society defined her self-value in relation to white standards of culture and worth. This poor little girl suffered from the impossibility of becoming a Shirley Temple. But suddenly the implanted spirit of God's love grips her and sends shivers up her spine. "She looked for a long time [at her real self] and suddenly a shiver ran through her." Her realization of herself, her conversion or born-again experience, forces her to say simply and profoundly, "I'm me . . . Me." Self-connectedness and self-love send her on an entirely new way and empower her. "Each time she said the word *me* there was a gathering in her like power, like joy, like fear." In the midst of this charismatic experience, she murmured, "Oh, Jesus, make me wonderful."[32] She gained power by gaining herself. It was like joy shut up in her bones, and simultaneously, a fear and trembling. In a word, God's liberating spirit was anointing her.

Though the divine spiritual gift of loving oneself comes from God's strength, it is not an easy task to self-connect and witness for oneself in the midst of a cruel and sin-filled world. Poor black women still have to continue the struggle against temptations of the Thing even as these women are caught up in the Funk's empowering spirit. For instance, even after Sula becomes armed with the value of self-connectedness, she faces at least four assaults on her womanhood—an indication that the Thing does not yield without a struggle. We detect this "battle" in a conversation she has with her grandmother, Eva. The latter matriarch instructs Sula in a question: "When you gone to get married?" Here the first temptation to attack womanist values of self assumes the form of patriarchy, a male-dominated marriage. The Thing, acting through Eva, tempts Sula with the seduction of false security and companionship supposedly guaranteed by a man. All Sula needs to do, from Eva's perspective, is give up herself to a husband who will take care of her and thus make it unnecessary for Sula to be connected with her own self.

Eva resumes: "You need to have some babies. It'll settle you." The second temptation tries to seduce Sula by playing with her maternal instincts. Eva knows quite well that Sula results from a line of independent women who strongly value offspring. Certainly Sula does not deny her desire to have children, just as she strongly wishes for male companionship. But Sula refuses to bow to any sugarcoated proposition, any false motherhood in which she bears children simply to "settle" the independence of self-connection.

Again Eva continues: "Bible say honor thy father and thy mother that thy days may be long upon the land thy God giveth thee." This third temptation, based on an incorrect interpretation of the Bible, appeals to blind submission to parental authority at the expense of denying the individual's self. After faltering with marital and maternal approaches, the Thing seeks to employ the Bible for divine authority. Finally, with the fourth temptation, Eva draws on folk religion: "Hellfire don't need lighting and it's already burning in you." Eva hopes to shock Sula into defeat by browbeating her with a common-sense type of Christian folk conviction.

Yet Sula remains connected to herself. She therefore responds with a clear understanding of who she is and what she is about. To the first two temptations she retorts: "I don't want to make somebody else. I want to make myself!" And in grand summation, she asserts all of her womanist selfhood against the Thing's encroachments: "Whatever's burning in me is mine! ... And I'll split this town in two and everything in it before I'll let you put it out!"[33] Womanist spirituality exists deep within the very marrow and sinews of her body and instead of yielding, it would rather torch wherever the presence of the demonic raises its head on earth.

Even if all else succumbs to the Thing's dominion, Sula pledges to stand alone with a liberated self-connectedness. In another discussion Sula immediately responds after her friend Nel cautions her about the danger of loneliness when a woman stands up by herself in the midst of oppression. "Girl, I got my mind," Sula asserts forcefully. "And what goes on in it. Which is to say, I got me." "Lonely, ain't it?" Nel quickly retorts. "Yes. But my lonely is *mine*," emphasizes Sula. She then gives Nel some sister-to-sister advice: "Now your lonely is somebody else's. Made by somebody else and handed to you. Ain't that something? A secondhand lonely."[34]

Results follow promptly for the poor black women who are self-connected in the stories of Toni Morrison. Ondine, the African American cook of the white capitalist male Valerian Street, challenges her boss by firmly stating: "I may be a cook, Mr. Street, but I'm a person too."[35] Here, Ondine claims her *somebodiness*. Similarly, Baby Suggs disputes Mr. Garner, another dominating white male figure, when the latter continues to call Baby Suggs by her slave name Jenny. "Suggs is my name, sir. From my husband. He didn't call me Jenny." Mr. Garner asks, "What he call you?" "Baby," answers Baby Suggs plainly; she decided which name fit her.[36] As a free self, Baby Suggs knows her own *name* and even the possibility of returning to slavery or other forms of oppression will no longer force her to accept another person's foreign titles.

In addition to the fruit of somebodiness and name—both expressions of cultural identity through redefined spirituality—that results from self-connectedness, poor African American women also achieve the right to control the areas around them (political self-determination in liberated zones). Pilate exhibits this benefit. Once she becomes fed up with all the obstacles she has confronted in her life, she realizes the need to realign herself to the world around her.

> She threw away every assumption she had learned and began at zero. ... Then she tackled the problem of trying to decide how she wanted to live and what was valuable to her. When am I happy and when am I sad and what is the difference? What do I need to know to stay alive? What is true in the world?[37]

The old self and way of life, strangled by the Thing's spirituality, meant others determining her coming and her going (all "that she had learned" as a poor black woman). Now, moved by a liberating spirituality, the new self starts at zero by taking care of itself—determining happiness, how to live, important values, and so forth. The discarded old-self dynamic and reborn new-self dynamic does not imply a debilitating inner mysticism. On the contrary, it spills over into the world around Pilate, but now she acts independently in her environment with her own assumptions.

Ultimately the value of self-connectedness empowers poor black women to re-create themselves away from the dictates of whiteness, the limitations of poverty, and male chauvinist demands and toward the self-authority to be free granted by God's spirit. At one point in their lives Sula and Nel claim this new reality. "Because each had discovered years before that they were neither white nor male, and that all freedom and triumph was forbidden to them, they had set about creating something else to be."[38] Thus to connect to themselves in a positive, loving way results in the creation of a new being.

Connectedness to Her Immediate Community

African American women's spirituality also expresses itself practically in black women's connectedness to their immediate community—their families, their relation to other black women, and their intimate dynamics with black men. Womanist spirituality refuses to bend to the pressures of harmful forces that would isolate black women from those whom they cherish in their close spiritual bonds. Black women in Toni Morrison's stories display a resilient will to involve themselves in liberated relationships, despite the continual presence of the Thing's spirituality (that is, the evil and damning forces of gender, racial, and economic discrimination). Thus connectedness to her immediate community signifies a sacred bond that a poor black woman maintains with those in her immediate setting.

The spirit of connectedness and love of family surface in the story of Eva Peace. As a single parent owning nothing but "$1.65, five eggs, [and] three beets" to feed her three children, Eva drew on her inner drive to create a life for her family. In fact, she gave part of her body and self as a sacrifice for the life and freedom of her family. One day she simply dropped off her three children and returned eighteen months later with one leg. Upon her arrival, her first act was to reclaim her children and later she began to build a house for them. No one openly questioned her about the disappearance of her leg, but it was rumored that she had "stuck it under a train and made them pay off. Another said she sold it to a hospital for $10,000."[39] In spite of the mystery, everyone knew Eva had departed in order to develop means for the survival of her family. The missing leg, along with the newly acquired money, indicated a deep love for her own offspring.

Not only did Eva have a spirituality of dynamic relatedness to her blood ties, she also defined her immediate family to include parentless children in her neighborhood. She became a mother to the motherless and provided a family for the homeless youth in her community. Many children had become victims of society's cruelness; they suffered from the spiritual sickness of a world that bred hunger and lack of compassion. But Eva's big heart stretched out to them and provided a home. In this sense, her connectedness to family moves her to care for other people's children as if they were her very own. Thus womanist spirituality accents the survival and freedom of the family in the development of black theology today.

Sethe, in *Beloved*, makes this point even more forcefully. Her relation to her family frees her both politically and culturally after she smuggles her children out of slavery. "It felt good. Good and right," she reflects about sending her children on the Underground Railroad to freedom. "When I stretched out my arms all my children could get in between." But recalling the previous years with her children under the oppressive restrictions of slavery, she pauses and concludes: "I couldn't love em proper . . . because they wasn't mine to love."[40] Spurred on by love of family, Sethe boldly confronts the structural powers of slavery. She risks the death of herself and her family in order to determine where on earth she will gather up her children; hence she makes a political act for the family. This fight for freedom against the political system of chattel that prevented her from deciding the family's future ("they wasn't mine to love") claims a free space outside of slavery where she can now define her love of her liberated family. Now she can affirm and define her family in a complete lifestyle of love—

an act of culture—because she fought for a spot on earth where "all my children could get in between" her outstretched arms. For Sethe the answer is clear: the cultural and political connectedness to her family permeates the depths of her spirituality.

In addition to the family, the immediate community in womanist spirituality includes black women's relation to other black women. Morrison's portrayal of black women to black women connectedness uncovers a profound instance of women defining themselves and creating a room for their own space. In the face of the ever-present demonic spirituality in society, black women know that an oasis of relief resides "just a sister away."[41] No other characters exhibit this dynamic better than Sula and Nel in *Sula*. Both women cooperate in a harmonious healthy relation in contrast to interactions between any other two persons in the novel.[42] "They never quarreled, those two, the way some girlfriends did over boys, or competed against each other for them." This black woman to black woman bonding was like "magic." After Sula leaves her local community and returns, Nel feels as though she has regained the use of an eye or had a cataract removed. Sula made her laugh and see old things with new eyes. With the return of Sula, Nel experiences a cleverness deep within. The Funk relationship between the two women gives her a gentleness and a "little raunchy" tingle. Indeed, "talking to Sula had always been a conversation with herself."[43]

Woman-to-woman connectedness—a spirituality greater than both women—teaches Nel and Sula how to be with someone else and not smother the person in the process. Such a liberating relation frees each one from the confines of a cutthroat competition in which victory for one meant defeat for the other. In contrast, womanist bonding presents an alternative; instead of a gain for one resulting in a loss for the other, when Sula wins so does Nel, and vice versa. Such a dynamic in poor black women's spiritual bonding suggests to black theology a new way for all human development. If such spirituality acts as an informative source for theology, then the depths of human togetherness should reflect a conversation with oneself. Just relationships succeed when two people see the goodness of themselves in each other and the goodness of the other in themselves.

Toni Morrison pushes the importance of black women loving black women beyond the encounter between two adults like Sula and Nel. Most "colored girls" require an entire system of black women to black women connectedness from birth till death. This web of interactions serves to shore up poor black women daily and frees them to continue the struggle demanded by the Thing's spirituality. The heart of womanist spirituality, then, remains the practical incarnation of God's liberating spirit, which yields strength to define and determine black women's selves.

In *Song of Solomon*, by negative example, we discover how Hagar lacked an intricate system of women bonding as women.

> She needed what most colored girls needed: a chorus of mammas, grandmammas, aunts, cousins, sisters, neighbors, Sunday school teachers, best girl friends, and what all.

Because Hagar suffered from a lack of healthy black women in her development, she becomes addicted to a blind love for a black male character, Milkman, and continues unsuccessful attempts to murder him. Ultimately her negative and wicked spirit of possession for Milkman contributes to her own tragic death. Hagar never realized in her life or death that she required a "chorus" of black women "to give her the strength life demanded of her—and the humor with which to live it."[44]

Here the full extent of womanist spirituality (in woman-to-woman relations) provides strength for life's journey and the gift of humor to heal one's soul and live life to its fullest. A black sister's concern for another sister demonstrates spiritual power to laugh and be in this world as God intended for all the poor. The spiritual and medicinal power of laughter, then, must become part of a black theology today. Why? Because the spirituality of black women teaches us that laughter keeps the victims of society from going insane. The poor need desperately to dig down deep and laugh at the absurdities of their environment in preparation to assert their God-given humanity in this world.

Finally, connectedness to the immediate community comprises more than poor black women's love of their families and other black women. It includes a healthy and self-affirming relation to black men. Sula, for example, eventually creates a connectedness of equality with Ajax, a black male friend. In the course of their dating and intimacies, she realizes that "her real pleasure was the fact that he talked to her." She experienced genuine conversations in which Ajax neither asked stupid questions about her life or insulted and bored her with monologues about his own exploits. Instead, he made her feel brilliant and "she delivered."[45]

It is this issue of brilliancy that womanist spirituality brings to the fore for black theology. Black female-male relationships, Toni Morrison's characters seem to suggest, will remain skewed and oppressive for African American women until the full brilliancy of their role in the inter-gender conversation surfaces in all its brightness. Part of this unrecognized and smothered brightness will shine due to the unyielding persistence and unapologetic initiative of the Funk. At the same time, black men must grab on to black women's rays of liberation and embrace, nurture, and encourage them on an equal par.

The protagonist Milkman (*Song of Solomon*) reaches this level when he finally (with over 90 percent of the novel completed!) sees a poor black woman named Sweet as another human being whose created purpose in life is not a one-way street of emptying her brilliancy for the whimsical, unresponsive desires of a black man. Just the opposite, when Milkman allows himself to participate equally in Sweet's creative, full, and human-to-human connectedness to him, he becomes a new being. By participation, Milkman dances a duet of mutual love and open relationship in which he and Sweet do for each other out of respect for each other.[46] Not only does womanist spirituality transform poor black women from their old self-connectedness to their new self-connectedness, it also has the potential, with the just cooperation of black men, to foreshadow a new example of black female-male vibrant complementarity.

Connectedness to the Broader Community

African American women's spirituality extends beyond the immediate community and expresses a love for and connectedness to the broader community—specifically ties to the folk and the ancestors. The folk includes the larger poor black community. Though blood ties are part of it, the focus is mainly on non-family members. Black women in Morrison's novels pour out a spirituality of compassion and pool their meager resources for black folk's survival and liberation. Visited by a divine spirit of justice—an empowering force that unglues them from a narrow self and pushes them beyond their immediate selves, these women feel a specific mission, sensitivity, and calling to aid the community when it is ailing physically and spiritually. Consequently, the communal well-being deeply affects the individual black woman's way of life. If there is a mouth to feed or a child without a home or a bad spirit harassing a family, these black women will pull together, activate their networks, sacrifice what little they have, and produce concrete results for the larger African American interests.

Yet this emptying of themselves for the overall good does not mean a blind act in which black women harm their own spiritual health; this would contradict the essence of womanist spirituality. In reality, their laboring for others simultaneously lifts their own spiritual individuality. The communal success, therefore, defines the personal state of being, and the personal completeness, in turn, benefits from the positive survival and advancement of the community.

A classic example occurs in *Beloved* when the African American women of the community unite to save Sethe and her daughter Denver from a negative spirit in the latter's household. Beloved, the demon spirit, is Sethe's daughter, who has returned from the dead to seek a ruthless revenge against her mother. In the process of this hellish retaliation, the ghost Beloved slowly attempts to drive her mother insane and also starve her to death. Beloved consumes all food, as well as emotional attention, in this household of three black women. The other daughter, Denver, finally acquires enough courage to venture out of the possessed house and into the surrounding black commmunity. Her act of courage and determination to get help to save her mother from the dwelling of the damned and liberate their house from the devilish spirit alert the community's African American women. Two days after contacting one of the women in the neighborhood about the battle for life in her home,

> Denver stood on the porch and noticed something lying on the tree stump at the edge of the yard. She went to look and found a sack of

white beans. Another time a plate of cold rabbit meat. One morning a basket of eggs sat there.

With each gift of food, Denver discovered little notes describing the sender of the various dishes. The contributors were all black women from the surrounding area. They left their names "to let the girl know, if she cared to, who the donor was."[47] The names symbolized hope and a message telling little Denver that she and her mother were not alone in combating the demonic spirit in their house. The names conveyed information: Be strong; the women are gathering up their forces because the presence of an evil spirit affronts the entire folk in the broader community. Thus these elderly women passed their unified benevolent spirit to Denver, trapped by the wicked witch Beloved.

Similarly, Lady Jones, another black woman in *Beloved*, dedicates her life and career to the African American folk, particularly the youth. She looked almost white and possibly could have "passed" with her gray eyes and yellow hair. Because of her light skin, someone had picked her to attend an out-of-town school. Such a unique education could have jettisoned her into the black bourgeoisie or the white middle class. Instead, she pledged her rare education and benefits of skin color "by teaching the unpicked"[48] and giving her real affection for these poor black children of the folk. For her, the freedom of her own spiritual definition suffered if the collective spirituality of these faceless black youth languished in ignorance and poverty. Indeed, Lady Jones saw a direct connection between self-affirmation of her whole being and the future generation and hope of the black community. She *chose* to undertake a seemingly holy crusade of emptying her privileged energies into youth cast aside to society's extreme margins.

Despite a certain degree of ambiguity regarding her role in her own community, Sula also brings positive effects to the folk of her black neighborhood. Instead of vicious competition with others, she simply helps them to understand and define themselves. When confronted with Sula's presence, people open themselves up and turn "their volume on and up." They become in tune with themselves and feel compelled to express themselves vocally and loudly. But "more than any other thing, humor returned" to the community when Sula appeared.[49]

Here womanist spirituality of connectedness to the broader community empowers the folk to strive for a harmonious extended family, a new reality. In the process the folk spill over with genuine interactions of deep and loud self-expressions. But above all, laughter and a sense of humor restore them for the community. Again, even in black women's relation to other black people, the grace of humor blesses the gathering. It relaxes them in the midst of a worldly, adverse spirituality; it opens them up to their own inner voices and volumes. Certainly, a first step in any liberation process takes place when the oppressed become in tune with themselves and their identity. Self-expression is, in fact, a declaration against demonic chains of silence.

Furthermore, the immediate community in womanist spirituality focuses on poor black women's ties to their ancestors. Throughout *Song of Solomon* Pilate periodically communes with the spirit of her dead father, who instructs and counsels her about major and minor decisions about life. "I see him still," confesses Pilate. "He's helpful to me, real helpful. Tells me things I need to know." Similarly, when Denver, in *Beloved*, reaches an indecisive point and hesitates to get help for her mother against the devilish spirit of the returned Beloved, the guardian spirit of Denver's grandmother envelops and advises her to move from her house and seek the women in her broader community. The benevolent spirit of her grandmother commands her: "Go on out the yard. Go on." When she heeded her grandmother's counsel, "it came back. A dozen years had passed and the way came back." Spiritual power, revealed in a poor black woman, shattered the scales of indecision and fear from the eyes of a little black girl. Consequently, Denver inhales enough strength to seek help from the folk in order to liberate her house, her mother, and herself from the deadly grip of an evil countervailing spirit. Communion with the ancestor's spirit made "the way" come back.[50]

In sum, the womanist spiritual value of the broader community teaches black theology that the latter's spirituality dimension must lift up and promote the positive aspects of the extended family. Responsibility does not limit itself to the individual or blood ties. A holistic and healthy spiritual attainment also accents the love, compassion, and harmony in the broader African American connections. More specifically, freedom and well-being of the poor sector of the wider neighborhood of black folk set the tone for all who claim membership among the folk.

As a model for individual-collective relations, moreover, black women's religious values dictate that individual and communal spirituality progress together in a mutual, complementary process. Linked closely to this "I am because you are" and "you are because I am" lifestyle, we find the importance of humor for the extended community. Humor for the folk is both a healing of spiritual sickness and an act of self-expression against the harmful effects of evil. Hence humor aids the folk with laughter, to keep from a paralyzing crying. In that laughter, they keep on struggling.

Last, the power and authority of the ancestors occupy a prominent seat in black theology's spirituality statement. African American (and African) spirits should ever remain a crowd of witnesses guiding the people, the church, and all endeavors of the African American experience. Within the accumulated historical, religious, and spiritual wisdom of those parted but not forgotten, black theology gains an infinite resource of spiritual depth and counsel. The ancestors persist as an accessible deposit of black history, knowledge, and advice regarding contemporary and future decisions for the broader community. Because physical death has put them closer in proximity to God's spirit, they facilitate the imparting of the divine freeing spirit among poor black women.

Connectedness to Nature

Related to love of herself, and of the immediate and broader communities, is the final spiritual value: poor African American women's connectedness to nature. Just as womanist experiences recover the novel place of the ancestors, so too do black women's spiritual roles in Toni Morrison's stories convey the creative and resourceful input of nature to the development and doing of black theology. Nature personifies and sides with the hopes and aspirations of the poor, particularly in sympathizing with and guiding the affairs of the poor. Nature also serves to unveil God's freeing spirit in poor black women because God has created nature with purpose. Through God's liberating spirit, all the created order testifies to what a just divinity has done for poor humanity. Nature cannot carry on the affairs of this world in a neutral, silent, or business-as-usual manner and simultaneously share God's spirit. Quite the contrary, nature grabs and points people in particular directions or embraces people deep into its breasts with the purpose of placing the folk on a liberation journey. Hence nature cannot be a faceless or absent character in black theological development. There exists a sacred expression in the natural creation, and poor black women's connection to nature manifests this divine gift of emancipation.

For instance, nature's love and compassion for the integrity of Pecola's spiritual essence demonstrates itself when Pecola's father rapes her in *The Bluest Eye*. Besides the sympathy displayed by her two girlfriends Claudia and Frieda, only nature cries out in protest against such a dastardly violation of a poor black girl's life. Specifically, no seeds yielded fruit in the entire community the year of the violent rape. Mother Earth halted the normal functioning of planting and harvesting to assert a resounding No!, and thereby linked the ravishing of Pecola's spiritual nature to the disruption of everyone else's natural rhythm of growth and fruition. Commenting on nature's connection to Pecola, Claudia narrates:

> Our seeds were not the only ones that did not sprout; nobody's did. Not even the gardens fronting the lake showed marigolds that year. ... It never occurred to us that the earth itself might have been unyielding.

All of nature cried out in disgust and revulsion. Even the green land around lakes refused to give birth to marigold flowers the entire year.[51] The natural rhythmic flow of the changing seasons ceased in order to side with Pecola's plight, and God's disrupting word against oppression spoke to the entire community. An evil act against Pecola's personhood draws the full attention of a just divinity who, in turn, summons the full force of the naturally created order. Indeed, a plague comes and devours the land and no seeds sprout; the food products that are vital for human consumption and development do not appear, nor do the oxygen-producing plants, which are needed to sustain human life. In a word, womanist spirituality's connection to and embodiment of nature parallel the success or failure of human living.

In *Beloved* nature also sides with Sethe in her struggle for life against a potential white slavecatcher, who would deny her right to political self-determination. Pregnant with her daughter, Sethe pauses in pain while she desperately and agonizingly labors to cross the Ohio River to free land. A deep groan leaves her aching body and inadvertently alerts a passer-by who she thinks is a white boy. She begins to succumb to the pain and wear and tear of her forced journey; she starts to yield to the spiritual if not physical death that the male intruder would inevitably bring. Yet immediately earth sends her a full jolt of strength to fight for her life and claim her space along freedom's road. A *"something* came up out of the earth into her — like a freezing, but moving too, like jaws inside. . . . Suddenly she was eager for his eyes, to bite into them; to gnaw his cheek.''[52] Out of the bowels of the earth, nature gives her the spirit and force of liberation to struggle against a potential power that would have dragged her back into the political system of slavery. A larger empowering force or being, through nature, infuses life-sustaining, rebellious energies into poor black women even when the latter become temporarily resigned to fatigue and physical pressures. Natural spiritual power can vivify and resurrect the near-dead.

In addition to relating to black women politically, nature also confronts them with the necessity for an African cultural identity. Jadine substantiates this point when we discover her struggling to extricate herself from a muddy swamp in *Tar Baby*. As she tugs back and forth, the surrounding trees are personified as wise women of nature ("women hanging in the trees looked down at her"). At first glance the nature women smile in approval at the sight of the entrapped Jadine, for they initially revel in delight, "thinking a runaway child had been restored to them." But, in dismay, the nature women quickly realize that Jadine attempts to run not toward but away from them and, in the process of escape, from her own divinely bestowed natural self-awareness. In contrast, possessing absolute clarity of cultural identity and origin, these women of nature were mindful of

> their exceptional femaleness; knowing as they did that the first world of the world had been built with their sacred properties; that they alone could hold together the stones of pyramids and the rushes of Moses's crib.

By negative example Jadine turns her back on the grace of black women's connectedness to nature offered by God's spirit. If she had accepted freely given womanist grace, Jadine would have experienced these tree-hanging women's knowledge of the African female self. Specifically, the nature women here exhibit a perceptive truth about the exceptional femaleness of African women and women of African descent. Why? First, African women gave birth to all of humanity. Archeologists concur that humanity springs forth from the womb of Mother Africa. Thus the original world—"the first world of the world"—results from black women's labors. Second, the wisdom and strength of African (Egyptian) women assisted in the engineering of the Egyptian pyramids, a testament to a highly advanced scientific and cultured society. Third, African women (the ancient Hebrews) served in the roles of savior and deliverer when they spared the life of Moses and sent him to freedom in his crib. Finally, the nature women's embodiment of African history and location, particularly the Egyptian accent, confirms the New Testament truth that Jesus, an African mixture, was born of Mary, a north African woman impregnated with God's spirit of liberation.[53] Accordingly, black women's link to nature reveals a profound reclaiming of the exceptional femaleness of black women's African cultural identity, indeed, their essential *sacred* properties.[54]

Finally, in *Beloved* nature becomes the liberated religious and theological space pastored by the poor black woman folk preacher, Baby Suggs. Ordained only by God's spirit, Baby Suggs claimed a space in nature and called it the Clearing, "a wide-open place cut deep in the woods."[55] The Clearing served as the pulpit from which Suggs's homilies exhorted black folk about God's calling to love their African American selves. In this sense Suggs's relation to nature brought together three elements: the theological, that is, her religious interpretations of God from the perspective of the bottom of society literally in the woods; the political, that is, her settling on a piece of earth where African American people could self-determine how they wanted to be in this world; and the cultural, that is, her preaching proclamations of love of the poor black self-identity.

And so, in womanist spirituality the value of poor black women's relation to nature instructs a constructive black theology to charter new ground in the virgin terrain of God's created natural order. A holistic comprehension of God's love and freedom for all humanity through the poor's plight necessitates an unearthing of the freeing spirit offered to all people in ecology. In the stories of Toni Morrison we find ample testaments to the interlocking survival and fullness of nature and humanity. A black theology, then, must accommodate theological, political, cultural, and spiritual expressions of nature in womanist spirituality; that is, the sought after wholeness of life concerns both the health of the poor and the health and compassion of the earth.

We have reviewed womanist spirituality contributions to black theology in four broad areas of values of connectedness—a poor black woman's connection to herself, to her immediate community, to her broader community, and to nature. In Morrison's novels African American women hold certain values dear and these cherished values—"sacred properties"—help anchor women's spiritual vessels, in which a divine freedom spirit dwells. These various theological worths fundamentally infuse, glue together, and filter women's understanding of theology, politics, and culture. Thus values of connectedness, a complex of interweaving complements, push black theology toward the search for a more complete theology of liberation. We now turn to the last general area that makes concrete the liberating dimension of African American women's spirituality, namely traditions of embodiment.

TRADITIONS OF EMBODIMENT

Like the values of connectedness, traditions of embodiment unfold around four similar categories: traditions of embodiment in poor black women themselves, in their immediate community, in their broader community, and in nature. Traditions are theological and spiritual deposits of wisdom shared with and passed on from woman to woman in the interest of all people. Put differently, sacred knowledge of survival, struggle, and freedom accumulates and stretches from woman to woman, thus sustaining an immortal body of traditions that surpasses and amplifies the strength of each individual woman.

Embodiment in Herself

Within themselves, Toni Morrison's black female characters manifest the tradition of conjurer. Conjurer women are usually associated with spiritual activities that do not signify Christian practices. Yet a timeless spiritual power of liberation reflects itself in the religious functioning of these very same women. Thus, the traditional embodiment of conjurer, vivified by poor black women, challenges black theology to recognize and create a space for a non-Christian reality of God's freeing representations. Will black theology acknowledge conjurers as legitimate sources for the actual doing of theology?

Put differently, the Christian church comprises the largest organized form of religion within the black community. For Christians who develop black theology, Jesus the Christ—the anointed one—remains the decisive revelation for our liberation faith encounter with God. However, at the same time, a liberating African American theology must perceive the possibility of conjurers, an important part of womanist spirituality, complementing the Christ and enhancing the liberation and formation of the new humanity. God's love for the poor brought forth the Messiah, yet the power of God's love for freedom did not and has not ceased in those places where the name of Jesus remains unknown. In those places God has provided an anointing and revelation of a just spirit through other instruments of divine purpose.

In general terms the conjurer women in Morrison's stories act as natural healers and saviors.[56] While drawing on God's spirit in nature and the collective might of other poor black women, they work alongside Christians. Several women in Morrison's novels will suffice to elaborate the conjurer as a tradition of embodiment within black women themselves.

In *Song of Solomon* Pilate learns the wisdom and practices of conjuring from a black female migrant worker in New York, who initiates and trains Pilate in the intricacies of root work, human relations to nature, and the untapped power within the human self. When asked why she remained with a band of migrant bean pickers in New York, Pilate claims her conjuring apprenticeship as the primary reason. "The main reason I stayed on," she relates, "was a woman there I took to. A root worker. She taught me a lot." Pilate opts to absorb a freeing spiritual craft in order further to define her female self-identity and thereby accomplish an act of cultural assertion.

The mentoring between this experienced female conjurer and Pilate displays, in one sense, the ability for veterans in the field consciously to train other poor black women in the expertise of dealing in spirits. However, the initiate must also have a special and natural relation to spiritual matters. The power and gift of divine spirituality has to set her aside, in other words. Like Christian prophetesses and priestesses, conjurer women work on behalf of the people, yet they are not quite similar to those for whom they struggle. Accordingly, Pilate

> was a natural healer, and among quarreling drunks and fighting women she could hold her own, and sometimes mediated a peace that lasted a good bit longer than it should have because it was administered by someone not like them.

Thus a natural conjurer lives to serve the community and move it toward peace and justice. Pilate immerses herself within the conflicts of people around her and, due to her special anointing, renders a healing peace to the lowly in society. Her power to resolve contradictions among poor folk originates from her spiritual set-asideness exemplified in her chosen being; that is, the "someone not like them" marks her ability to have a justice interest in the affairs of her people.

Indeed, particularly relating to saving life, conjurers in Toni Morrison's stories seem to labor for goodness wherever there exist evil spirits who would attempt death. For instance, when Macon Dead the elder attempts violently and viciously to cause his own wife to have an abortion, the wife seeks out Pilate to save herself and the life of the fetus. For the strength of the mother and the child developing in her womb, Pilate prescribes crunchy foods (such as cornstarch, cracked ice, nuts). For Macon Dead the elder, Pilate positions on his chair a small "doll with a small painted chicken bone stuck between its legs and a round red circle painted on its belly." Consequently the expectant mother grew stronger and gave birth to a healthy baby boy who, as Macon Dead the younger, carried on the lineage and thus the life of the Dead family.[57] The right to determine life through conjuring spirituality highlights Pilate's fierce passion to promote the growth of victimized black folk and their right to decide space around them—an act of politics.

Oftentimes, the community in which the conjurer woman functions feels threatened due to its incorrect understanding of God's manifestation of God's spirit through diverse human channels. This particularly applies to insecure Christians who pit God's decisive ultimacy for liberation revealed in Jesus Christ over against the same spiritual ultimacy discovered in others. Even when the conjurer woman brings sustenance and life within the community (similar to the nourishing of Jesus), she risks potential isolation from her own benefactors. Baby Suggs experiences the effects of this blind, narrow type of Christianity when she increases food for the poor black community she loves and is a part of.

[For Baby Suggs] to take two buckets of blackberries and make ten, maybe twelve, pies; to have turkey enough for the whole town pretty near, new peas in September, fresh cream but no cow, ice and sugar, batter bread, bread pudding, raised bread, shortbread—it made them [her neighbors] mad. Loaves and fishes were His powers—they did not belong to an ex-slave.[58]

The conjurer ventures such potential recriminations and possibly precarious acts of healing and saving in community because she has received an unsought-after ordaining by the spirit of God's word. At one point Baby Suggs struggles against her calling due to the death and injury caused by white slaveowners and a slavecatcher coming on her property. But her colleague, Stamp Paid, reminds her: "Listen here, girl ... you can't quit the Word. It's given to you to speak."[59]

Finally, conjurers in womanist spirituality (a tradition of embodiment within poor black women themselves) complement the spiritual power of Jesus Christ. For instance, Baby Suggs is both a Christian ("I did get to church every Sunday some kind of way") and an unconventional "unchurched preacher," whose compassionate heart swells from God's spirit in nature (she preaches at the Clearing, her sanctuary deep in the woods). In a similar fashion, when black women come to exorcise the she-devil spirit called Beloved from the black community:

Some brought what they could and what they believed would work. Stuffed in apron pockets, strung around their necks, lying in the space between their breasts. Others brought Christian faith—as shield and sword. Most brought a little of both.[60]

Furthermore, the complementary nature of Christian spirit and conjurer spirit in the act of saving and healing engages us in *The Bluest Eye*. In one part of the story, an Aunt Jimmy borders on death. To halt the slow decline of their friend, her neighbors read her the Bible, but to no avail. Finally, they summon a male Christian preacher and a female healer-savior named M'Dear, who approach Aunt Jimmy's bedside together. M'Dear dwelled quietly in a shack near the woods. "Any illness that could not be handled by ordinary means—known cures, intuition, or endurance—the word was always, 'Fetch M'Dear.' "[61] The conjurer woman, in this instance, provides the cure, which temporarily saves Aunt Jimmy's life. Though the Christian preacher remains outwardly silent, in fact, the combined spiritual strength of both Christian and conjurer shores up the ailing Aunt Jimmy.

Embodying within themselves the tradition of conjurer, poor black women thus offer a valuable and untapped resource for creating a constructive black theology. To fulfill God's plan of liberation for the African American church and community, a black theology today does well to hear the "unorthodox" (and hence seemingly threatening) voices and to seek out vivifying syncretistic practitioners of divine spiritual healing and saving.

Embodiment in Her Immediate Community

The tradition of a mother's relation to her daughter, in Morrison's novels, encompasses the essence of embodiment in a poor black woman's immediate community. Women share a particular connection to their female children through nurturing from sickness to health, protection, passing on knowledge, and providing the nutrients of life. In *The Bluest Eye* Claudia harbors fond recollections of her childhood autumns due to the doctoring role of her mother. Unable to summon a professional doctor, who would charge money for his services, Claudia's mother repeatedly attended her bedside during bouts of illness. The hands of motherhood literally nurtured the illness out of Claudia's weak body. She reminisces about the healing hands of her mother during the late hours of the evening: "When my coughing was dry and tough, feet padded into the room, hands repinned the flannel, readjusted the quilt, and rested a moment on my forehead." The closeness of the mother-daughter spiritual touch during sickness sketched such a graphic and indelible imprint on Claudia's consciousness that the coming and going of the seasons now correlate with the medicinal hands of her mother. "So when I think of Autumn," resumes Claudia, "I think of somebody with hands who does not want me to die."[62] For Claudia, then, a mother's powerful hands resurrected and delivered her from death's brink.

Furthermore, mothers not only ward off the threat of deadly diseases from their little girls, but, especially when men attack their daughters, mothers also draw on latent reserves of spiritual strength and risk bodily harm to themselves. Such a "foolishness" of a mama's protectiveness motivates Pilate to draw a knife on a man who has wrongfully slapped her daughter. Slowly Pilate approaches the male aggressor from behind, whips her arm around the man's throat, presses a knife against his heart, and waits for him to feel the knife blade. The man checks the rhythm of his breathing for fear he might cause the steel to sink in. Now, with the might of the man neutralized by the touch of near-death, Pilate calmly informs him about the spiritual bond between mother and daughter.

> Women are foolish, you know, and mamas are the most foolish of all.
> ... First real misery I ever had in my life was when I found out somebody—a teeny tiny boy it was—didn't like my little girl.[63]

If the initial real pain and misery suffered by Pilate in her life resulted from a little school boy not liking her daughter, then her spiritual whirlwind to protect her now adult daughter could possibly drive her to unknown acts of "foolishness." Grasping quite clearly Pilate's words, the former male attacker runs down the road when released from her grip.

Black mothers pass on vital knowledge to their daughters, important information such as how to be a woman. Mothers train their daughters to survive in a hostile world bombarded with demonic spirits of racial, gender, and economic oppressions. In order to make it to womanhood, daughters have to possess a wisdom of survival that engenders the maintenance of their lives and the attainment of their freedom—both the free ability to name their own nature (the cultural self) and to move about based on their own decisions (the political self).

To this end Jadine receives the following counsel from her surrogate mother, Ondine, in *Tar Baby*. "Jadine, a girl has got to be a daughter first. ... And if she never learns how to be a daughter, she can't never learn how to be a woman." In the very mix of the mother-daughter tie flows information, tradition, strategy, perspective, and the particular instruction that transforms a daughter into a woman. But this wisdom of womanness comes only when the daughter cares about her maternal roots. Accordingly, accountability accompanies the acceptance of the answers of womanhood imparted to daughter from mother. Continuing her maternal role, Ondine states: "A daughter is a woman who cares about where she come from and takes care of them that took care of her."[64] The female child blossoms into an image of her mother, because the daughter's acquired spiritual substance (her political and cultural being as a woman) activates in proportion to self-acknowledgment of her female lineage.

In addition, mothers defy the clutches of death so they can provide the nutrients of life for their daughters. For example, Sethe, without assistance, escapes from the lethal snares of slavery only to find herself on the edge of dying before she can cross the Ohio River to liberation. Though burdened with swollen numb legs and with bloody whip wounds drenching her back, she still is able to call on the spiritual strength from within to carry her nutrients of life to her baby daughter. "All I knew was I had to get my milk to my baby girl," exclaims Sethe. The drive to give milk, the only life sustenance for her daughter, empowers her and focuses her mission. No thing, not even the boundaries of death, or nobody could have entrapped her. Because she knew only one reality—the possession of liquid life for the survival of her female baby's physical life—Sethe passionately concludes: "Nobody knew that but me and nobody had her milk but me."[65]

Finally, in certain cases adverse circumstances force little black daughters to assume the role of mother when a negative spirituality slowly sucks the life and vivacious spirit for survival and wholeness out of their mothers. The evil intent of the returned she-devil, Beloved, does exactly this. "Beloved ate up [Sethe's] life." She sat around and ate up every piece of food in the house, while her mother starved herself in deference to the she-devil spirit. Sethe, the mother, began to resemble a "teething child." Even after the black women of the community exorcise Beloved from their neighborhood, Sethe still suffers from physical and mental weaknesses. Therefore, to protect her mother against the effects of the devilish thing, Sethe's other daughter, Denver, takes on two jobs.[66] In situations of crisis, the dynamic of mother-daughter can produce a reversal of roles whereby a childlike state in the mother compels the daughter to become substitute mother. Nevertheless, the substance of the tradition of embodiment in her immediate community, expressed with the mother-daughter association, remains the same.

Embodiment in Her Broader Community

African American women's spirituality also presents another tradition of embodiment for black theological development: the broader community. We look now at the powerful imagery of Africa, which signifies poor black women's broader community.

Though removed from the distant shores of Africa, poor black women display a special tradition of affinity to Africa, the mother continent. The power of Pilate (her conjuring abilities, clarity as a woman and as mother, love of the folk, veneration of black ancestors, courage to move about, and so on) derives from her being the link between those living in her family and their origins in Africa. Besides her strong female spiritual qualities suggesting an African origin, her very physical features confirm that African tradition planted, incubated, nurtured, and bore all her wisdom. Confirming this certainty, Macon Dead the elder tells his son, "If you ever have a doubt we from Africa, look at Pilate." She lives in testimony to Africa. Somehow the tradition from Africa to African America comes by way of a female linkage. Not that black men play no part in the dark tracings from the mother continent. Rather, black women's spirituality burgeons with a gripping sense of who they are and where they come from. Accompanied by such potent exactness in ties to the broader African diaspora, women's spiritual experience then permeates and aids the vitality of the entire black environment.

As a child, Sethe likewise receives knowledge of her own link to Africa. Nan, who cared for her because white men hanged her biological mother, explains how she and Sethe's mother "were together from the sea." Both her mother and Nan spoke an African language, which Sethe understood in her early childhood days. But since Nan's death and slavery's burdens, she has forgotten the specificities, sounds, and syntax. What remains in Sethe's consciousness is "the message—that was and had been there all along." The historical consciousness that poor black women have regarding their African relationship is not a mere infatuation with things long dead. Rather, Africa, with its forgotten language, yields significance for today. Specifically, the exact memory of origins still suggests to the descendants of memory that they have a place of beginnings defined not by their contemporary oppressive constraints, but by divinity. Therefore, a free place of origin implies a historical moment in which both self-identity and self-determination prevailed as the norm. And so, knowledge of a fighting and survivalist spirit from Africa, the message, becomes a tradition passed from one female generation to another.

In fact, the resurrection of the African consciousness in all its coded and shadowy meanings comes to Sethe when she relates to her daughter, Denver, the story of her hanged mother. No doubt Denver too will link her own future daughter into the traditional web of intergenerational bonds to Africa, and the cycle of story-Africa-tradition will continue from woman to woman. Black theology needs to look into sources of liberation embedded in a spiritual tie to Africa. And the intergenerational lineage that poor black women have with Africa presents one important place to discover the liberating spirit from that continent.

Another dark-skinned, tar-baby-looking woman suggests the strong African tradition of poor black women. We find her in a Parisian grocery store, where her striking African presence disrupts the normal activity of this food establishment. Her skin like tar contrasted with her dazzling canary dress. Wearing many-colored sandals and sporting family markings engraved in her cheeks and a gelee wrapped around her hair, this African epitomizes a positive femaleness. She is a "woman's woman" and a "mother/sister/she," endowed with "unphotographable beauty." In fact, her beingness is summed up in the word "she." She owns womanist values and traditions; that is, she connects with herself, and with her immediate and broader communities. Because colors and body qualities help to define her, she embraces nature. She is extremely clear on her identity, and she moves about Paris, indeed the world, with grace, ease, and self-determination.

This African character suggests a treasure of spiritual self-determination and self-identity. Drawing on her own spiritual self-sufficiency, she teaches a black theology whose very existence and persistence challenge the status quo and disrupt those who would define an oppressive human relationship in their own image of privilege. Why? Because the African spirituality of today's black theology helps it draw on the depths of its foundational identity, despite the attempts of European and Euro-American theology to desecrate black Americans' African survivals. The reality of an African presence is therefore a critique and refutation of the supremacy and normalcy of white theological language. The survival of African identity testifies to a createdness by God "in the beginning." And black theology's acknowledgment of God's first creation of African Americans serves as acceptance of self-identity.

Self-identity then fosters an awareness that all things are possible when one opens oneself to God's power in creation, even the possibility of black people reclaiming the space around them. Accepting an African spiritual presence, particularly the symbolic mediating role for this presence displayed by the African woman in Paris, can give black theology courage and vocational focus to stay the course for both cultural and political liberation.

Unfortunately Jadine, the major black female protagonist in *Tar Baby* (the woman who flees in fright from the swamp women), attempts to escape from this African woman in Paris and thereby break a connection to her extended community. The mere presence of the tar-baby beauty runs Jadine out of Paris. Furthermore, Jadine feels derailed; she feels lonely and "inauthentic." Her emotion derives from deserting Africa and the broader community. Her derailed depression comes from a lack of self-conscious personality.

More specifically, Jadine grew up in a poor working-class family in Baltimore. But a white male capitalist patron turned her into a white-black middle-class woman. Jadine's profound schizophrenic racial identity can only achieve a healthy resolution when she feels authentic. Yet her authenticity will ensue only when she names and claims her tradition of embodiment in Africa; the fountainhead of African American female spirituality is Africa.[67]

Embodiment in Nature

Finally, black women's embodiment in their natural bodies concludes this overall section on traditions of embodiment in women's spirituality. Poor African American women regard the natural state of their bodies as a sacred temple of self-love, normal physical-emotional expression, and a gift to God's spirit in worship. In *Beloved* Baby Suggs pastors a congregation of poor black folk in a section of the woods they call the Clearing. Here this unchurched preacher woman exhorts her "church" to love the flesh of their bodies and to give full play to their natural appetites for crying, laughter, and dance. Put differently, this Christian-conjurer calls on her people to lift up their spirits, through their bodies in liturgy and supplication, to divine spirit.

First, church service begins with Baby Suggs's sermon on self-love of their sacred flesh. "Here," preaches Baby Suggs, "in this here place, we flesh; flesh that weeps, laughs; flesh that dances on bare feet in grass. Love it. Love it hard." Why does she stress the specific passion of love of the body in her sermon? Suggs speaks within a concrete and historical context of white racism, a context quite familiar to her congregation's memory and to their daily, and dehumanizing, relation to whites. Resuming her spiritual sharing of the body's importance, she reminds her folk that "they" (white cultural and political norms) despise poor blacks' "eyes" and "the skin on your backs"; "they" do not love black hands; and "they ain't in love with your mouth." Instead, her congregation must love their flesh; stroke their hands and touch other black folk with them; grace their necks; support their backs; provide strong arms for their shoulders; and love their inside parts. Above all, climaxes Baby Suggs's speaking truth, "hear me now, love you heart. For this is the prize."

The heart stands as the ultimate part of the body because God has granted poor blacks the ability to love each other, non-blacks and themselves. But in order to be human — to take God's grace of love, planted spiritually within each heart, and love the rest of humanity — black folk have to go down deep in the depths of their black hearts and love the blackness of their physical being. Self-love, coming to terms with the natural created love of God in human hearts, sets the context for resonating with love of others, even feeling compassion for one's enemies. Thus the natural bodies reflect sacred temples of self-love.

In her church services, moreover, Baby Suggs calls out the spirit through the normal physical-emotional expression of her congregation. With sacred authority she summons forth the children and instructs them to laugh before their parents. And the children's bodies, which they loved, filled the trees with laughter. She then orders the men to step forward and dance before their wives and children. And "groundlife shuddered under their feet" as the trees rang with the ongoing sounds of children's laughter. Finally she designates the women and tells them to cry for the living and the dead. It began with clear roles for each segment of the folk, but then everything and everybody intertwined and intermixed.

> Women stopped crying and danced; men sat down and cried; children danced, women laughed, children cried until, exhausted and riven, all and each lay about the Clearing damp and gasping for breath. In the silence that followed, Baby Suggs, holy, offered up to them her great big heart.[68]

In summary, Baby Suggs offers the spirituality of the individual and communal body in worship. Love of self, granted by God's spirit of love and implanted in the heart, enables one's spiritul self-identity (a cultural claim), which in turn helps one to fight off the "they"s of the world (a political claim), even to the point of compassion for the adversary. In addition, one returns God's spiritual love through a demonstrative display of the body's natural activities of laughing, dancing, and crying. Therefore, Baby Suggs pulls together the necessity for black theology to develop a spirituality of the body. In worship, more exactly, poor black women's spirituality transmits spiritual *wisdom* — the tradition of embodiment in poor black people's natural bodies.

CONCLUSION

In Toni Morrison's novels poor black women's spirituality — an immortal, thus divine, spirit of liberation incarnated in poor African American women's values and traditions — teaches a constructive black theology of liberation that God is a holistic divinity, whose power of liberation manifests throughout the African American church and community. God's power of loving the poor through justice and freedom knows no boundaries. Consequently, a black theology of liberation must open its heart and mind, ears and eyes to wider resources in the total African American spiritual experience. The novels of Toni Morrison, then, provide one source for broadening our openness to God's spiritual involvement in human affairs.

Poor African American women's theological contributions to black theology prove that at least one vital role for poor black women's voice is sharing their engagement with God's free spirit. This spirit breathes in cultural and political expressions of vibrant values and traditions; hence an intergenerational process, a material and immaterial lineage of self-identity and self-determination appearing and reappearing in presentations and representations. Consequently, spirituality contains definite acts where cultural claims of self-naming empower oppressed individuals and communities to then subvert unjust social relations in order to control political places for liberation.

Poor women's spirituality includes Christian and non-Christian thought and action. Such reflection-action does theology because it witnesses to God's liberating spirit wherever God chooses to reveal God's Christian and non-Christian self. Similarly, African American women's spirituality embraces the religion of the institutional church and the non-church. It is religious because an unrestrained divine initiative among humanity expresses itself both within the church institution and, at the same time, within the broader African American women's community. This community, of course, links to the rest of black folk and indeed to all of poor humanity. Hence black theology has to open its eyes to see other institutional forms of black women's spirituality outside the recognized black church structures.

If God brings freedom for all humanity, then this universal liberation will result from freeing poor African American women from gender-race-class oppression. Put differently, the more poor black women have the ability to define themselves and determine the space around themselves, the closer all humanity approaches the future new reality that God, through

Jesus, offers to all. In this sense black theology must take seriously the reality and possibilities of poor African American women serving a salvific role for the black church and community—indeed, for entire humanity.

God's liberating spirit embodies itself and incarnates itself within poor black women's values and traditions. Thus methodologically one cannot begin with preconceived theological traditions (from above) and thereby restrict the multicolored garden of poor black women's religious experience. Out of the soil of such spiritual realities a constructive black theology will harvest new theological language, thought forms, metaphors, and categories.

Briefly, women's spirituality teaches black theology the following: The more completely black theology accepts the richness and many voices of indigenous theological sources found within the African American church and community, the better are chances for constructing a holistic black theology of liberation movement that will suggest freedom not only for blacks, but for all of suffering humanity. Poor African American women's encounter with the Holy challenges black theology to pursue a basic reorganization of interpersonal relations and to forge *systemically* a new social order.

Furthermore, to do theology from black women's literature is precisely *theology*. Why? Because the God of justice and love presented and discovered in African American religious values, tradition, and contemporary witness is the same God who freely chooses to reveal an emancipatory spirit in black women's stories. Admittedly, Christianity does not consistently serve as the explicit primary location for divine spiritual presence in Toni Morrison's novels. Still, the liberating appearance of God's spirit in non-Christian revelations, through story, complement God's spiritual descending upon the decisive Christian revelation of Jesus the Christ ("The Spirit of the Lord is upon me"). God, as a result, grants a unique revelation in Jesus the Christ as well as a general revelation in all of creation.

Again, a fundamental theological and methodological issue is at stake here: Can poor African American women's values and traditions be authentic theological birthers of divine freeing spirit? Black theology must respond with a resounding Yes! (perhaps through laughing, dancing, crying, and loving its sacred body in the spirit). Indeed, the originality of black women's spiritual experience and story must be taken seriously precisely because a black theology of liberation receives and participates with an *incarnational* God who tabernacles with the poor. For black theology, one of the locations of the poor is the gender-racial-poverty reality of African American women.

And while attending to the fight against wicked spiritualities, we also open ourselves up to the multiple positive, creative, and spiritual laughter, tears, dance, and *thinking* of the women. Womanist spirituality is a holistic political and cultural Funk.

3

"Now, You Gointer Hear Lies above Suspicion"

But then there are the low-down folks, the so-called common element, and they are the majority—may the Lord be praised! ... They do not particularly care whether they are like white folks or anybody else. Their joy runs, bang! into ecstasy. Their religion soars to a shout. ... They furnish a wealth of colorful, distinctive material for any artist because they still hold their own individuality in the face of American standardization.

Langston Hughes[1]

Like a natural spring in the rich soil of the Black Belt South, theology in African American folk culture gushes forth in all directions. Waters of self-identity and self-affirmation spew out and blanket the black earth. Poetry, plays, work songs, folk tales, blues, short stories, autobiographies, sermons, toasts, ballads, personal narratives, and protest literature blossom. Here, showered with "a wealth of colorful, distinctive material," a poor people name and claim themselves with the flowers of new definitions and positive assertions. The vibrancy of a multidimensional faith in a culture of liberation covers the pregnant land. This faith in freedom of the collective self continually plants and replants a vast garden of total African American life. Black folk culture is a powerful source for the harvesting of a black theology.

WAY MAKER AND WAY MADE

The ultimate power in African American folk culture is the Way Maker, a being so infinite in abilities that anything is possible. Similarly, the ultimate destination of these folk's aspirations is the Way Made, a place or condition fulfilling the basic desires of life. The Way Maker–Way Made being-space finds itself in the following honor given to God when a black folk character approaches the divine throne in heaven. "Oh Lord and Master of the rainbow. I know your power. ... I know you can hit a straight lick with a crooked stick."[2] The Way Maker can take a crooked stick — the problems of life, the oppressed conditions of the poor, the humanly impossible — and hit a straight lick, a correction of all the ailments and infirmities suffered by society's victims. The Way Maker takes the frailties of the human condition and out of that which is ill-formed changes human relations into a dreamed-of newness.

Likewise, the Way Made, in the minds of the folk in their culture, stands as the reality in which poor black people can name themselves in a place they have claimed. The Way Made means finally accepting the self and being accepted by others.

The Way Made is also a place where a way is made out of no way. In substance it is the same as the result of a straight lick being hit by a crooked stick. Consequently, the Way Made and the Way Maker share functional equivalency. Initially one finds one's self in an unbearable situation with an excruciatingly painful life or dreams unattained. But the Way Made becomes the focus of all one's visions and plans, sometimes realized and sometimes a distant hope that soothes aches of present existence while spurring on persistent efforts toward the Way.

Both the Way Maker and the Way Made are the foundational beings or places to which black people dedicate their lives in African American folk culture. Theologically both are ultimate concerns and life-and-death pursuits of faith. Beginning with the Way Maker and then the Way Made, we will see different steps that the folk take toward their belief in the most powerful being and place. Because it is their story and language about something greater than human capabilities, we have to open ourselves to the affirmation of black poor folk. The Way Maker and Way Made, in other words, grow organically out of an African American culture and a style of faith.

Creator Way Maker

Folk culture believes the Way Maker has the power to create human beings, specifically women and men. In fact, the name Way Maker indicates that one of the divinity's primary functions is to make or create new realities and new lives out of nothing. In the folk tale "The Man Makes and the Woman Takes," the storyteller provides an African American interpretation of the origin of male-female relations in the book of Genesis.

> You see, in the very first days, God made a man and a woman and put them in a house together to live. Back in those days the women were just as strong as the men, and both of them did the same things.[3]

The narrator relates an inherent quality of the Way Maker as gender equality. The phrase "in the very first days" tells the listener how God placed the highest priority on establishing male-female relations correctly.

Therefore the making of man and woman with similar strength and the same work responsibilities occupied divine deliberations from the dawn of creation. Because God made and put human beings together, just relations in the area of gender fall within the sacred domain. Prior to any person or thing having a say, God set up the proper interactions during the first days of human existence. So whatever men and women do to themselves today has to be judged on the standard of sacred creation.

Not only does the Way Maker's trait of created gender equality arise in folk tales, it also comes out in true stories experienced by the folk in their everyday lives. Zora Neale Hurston, a renowned African American folklorist and cultural anthropologist, recounts living with poor black people in rural Florida. One evening, after she and others had fried and eaten fish and begun preparations for the evening's partying and games, "three figures in the dusk-dark detached themselves from the railroad track and came walking into the quarters." The main character was a traveling unlettered preacher, called a "stump-knocker," who immediately commenced to preach a sermon on "Behold de Rib":

> Behold de rib!
> Brothers, if God
> Had taken dat bone out of man's head
> He would have meant for us to dominize and rule.
> He could have made her out of back-bone
> And then she would have been behind us.
> But, no, God Amighty, he took de bone out of his side
> So dat places de woman beside us;
> Hah! God knowed his own mind.
> Behold de rib![4]

The stump-knocker first addresses the men in the crowd, indicating their lack of knowledge about the original gender creation. In fact, the preacher parallels the parts of the human bone with how many of the poor women are treated by men. He emphasizes that "God Amighty" took the rib and placed "de woman beside us," proving that men had no active role in the creation of women and their relation to males. Furthermore, God "knowed his own mind." Having created men's bones, the Way Maker was well aware of the implications each bone conveyed. The choice of "de rib," then, carried deliberate and decisive divine choice. The status, purpose, and law of creation called for equality between poor black women and men; any other arrangement would seek to abrogate God's making power.

God's ability to create and make out of divine desire did not limit itself to gender equality. The Way Maker also held an infinite power to make all of nature and the universe simply by movement of divine body parts. We discover these qualities in the following folk tale concerning human praise of God:

Old Maker, with the morning stars glittering in your shining crown, with the dust from your footsteps making worlds upon worlds, with the blazing bird we call the sun flying out of your right hand in the morning and consuming all day the flesh and blood of stump-black darkness, and flying home every evening to rest on your left hand . . . [5]

God exists as the all-powerful originator of total creation by merely walking in space and time; wherever dust of divine tracks arose, worlds appeared out of the imprints. The sun resulted from the extension of God's right hand and returned to the "Old Maker" after doing a sacred day's work of lighting up the universe. The stars grew out of God's head; they received their glitter from the eternal shining of the divine crown. Stump-black darkness and light went forth and came back, mornings and evenings; everything started with God in the very first days.

Not only do God's being and body contain and give forth creation, the Way Maker also creates things perfectly, logically, and with consideration. For instance, one folk character humbles herself before the heavenly throne with these words: "O Lord and Master of the rainbow. I know your power. You never make two mountains without putting a valley in between."[6] God's efforts portray the craftsmanship of a supreme architect; every major joint and minute trivia dovetail exactly. The resulting handiwork makes sense too. God provides bridges for humanity to cross life's rivers with success. Otherwise the Way Maker would suffer from an irrationality threatening the divine laws that enable human beings to "get over."

Likewise, God takes care of life's details. We have valleys to enable us to descend one height and climb another peak. Without ups and downs, life would seem like a static plateau lacking the exhilaration of accomplishments, the challenges of new horizons, and the strengthening of character caused by valleys of despair. In this manner God makes, shapes, and takes into consideration the particularities and needs of divinely created order.

The Devil and his role are closely aligned with the Way Maker's power of creator. Whenever God goes about the holy business of originating something new and granting that living product a specific role in overall creation, the Devil either intervenes or is called on to play a role in the further work of the created product. In African American folk culture, the Devil inevitably comes into the midst of God's creation. However, the power of the Devil is not one of fundamental evil. Rather the Way Maker and the Devil signify two powerful forces of authority, wisdom, and ability. God, of course, retains the ultimate hand in the final analysis. In the folk tale "The Man Makes and the Woman Takes," the man disrupts the gender equality by asking God for more strength than the woman. To compensate, the woman approaches the Devil who instructs her to request certain keys from the Way Maker. These keys allow the woman to regain her equal status with the man.[7] Here God and the Devil display similar authority in creation, with God still having the last word.

Though the Devil isn't portrayed as absolute evil and terror, he does meddle in the affairs of creation, often attempting to derail the intent God has infused in the created arrangement. This occurs when God first makes tadpoles and tells them to pull weeds while he continues to create other beings. The Devil steps in and convinces the tadpoles to delay their chores and go swimming in a water hole. God, in turn, changes tadpoles into frogs as a reminder of their original disobedience to their initial created purpose.[8] Thus the Devil can momentarily deflect sacred intent, only to have God re-create new realities within the divine strategic plan. In this sense, the Devil exists to underscore God's creative and re-creative power.

A Co-laboring Way Maker

In addition to the divine function of creator, the Way Maker plays the role of co-laborer in divine existence. God does not wish to go forth and work alone without other living realities aiding in the acts of creation, survival, and liberation. We meet these qualities of the Way Maker in the work of James Weldon Johnson, who rendered a folk sermon into poetry and titled it "A Negro Sermon."[9] "And God stepped out on space/And He looked around and said/'I'm lonely—/I'll make me a world.'" Clearly, in African American folk culture, God could be lonely; thus God is not and does not live in God's self but is fully divine and satisfied with the divine self only when God makes various creations to accompany sacred activity. The Way Maker steps out onto the darkness of eternity to fashion living products in nature who complete God's purpose for being the ultimate power—that is, God's fundamental plan calls on the Creator and creation to live together and co-labor in the ongoing process of unfolding new realities and novel possibilities. Thus God's reality remains somewhat obscured prior to God placing divine steps out on space.

In a certain perspective, then, the Way Maker's totality of revelation happens only through God's self-revelation known to and through God's objects and co-workers. The folk are not so much interested in the unsolvable mysteries of God's previous oneness in isolation. The culture shows poor people theologically grappling with God's doing and doing it with them.

In this sermon/poem of Johnson's, God smiled and broke the darkness, rolled light around in his hand until he made the sun, spangled the night with the moon and stars, spat out the seven seas, and appeared to have completed his work and, therefore, quenched divine loneliness. Yet God realized, "I'm lonely still." Admiring all the beauty that lay before the heavenly throne, God sat down to think, "Till He thought, 'I'll make me a man!'" The Way Maker's sense of aloneness completely disappears with the final creation. In fact, this last living product, humanity, soothes God's need and desire because God finally establishes a body in divine initiated reality where a part of the divine self-image becomes ingrained in the definition of the created. In the face of humanity, God viewed God's own likeness and creative abilities. The Creator enjoyed the existence of its own co-creator.

So, in the folk's faith, the image of God breathed into human form signifies God's giving of divine self-identity to humanity. To be at one with the Way Maker and one's self is to hold to the divine identity implanted in human creation, which defines the human self-identity to co-create, with God, a new reality out of the given human predicament. Accordingly, the image of God in humanity means the birthing of a co-laborer and co-maker with the Way Maker.[10]

Furthermore, God does not remain an absentee or distant co-worker in the vineyards of life. The Way Maker actively and physically participates with human beings who struggle to bring fruit and crops from a living soil. A preacher-farmer folk tale shows this dynamic nearness. Two brothers, one a preacher and the other a farmer who "ain't nevuh set foot in a chu'ch house in his life," had a discussion about the successful crops on the non-church-going brother's farm. After examining each vegetable and marveling at his brother's achievements in farming, the preacher brother condescendingly repeats the refrain "by de he'p of de Lawd." Finally the farmer brother becomes impatient with the overbearing Christian brother's one-sided understanding of God's ways in the world with God's creation and responds emphatically, "Yeah, but you oughta seed hit [the farm] when de Lawd had it by Hisse'f."[11] Despite the Christian preacher's claim of theological superiority and in spite of his authority clothed in the status of pastor, he fails to comprehend how the image of God planted in all creation, Christian and non-Christian, means a reflection of divine co-laborer and co-creator. In other words, God does not work alone.

The farmer brother represents a non-institutional folk theology critiquing the shortcomings of the church pastor. The farmer realizes from his common-sense wisdom born out of the divine image in him that God does not do anything in and of God's self. The Way Maker is a relational power that has to use human instruments to materialize the sacred will. More than a general helper, God works directly in a physical effort and digs in the black dirt of life with toiling humanity. In particular, God works with and through poor working people to achieve results of a continued dynamic re-creation.

We also note the Way Maker co-laboring with enslaved black victims in a personal letter sent by Frederick Douglass to his former slavemaster. Douglass's writing exhibits the thankfulness of one with whom God has worked literally to break chains of bondage and usher in liberation. "Thanks be to the Most High," pens Douglass in 1848,

> who is ever the God of the oppressed, at the moment which was to determine my whole earthly career. His grace was sufficient, my mind

was made up, I embraced the golden opportunity, took the morning tide at the flood, and a free man, young, active and strong, is the result.[12]

Because the Way Maker is a God of voiceless humanity, those violently and institutionally forced to the margins of the dominant mainstream society will never lack the accompanying presence of God. Indeed, the empowering nearness of "God of the oppressed," the resolute mind of the victims, coupled with determined activities toward freedom define the substance of grace. In particular, God enters Douglass's career at the decisive point when he needs both clarity in decision making and a chance freely to define himself as a human being. Divine grace influences the determination and vision of those exploited so that their minds stay on freedom. The Way Maker makes a way at the irreversible moment ("the golden opportunity" of *kairos*); with God working to provide a path, Douglass rides the flood to emancipation. Hence God renders sufficient grace alongside struggling humanity.

Moreover, the Way Maker extends the created co-laboring power beyond human beings to the entire cosmos and ecological sphere. Nature can also serve as a co-worker with God or God's Spirit. In an interview a Mrs. E. L. Smith narrates how she was hoodooed by an apparently jealous enemy, and the Spirit informed her about the proper cure: "I was hoodooed in Chicago in 1933. I felt it in my feet first—it drove me crazy. . . . So I prayed, and the Spirit told me to smoke cigars." Later she had a dream in which she drank water from a spring and "felt healed." Soon after, she actually bought a house that had a spring in the backyard. Just as in her dream, the real spring relieved her hoodoo-inflicted illness as well as other types of afflictions. "The water in that spring," concludes Mrs. Smith, "comes from the Lord and it can cure anything caused by the Devil," including complaints and cancer.[13]

In this example, the demonic manifests in the realm of bad hoodoo and the wicked use of nature for bodily harm. To exorcise evil out of nature, God sends the Christian Spirit and also a vision in a dream to the hoodoo victim. Both cigars and spring water carry the divine power and work with the will of the faithful Christian to defeat the machinations of devilish hoodoo. Theologically, Mrs. Smith believes in the potency of hoodoo and the inevitable triumph of Christian faith. Specifically, she has faith in a God who answers prayers and utilizes nature to help the folk during their trials and tribulations. The Way Maker is a God in nature who makes your enemies your footstool.

We witness a similar triumph of a supernatural good force in nature over a supernatural evil in the "Barney McKay" folk tale from the South Carolina Sea Islands (the Gullah Islands). The story's main characters are the "very, very poor" siblings, Jack and Mary and "an old witchcraft." One Christmas the children's parents give them three dogs (Barney McKay,

Doodle-Dee-Do, and Sue-Boy). The siblings receive permission to take a walk and Jack, "a very wise boy," puts four grains of corn in his pockets before leaving. Eventually the children meet "old witchcraft," and Jack uses his corn grains and sings a song to call the three dogs in order to escape death. The successful escape of the economically poor victims results from the children's confident faith in a supernatural power incarnated in the corn grains, the song of liberation, and the three dogs who finally kill the witchcraft. Thus we have the wisdom and bravery of the children, who call on a supreme benevolency through singing and operate with nature's animals and plants for emancipation.[14]

Release from harmful death, then, can be achieved by calling on and toiling with the infinite possible representations of divine goodness in nature and song. In contrast, preconceived notions and sterile doctrines about where the forces of good reside blind us to the grace of an all-powerful partnership for freedom. Actual resources for combating the demonic are immediately at hand for those willing to accept and to fight in concert with the ever-present conceivable gifts of divine favor. Nature's good accompanies the poor against evil.

A Stormy but Tender Way Maker

Though the Way Maker creates a co-laboring humanity, nature, and song, and presents an emancipating grace for society's oppressed, the folk culture's God can also provide stern lessons against the unfaithful who refuse to acknowledge or accept divine offerings. Rev. A. C. W. Shelton composed a song ("Wasn't It a Storming Time?") about one of the worst storms (1915) in New Orleans' history. Theologically, the tune depicts the taskmaster and disciplinarian nature of God when applied to the non-believers and non-seekers of the Way. "You want [won't] serve God, Men and Women/You are wicked and you seldom Pray." This contrasts clearly with the above-mentioned experiences of Mrs. Smith, who sincerely prayed to God and received the blessings of the Spirit. Instead of the prayerful and faithful pathway to freedom, the New Orleans community suffered the ravages of God's wrath through nature. Furthermore, this wicked people rebuffed the preliminary signs of impending doom from heaven: "I have warned you by Lightning." And even as the rains of destruction commenced and some did cry out to God, they persisted in doing evil: "People mourning, weeping did Pray/Just keep on with your sinful ways/I am able to stop you People's way." The Way Maker will break the backs of the people's evil will in order to stem all rebellions against their created purpose of working with God for new earthly social relations.

To resist the Way Maker's plan yields devastation and defeat. "People of New Orleans they did Run/God broke the Power and Cars couldn't run." At stake are the attributes of God's status shown by the terrible storm's disintegration of all aspects of human support and, indeed, human life itself.

Waters from heaven rained down on the very infrastructure of the city; "Telegraph and Telephone Wires" washed away. The flimsy symbols of human-made speech bowed to God's talking storm in nature. Likewise cars, artificially created means of transportation, could not run while the hurricane "was making eighty miles an hour." Commerce initiated by people halted all activities, but the "weight of the Gale everybody felt." In the song's words, God said: "I am able to stop you People's way." More specifically, the struggle fundamentally took place over retrogression along the "People's way" or progress along that of the Way Maker.

Consequently, God felt compelled to level the oppressed people's community so that they might once again acknowledge through practical faith their created calling to a supreme Way Maker. In the final analysis, the premier refuge in the critical times of lethal storms resides in God's status and direction. Any veering away from that fact will attract havoc and ruin of sinful lifestyles until the folk's culture of living realigns itself with the Way of their Maker.[15]

But the storms of God's righteous rage eventually blow over into divine tenderness. Judgment transforms into mercy. In his revealing poem "Black Mother Praying," poet and novelist Owen Dodson uses the voice of a poor African American woman wailing out for help. The mother beseeches God to end one of the world wars to which she has sent sons who will only return to the United States to suffer racial discrimination and lynching. Despite the terror of white people rioting against defenseless blacks domestically while the war is being fought for "freedom" abroad, this black mother persists in prayer because she understands that the Way Maker will not permit trouble to last always. Knowing that a secure lifeboat has to float her way, her humble plea goes out as from a shipwrecked victim amid a raging tempest:

> My great God, You been a tenderness to me,
> Through the thick and through the thin;
> You been a pilla to my soul;
> You been like the shinin light a mornin in the black dark,
> A elevator to my spirit.[16]

The tenderness of God implies a multilevel dimension to divine greatness, from steadfastness to bright lamp and leaven for the spirit. A tender divinity inherently grounds its mercy on rock-like dependability. God has to possess the qualities of a solid, immovable lifeline, which undergirds God's soothing nearness for the victims who are tossed to and fro. Regardless of the unpredictabilities of life, the oftentimes unworthiness of other human beings, and the approach of enemies from all sides, without doubt or hesitation one can always place the soul's heavy burdens upon the Way Maker's soft reliability. God's pillow contains the durability of satiny sympathetic materials, which are constructed for the weary weight of the innocent who cry out with pain.

A tender divinity inherently shows forth a burning torch's brilliance as a high-beam light during one's thick confusion and dense difficulties. For instance, this "black mother praying" finds herself in a confusing dilemma. On the one hand, she has bid all her sons goodbye, possibly to die on foreign soil for the freedom of another country. On the other hand, as a citizen in her own land, she encounters lynchings and intentional violations of her human rights by those who preach a patriotic war abroad. But since she has personally and historically experienced God's steadfast nature, she also knows that life's opaque obstacles will prove temporary before divine paths of resolution. In other words, faith in and encounter with God's steadfastness encourages her to expect visionary light out of severe adversity. Therefore steadfastness and light are the concrete bases for the elevation of depressed and worn-out spirits. Thus, too, a tender divinity spiritually lifts up the innocent prey trapped and held down in unjust social relations.

Way Maker Will Deliver

Above all, deliverer stands at the forefront of the Way Maker's nature in African American folk culture. Indeed, the interpenetrating thread weaving God's tapestry of creator, co-laborer, and stormy-but-tender being is the unquestioned certainty and predetermined victory of God's releasing the victims on time. The essence of the Way Maker, then, is definitely the highest deliverer, because God's name means the ultimate one who makes a way. Naming one's self and claiming one's identity carry profound theological importance in poor folk's way of living. In this manner, the theology of black culture contains the potency of liberation in the divinity's actual name.

In a recorded sermon, a southern African American folk preacher utilizes the metaphor of post office to amplify the Way Maker's paramount deliverance characteristic: "And whatever fer yer all, yer git it [from God]. Kinda like a mail-carrier or post office; give yer whatever fer you."[17] For the listeners of this sermon, the image of mail-carrier immediately registers pictures of the inevitability of God being there through all types of weather. The ultimate mail-carrier or post office will never fail to take your mail and deliver it on time, as well as ensure your receiving whatever has your name on it. In addition, the deliverer is someone you know by name, who asks about your family and stops to talk awhile before heading to the next mailbox. Because the carrier knows each name on the route, an attentive and good mail-carrier will deliver your goods even when someone has misspelled your address.

Similarly, in two "John and master" tales we witness God's special deliverance of freedom for the oppressed. In the first, master catches John, who has stolen hams, and threatens: "I'm still going to kill you John, because I know that's my meat." Refuting master, John argues that God gave him this food, and he aims to substantiate his definition of stealing and receiving. John tells master to meet him later under a persimmon tree to talk with God about the entire situation. By the time they reach the tree, John has already hidden his partner up among the persimmons. Each time John offers a prayer to God, his cohort rains persimmons down on master's head. But when John calls on God to drop flour and ham and they both "hit down on top of Old Boss's head," Boss cries out: "'I'll give you a forty-acre farm and a team of mules if you just don't pray no more. . . . From now on you can go free.'"[18]

Here the Way Maker realizes freedom from death for John and also makes the oppressor provide means for maintaining a quality life. God grants food to the poor from the storehouse of the rich; then, as part of the deliverance act, ensures the independence of the victims with adequate resources and capital. Therefore God establishes relationships out of injustice; the land and mules rightfully belonged to John, because he had worked it all his life. Admittedly one could raise the question of whether God or John's partner responded to the poor's supplications. However, the point is that John's perception of God is reflected in how he prays and the life-giving results he receives from the being to whom he turns.

The second "John and master" story underscores the Way Maker's deliverance work. In this instance, the master places two little boys in a tree to fool John. Master had promised John $100 for Christmas, but when John prays for the money underneath a tree, the two little boys drop a sack containing only $99.90. Returning to master, John counts out the sack's contents and comes up short. The master immediately begins to take the money from John because the original bargain denied John all monies except the exact $100 figure. But John had faith that his God would not be undone and would deliver both the money to him and him out of this quandary. John, therefore, responds: "That okay Boss, [God] did what he said he did, but he charged me a dime for the sack."[19] For John, God has the final say over the Boss's rules and guidelines and also determines the distribution of resources for the poor.

Finally, the Way Maker as deliverer will cure imbalance within the oppressed community (for example, delivering the folk from harmful social relations) and accept the victims just as they are (for example, delivering them back to God). "How the Snake Got His Rattles" concerns the problems engendered by a broken community when one member's self-sufficiency threatens the survival of the entire neighborhood. Specifically, God gives the snake poison so he can protect himself from the other animals, who unwittingly step on him every day. Due to poor sight and smell, the snake cannot distinguish whether a friend accidentally or a foe intentionally crushes his body. And so his poisonous bite kills all who approach, thus depleting the number of innocent animals in the forest. At a town meeting on these increasing deaths, Mr. Rabbit exclaims: "It's that snake! We got to do something, and do it quick, before he kills us all off."[20] The Rabbit becomes a delegate for the rest of the animals and asks God to save the animal community from the snake's further killing. God responds by giving the snake rattles to use as advance warning signals for those who approach him. The rattle noise will ward off potential enemies and alert friends to introduce themselves and their harmless intentions to the snake immediately.

In the course of restoring balance to this community, God listens to both sides of the dilemma, weighing and understanding the snake's concern as well as those of the rabbit, the animals' representative. The Way Maker then employs a balanced delivery process within the oppressed community. God becomes available to all, hears the petitions of both sides, sympathizes with the shortcomings in the particular situation, utilizes wise judgment, and ultimately restores balance to an unintentional predicament of unequal social relations. Thus the snake no longer suffers from innocent acts of murder and reintegrates himself among his neighbors. And the entire group of animals can conduct their normal affairs without fear.

Furthermore, the Way Maker delivers us back to itself (our creator) without preconditions or petty pretensions. Rather, a major criterion for emancipation is the poor's acceptance of their own identities regardless of how the larger society grades acceptable or non-normative behavior. Self-acceptance and self-naming, both cultural questions, have an impact on one's liberating return to the Way Maker.

Drawing on the come-as-you-are emancipation theme deep within black folk culture, the renowned preacher C. L. Franklin chose the widely known biblical story of the prodigal son to elaborate this theological point. Franklin unfolds the story of an adventurous son who departs from his father's home into the far country. Eventually the boy eats and cohabits with pigs, indicating an absolute demise. But when the prodigal son realizes who he is in the midst of rags and pig dung, he discovers a return path to his father's house. "You see," Franklin preached, "this young man didn't find himself until he had gone all the way from a palace to a pigpen." Then and only then could the youth find deliverance back to his father's safe home. Deliverance, then, hinges on a rediscovery of individual identity (to name) and an intentional confession of one's sinful plight (to claim). Hence God is able to bring us home just as we are in life's diseased environment.

Indeed, the Way Maker transports us from our "finding" ourselves in pig slop to the divine domain through a profound and dynamic conversion metamorphosis. Initially, the arrogant departure of the prodigal son images humanity's stubborn pride along a pathway from God. Pursuing such a reckless adventure, we inevitably cling to and value material possessions, wealth, and individualism. But the Creator has imbued human purpose with a definitive end. In Rev. Franklin's words: "The ultimate end of man was to come to God." The implantation of this truth within humanity's natural (original) state provides the conditions for the prodigal son to rise up out of the pigpen and open himself for a liberating return. And when he converts back to the freedom path which he had left, the boy cries out to God: "Make me, make me one of your servants." Deliverance offers a conversion from a superficial identity to a stripped-down essential self, which fundamentally is our cry to be made into servants of the Way Maker. In a word, God frees us in our self-acknowledgment to serve in a liberation movement.[21]

Actress Ruby Dee deepens further the conviction of deliverance by coming as you are. She relates the story of her Aunt Zurletha, who dies but is criticized by Ruby Dee's father with the pompous testimony: "Too bad, though, she never planned time to get with God." The father upholds incorrect theological doctrine that rigidly claims the Way Maker brings "home" only church members. No salvation exists for those outside the church institution or the Christian religion in the father's skewed religious beliefs. But Ruby Dee, a child at the time, rebukes her father's narrow notions about "getting with God" and screams:

Yeah, but [Aunt Zurletha] will. And when she does, I hope she'll have on her red wig and her rouge and her fingernail polish with toes to match and all her jewelry, and kiss God with her greasy lipstick on. I bet he'll just hug and kiss her back, and tell her how beautiful she is.[22]

The little girl knows within her heart how God brings humanity to the divine self, each person as she or he is. Specifically, God loves the beauty of each person's lips, hair, and other body parts unaltered to imitate those who would establish normative aesthetic attractiveness. Furthermore, God's arms open up to and deliver both the saved and the unsaved, sinner and saint, as long as one appreciates one's own unique identity. In the case of Aunt Zurletha, she refused to wear the faith cultural dress of Ruby Dee's father, who, in actuality, tried to force superficial external trappings upon Zurletha's kind and giving personality.

Again, the Way Maker's freeing activities in the world confuse those believers in a deliverance aspiration grounded on foreign and, therefore, nihilistic theological doctrines. Whether one needs to sink to the swine level, in the case of the prodigal son, or layer one's lips with greasy lipstick, like Aunt Zurletha, God calls, hugs, and carries us wherever the Way Maker has made a way especially for us.

A Place Way Made

The ultimate destination in life can also be a free place, a beneficial situation, or a hoped-for transformed reality. From this vantage point, the Way Maker becomes a Way Made. Theologically, the sought-after new place attracts one's persistent faith and subordinates all other desires within the context of one's longing for the final, ideal space. Only at this point can one assume a true identity. The Way Made offers the supreme cultural location.

Langston Hughes's poem "Our Land" gives a feeling of a broad seeking for a land of ultimate allegiance found in African American folk culture. The first lines of each stanza depict the poet's symbolic yearnings for all of black folk: "We should have a land of sun," "We should have a land of trees," and "We should have a land of joy."[23]

With the final destination established, Hughes employs a contrast technique that fleshes out the focus of a displaced people's desires. The landscape of the new place will include plentiful sun, sweet-scented water, and soft twilight against the folk's anemic reality; "And not this land/Where life is cold." Oppressed black people cannot thrive and be who they are living in a frigid climate that kills abundant sunshine (a necessity for plant growth), negates fragrant water (a rejuvenation from thirst), and eradicates a kind twilight (a precondition for peaceful rest). Our land, the poem indicates, is brightness not cold, vibrant nature not death, merriment not sterility, and love-song not infertility. The poet's dialogue of opposites tells us that this land of now is not our home. It belongs to someone else, and we are temporary residents suffering and dying. We can never be our true selves until we find our own place of lodging.

Our land includes the basic elements needed for the physical body. But it also takes care of a free spirit by providing us with healthy emotions and commitments to others. And coupled with the carnal and spiritual, pure merriment and "wine" flow in abundance. Accordingly, the Way Made appears when poor black folk freely live in what the original Garden of Eden offered—a harmony among humanity, the Way Maker, nature, and bountiful joy. Here, then, the folk will no longer endure poverty and the forced conditions of perpetual reacting to outside domination. Instead, in their liberated zone, they will pursue complete creativity.

Our land often comes to life in a poet's longing and conjecturing of Africa. Arna Bontemps's "Nocturne at Bethesda" reflects theologically upon a black poet's crying out to the silence of the pool at Bethesda, now asleep where angels used to stir it; "now no Saviour comes with healing in His hands." The absence of a savior and the medicinal pool's impotency, in Bontemps's poem, represent death's strangulation of contemporary "black faces." Consequently, the "old terror takes my heart, the fear of quiet waters." Yet the future hope lies in the possible return of the dead poet (and oppressed blacks in general) to Africa.

> Yet I hope, still I long to live.
> And if there can be returning after death
> I shall come back. But it will not be here:

if you want me you must search for me
beneath the palms of Africa.[24]

Africa, the Way Made, offers the final destination for the folk and, simultaneously, the start of a new life, a revitalized "me." The poet hopes to live but has to die in order to commence again. Death to the present old life, which the poet refuses to revisit ("it will not be here"), paves the way for Africa's idyllic refuge. Such dying and rising again is the only passage from a situation where salvation and healing have dried up to the oasis of palm-tree living.

With this death-to-life process completed, we can discover the real "me" of the poet. "If you want me," writes Bontemps, "you must search for me." If we wish to know the poet's identity now, our vision would be blurred if we relied on past understandings and descriptions. To want this reconstituted artist, we are forced to search, to make an effort to decipher a new black being. Africa, then, is African American folk's reconfiguration territory.

In addition to our land, Africa, music can be the Way Made in African American folk culture. The poet who authors "Daybreak in Alabama" seeks to compose music epitomizing the fresh reality of the day's breaking-in in that southern state. "When I get to be a composer/I'm gonna write me some music about/Daybreak in Alabama."[25] The music composition, the Way Made, will include "kind fingers" (universal kindness); black, white, brown, yellow, and red hands (the dawn of racial harmony); "touching each other" (recognition and loss of fear of the other); and "natural as dew" (natural equality and human relations). Underscoring this latter point, the poet pictures Alabama daybreak with a series of nature scenes such as swamp mist, heaven, tall trees, red clay, and a field of daisy eyes. Placing nature's development with race relations implies that racial harmony develops naturally, "falling out of heaven like soft dew."

"Daybreak in Alabama" fosters a search for the Way Made on three levels. First, the *poet's intention* is to achieve the future Way when he eventually becomes a musical artist and creates an unusual social space and nature-human relationship in his composition. Second, the *poem's actual meaning* itself is already an illustrative canvas of the final aim. In fact, the final aim's description appears in broad strokes in the poem's own text. And third, the poem's effect on the *reader* provokes us so that we begin to imagine theologically our agreements and disagreements with both the poet's and poem's conception of the folk's ultimate destination. The reader becomes an interested and responsive partner in the visioning of his or her own Way Made. And so we have a multiplicity of theological engagements intertwining around the human quest for ultimate new living.[26]

Last, the short story "The Life You Live (May Not Be Your Own)"[27] defines black folk's life and death end point as a transformed reality here and now. While growing up in school together, the two main characters,

Molly and her girlfriend Isobel, never had their own ways. The young girl Isobel always lived in the shadow of someone else's independence. She stayed in her father's house, where he worked her all the time, never giving her any money "to spend on pleasure things." She performed "farm work and all the housework." He was "even stingy at the dinner table." Later Isobel marries, yet her husband treats her worse than her father by forbidding her any friends.

Molly had survived no better. When she eventually marries, her husband keeps her "lookin' kinda messy"—a "fat, sloppy-dressed, house-shoe wearin', gray-haired, old-lookin' woman." But both black women reach a crossroads where they have to rethink their present and future. Isobel's husband dies from a heart attack while having an affair with a seventeen-year-old girl. And Molly's spouse discovers a very slim girlfriend and asks for a divorce.

The husbands' departures open a window of opportunity to perceive and pinpoint a place neither woman had ever experienced. Finally attaining it brings them into their own peace. The blind scales of servile allegiance depart with her spouse's death, and a liberating act of renaming unfolds for Isobel. She testifies with power as an unoppressed widow: "Now that I am free, I can change my name if I want to! Change my whole life if I want to!" In fact, she switches her old name, Isobel, to Belle. Naming, for her, becomes life.

Likewise, after her divorce, Molly undergoes this profound revelation: "I learned a lot I did not know, just on account of my not stopping to think for myself. Listenin' to others, taking their words. Trusting them to THINK for me!" Thinking, for her, becomes possessing one's own place.

Next Belle vomits out her sick memories and claims an unadulterated healthy consciousness. Referring to her husband's house, Belle screams,

"Some of the worst times of my life was spent here! First I was glad to leave my daddy's house. Now I'm glad to leave [my husband's]! The next house I get is gonna be mine. MINE! I'll live in that one in peace."

The oppressor's house can only leave memories of a broken body in pain and turmoil. It is definitely not the Way Made. Thus soothing, genuine healing starts when Belle transports herself from her daddy's and her husband's spots to her own. After acquiring five acres of land on the edge of a lake, she exclaims: "I want to be alone. Don't want no man, woman, chick or child tellin' me what to do no more!" Ownership of her own dirt enables her to stretch out and not take orders from any creatures. Then she can embrace a living peace, lying on black earth.

Molly also pursues peace. As a liberated African American woman who now thinks, she makes up her mind to quit her reading clubs because all she desires is peaceful reading. Her clubs "wanted us to make reports on what we read. I didn't want to make no report! I just wanted to read in peace." Free thought means a self-declaration for Molly. Apparently, she had previously joined clubs to keep busy or by force of habit.

Finally empowered, she can now freely choose each of her current and future moves. Furthermore, acquiring peace for both women has a psychosomatic impact. A restful mindset in their own homes produces healthier internal bodies, attractive external looks, as well as an unleashing of creativity reserves. "Both Belle and me was lookin' better, healthier, and was more peaceful every day. She was taking painting lessons now and music appreciation." Not only do bodies and health mature into progressive states of calm, all of life becomes an inexpensive, beautiful peace. "Life can be beautiful!" declares Molly. "Peace don't cost as much as people think it does!" Peace is life and beauty removed from a dominating thought, house, and name. Ultimately, peace rests on the victim's freedom: "The main thing is I do whatever I want to, whenever I want to," Molly states.

For Molly and Belle, the Way Made has become a serene way of life, a state of dynamic being where they have excommunicated imposed antagonistic contradictions from various levels in their relational identities. This has paved the way for a new being and a new community alive in a new authenticity. In Molly's words, "I love myself now . . . and everything around me . . . so much." In this specific sense, then, the Way Made for all also resides in peaceful conditions whereby poor and working-class African American women can love themselves while controlling their own spheres of influence. These women have found the final space that has motivated their entire lives. Faith in such a freedom goal stands as hope for all who would surrender to their liberation dreams.

THE TRICKSTER INTERMEDIARY

Quite often in black folk culture the Way Maker or Way Made relates to humanity through an intermediary Trickster figure. On the one hand, the Trickster exhibits exceptional cunning, unbelievable bravery, and a special relation to the Way Maker or Way Made. On the other, this intermediary individual shares the ups and downs of the human predicament, whether in the form of human finitude, circumstances, or striving for the fulfillment of aspirations.[28] Some of the more prominent Trickster personalities appear as animals and fictional human characters.

Animals

One of the most renowned animal tricksters is Brer Rabbit. He acquires his divine-human status because he is usually the only forest creature who can outwit his peers. Yet, at the same time, God can still put him in his place. Therefore he spends his day-to-day awareness in unique contrasts. While Rabbit rises to overcome whatever contradictions or challenges he encounters with the forest dwellers, God always subordinates him to divine power.

For instance, in "Hankering for a Long Tail"[29] Rabbit continually tries God's patience with requests for a long tail. To test Rabbit's craftiness, God assigns him a series of feats to perform against his forest brothers and sisters. "I reckon I'll set you a task to see just how smart you are," God states. Rabbit does fulfill his instructions and returns to God's door with a "bold and loud knock" and "puffed himself up." Unfortunately, instead of humility and thankfulness Rabbit expresses pride and overconfidence before the Way Maker. Rabbit expects immediate reward but is dissatisfied with God's response to his arrogant achievements. Instead of receiving the desired long tail, he is asked to wait under a pine tree before God "can fix" him up. Rabbit grows increasingly afraid and eventually starts to run away from God's house. God looks out of his window and shouts: "You think you are so smart, eh! You are so drat smart! Well, get a long tail yourself!"

God recognizes Brer Rabbit's superiority over other forest animals when the latter accomplishes the seemingly impossible assignments, tasks beyond the average creature. But, at the same time, when Rabbit arrogantly pumps himself up before God's house, God defeats Rabbit's desires and sends him away in fear.[30] The Trickster leaves others dazzled by cunning; nonetheless, God remains the master schemer.

We might note that there are instances where another forest animal defeats Rabbit. In "The Quail and the Rabbit," Quail tricks Rabbit and ends up feasting on peas and plums. "So that's one time Mr. Rabbit was beaten."[31] Still, we can assume from the overwhelming evidence in black folk culture that Quail's momentary victory serves as a rare exception to Rabbit's qualifications of Trickster. We can also assume that Rabbit will return for a future engagement in a protracted war of trickery. Rabbit's temporary failure does not erase his persistence.

Though the Way Maker situates and subordinates Brer Rabbit beneath divine trickiness, Rabbit is still God's benevolent emissary to the remaining forest brothers and sisters. Rabbit proves his intermediary status in "Brer Tiger and the Big Wind."[32] Tiger, a ferocious hoarder of abundant food and water during a forest famine, threatens any animal who attempts to share in his delicious treasures. Indeed, all "the creatures backed off and crawled to the edge of the woods and sat there with misery in their eyes." But Brer Rabbit discovers this contradiction of poverty and abundance and says, "That's not right. .... It's not right for one animal to have it all and the rest to have nothing." In the role of Trickster, Rabbit takes responsibility to call all the forest animals together as one body. Next he educates, persuades, and organizes them to defeat Brer Tiger. This process of organization and strategizing of the collective body helps the weaker brothers and sisters realize that they can defeat the big bully of the forest by working together. A move toward a communality of the disadvantaged verifies the belief that in unity there exists strength.

Moreover, though all other creatures initially live in fear, the Trickster is the only one who dares to tie Tiger to a tree, thus breaking a reign of terror. Tiger's forced removal frees up the forest's formerly monopolized capital and resources for the democratic majority suffering from hunger and thirst. Rabbit's heroic action, then, results in a new day of equality and peace; abundant food and drink prevail for all. In the course of a painful situation transformed into plentiful sustenance, all the brothers and sisters perceive Brer Rabbit as a mouthpiece of the Lord. And rightfully so. Rabbit confirms his position by blessing the food: "Get all the pears and drinking water you want, because the Good Lord doesn't love a stingy man. He put the food and water here for all His creatures to enjoy."

Rabbit thus interprets God's intentions for God's created order. Democracy (the will and welfare of the majority), equality (proportional and representative sharing according to each animal's needs), and power (decentralized economic control of resources) are the divine purpose for the hungry, fearful, and poor.

Brer Rabbit is a servant-leader sent directly from heaven. After having their fill of basic necessities, all the animals praise the Lord for giving them such a crafty intermediary: "They all joined in a song of thanks to the Lord for their leader, Brer Rabbit, who had shown them how to work together to defeat their enemy, Brer Tiger." As a result, the forest animals lifted up thanksgiving to God for putting forth a shrewd and powerful intermediary, who leads them on a grand exodus out of fear into a place of "milk and honey."

In another part of the animal kingdom, Elephant and Whale hold a power meeting in which they selfishly decide to monopolize all resources on land and sea and, in addition, employ their own normative canon to govern the poor.

> The elephant said to the whale: "compere Whale, since you are the largest and strongest around in the sea, and I am the largest and strongest on land, we rule over all beasts; and anyone who doesn't like it, we'll just have to kill, all right, compere?" "Yes, compere," agreed the whale. "You keep the land and I'll keep the sea, and between us we'll rule everyone."[33]

Brer Rabbit overhears this cartel conversation and observes the power dynamics unfolding. After watching and listening to these plans to implement a brute-force dictatorship, he voluntarily decides to risk his life by siding with the oppressed and the weak. His intent is to remove the prey of Whale's and Elephant's skulduggery from objects of someone else's domination into subjects of their own living space and animal history. For trickster Rabbit, the meek should inherit the earth and its riches. Accordingly, the Trickster does not care about a formidable status quo. He astutely discerns the role of those at society's underside and has faith that the physically weak can use their higher knowledge of tricks: "Oh, I don't care [about Elephant and Whale]," said Rabbit. "I know more tricks than they do."

Likewise, he recognizes his calling to resolve unjust conflict between a powerful minority caste and the forest's unempowered majority. Resumes Rabbit, "I am going to fix Whale and Elephant." Eventually Rabbit devises a ruse, which has Whale and Elephant unknowingly employing their physical power against each other in a tug-of-war rope-pulling contest. The Trickster, therefore, turns the oppressors' own strength against them in order to thwart their physical hegemony on earth. Similarly, Rabbit plays on Elephant's and Whale's fear and, as a result, obtains an instantaneous advantage. Donning a deer's skin, the disguised Rabbit approaches both Elephant and Whale and whines, "Take care . . . for Rabbit can poison anyone he wants because the Devil gave him the power to do so." The stupidity of the larger animals becomes apparent when their fright makes them timid grovelers before the triumphant Rabbit.

For poor folk who hear and enjoy Brer Rabbit's exploits over Whale and Elephant, a new way of being can enter and change their lives. In particular, Rabbit's victory suggests a new style of living. In his concluding remarks Rabbit says, "No matter who's the largest, I'm still the strongest—at least when I use my head!" Here he fortifies the folk's inner feelings of visibility and invulnerability by telling them they possess worth through a calculating use of their intellect. Therefore, the poor gain hope and courage to view themselves and their situation in a revealed light. They simply must use whatever appears as weakness for their strength in order to bring to earth future possibilities of uninhibited safe habitat. In other words, the Trickster helps the black folk to get over to their ultimate goal. In this way the intermediary empowers and delivers the listeners of this folk tale from their current dangerous situation to an alternative tranquil condition.

The Signifying Monkey story also deconstructs power relations by utilizing the language of signifying, an artful form of trickery in black folk oratory.

> The Lion was supposed to be the king of the beasts, and the Monkey wasn't satisfied. He thought, well, maybe there was a lot of animals in the wood was more substantial than the Lion, so he thought he would get up a contest. So the next day he decided on the Lion and the Elephant.[34]

First of all, the Lion has claimed a "supposed to be" throne due to his swift speed, terrifying bite, and potent strength. More specifically, this is his meta-narrative, a unilaterally imposed discourse placing restrictions on jungle conversation. Fair competition for a leadership title does not reside in Lion's vocabulary; Lion's talk, on the contrary, is sheer might. But Monkey knows the power of language; words plus their enunciation and nuances can bring victory or defeat depending on the agility and fast tongue of the talker.

Second, Monkey renames and redefines what is "more substantial" to include many more creatures in the woods than the Lion. Monkey reclaims and steals the privilege of naming power. Once he re-signifies reality and sees the potential of how things can and ought to be, he is free to connive at the empowerment of the weaker animals at the expense of the "supposed" king of the beasts.

Third, Monkey commences to signify the new reality by planting words of disharmony in the Elelphant's ears. "I know you can't be friends," chatters Monkey to Elephant about Lion. "The way he talked about you is a doggone sin." Trickster Monkey initiates a deconstruction of power relations through a process of verbal hearsay; he has not accused Lion of an actual physical act of misconduct. The "sin" is merely Lion's alleged bad-mouthing against Elephant. Thus Trickster Monkey employs a signifying tool (talking bad about and stirring up trouble between two people) whose substance itself is also signification (Lion's sinful gossip against Elephant).

In addition, Monkey positions Lion's signifying on a moral and theological level with the word "sin." Now Elephant has no alternative but to confront Lion angrily because the latter has challenged his perception of right and wrong. Clearly, signification is the Trickster's reconfiguration of spoken worldviews by hoisting the conversation to an ethical plane.

Fourth, Elephant's eventual brutal rout of Lion provides the occasion for Monkey verbally to harass Lion about the original evil (Lion's false superiority), which initially caused the Trickster Monkey to enter the discussion. Mockingly Monkey retorts: "Your eyes all bloodshot, got the nosebleed, even your rear need a couple of stitches. You call yourself the King of the Beasts." Thus Monkey's contrived sin against Lion (Lion's supposedly talking bad behind Elephant's back) enables him to rectify the paramount sin—Lion's exploitative claims of hegemony—and verifies Monkey's signification that many more woods creatures have substance.

Signification is not the only Trickster medium for the expression of word power in African American folk culture. Tales of weak creatures trapped in life and death situations abound in which the potential victim simply speaks a few words to mystify and terrify the oppressor bully. Buh Goat's talk against Buh Lion stands as a Trickster example for the listeners of this tale. Goat, the innocent character, controls the potency of word associations and thereby teaches folk listeners how to get over to their own ultimate concerns and final places. In this story Buh Lion sees Buh Goat relaxing on a big rock, approaches him for the kill, and in the process queries Goat about his activities. As Lion closes in, Goat keeps a bold heart and speaks out: "Me duh chaw dis rock, an ef you dont leff, wen me done finish chaw um me guine eat you."[35] Goat repels Lion and certain death by warding off Lion with words that merely interpret reality differently from Lion's nefarious intentions and crooked sight.

To the story's audience, the narrator sums up the force of speech: "Dis big wud sabe Buh Goat. Bole man git outer diffikelty way coward man lose eh life." Buh Goat teaches us the decisiveness of the "big wud." It can make us the object of the oppressor's claws, or it can depict us with rock-eating teeth and, thus, create a new reputation for the oppressed. In fact, Intermediary Goat's talk carries the weight of stone and the boldness to send his enemies fleeing with a fresh respect for former prey. Again, not only does the Intermediary succeed by virtue of commanding unnatural, and thus supernatural, discourse, but the poor African American listeners of these tales are renewed by the strength of the "big wud." Hence the Trickster connects a disadvantaged audience to a power source, the word, greater than their knowledge and themselves.

A final example of the Trickster's engagement of the big word is the victim's utilization of and empowerment by biblical exegesis: who has the right to interpret and interpret correctly the Way Maker's "word." At a certain point, Bear has captured Rabbit, who in self-defense uses his own biblical interpretation to attain an "exodus."

"Oh, you know if you say your prayers before you eat me," [Rabbit tells Bear,] "you'll have something to eat all the time—that's what the Good Book says." Well, Mr. Bear shut his eyes and returned thanks. When he opened his eyes Brother Rabbit was gone.[36]

Rabbit has his own biblical analysis of the "Good Book," that is, to serve the activities of those captured. First, Rabbit's common-sense folk wisdom, which tells him to trick Bear into closing his eyes, inspires Rabbit to dare his own biblical interpretation. Next Brer Rabbit's wisdom opens him up to a true biblical message—the Bible is a faith document of struggle between incarceration and liberation. The biblical word says those ensnared shall go free, but dominators have hardened hearts and scales on their eyes that impair their perception, reception, and digestion of the Good News. Basically Rabbit signifies to other animals, and the story symbolizes to its listeners, that the Bible is the privileged domain of the poor. Such a privilege gives them the authority, audacity, and revelation to interpret for their own majority experience.

A guardian angel theological role concludes this discussion on Tricksters found in animal characters. For example, a series of tales highlighting the protection of a white dog over poor people in real or potential danger depict the Way Maker's unending and diverse revelations on earth.[37]

An old black man walks home from a baseball game late at night, sights "a great big white dawg wid red eyes," and runs in fear, with the dog trailing behind. His wife tells him the dog is a spirit of a good Christian friend who came from the grave to bring him good luck and protect him on his return home. Another "true" story finds a fiddler leaving his younger brother in a cotton-seed house while the fiddler temporarily finds work. "A great big white dawg" appears at the foot of the younger boy's makeshift bed. The older fiddler brother explains later that the dog was "de li'l boy's mama, what done comed back from de grave to keep a watch ovuh de li'l felluh." A similar factual account narrates the ill plight of a little black boy who refuses to eat food and becomes sick. Fortunately, "a big white dawg" comes " 'bout twelve o'clock" and "staa'ted coughin' up tea cakes," which the little boy ate and loved. The boy's father states that these life-saving tea cakes were exactly like those his wife used to cook for their son.

Last, a tired black woman, Effie, heads home along the railroad tracks at night after working since dawn for a white lady. The Ku Klux Klan approaches her and she falls to her knees in prayer:

> My Lord, my Lord, please help me! . . . There on the tracks was a huge white dog. . . . The Klansmen were near. . . . As she stared at the dog, a soothing warmth enveloped her. . . . From within the silence came "Effie, keep walking." . . . She glanced back in wonder at the dog and felt the thought, "Walk, Effie, I am with you." . . . Effie passed within inches of the white-shrouded figures, between them, in front of them. They did not see her. . . . Effie slowly smiled and whispered, "Thank you, dear Lord."

The intermediary white dog (part animal and part divine) serves as God's guardian angel, who provides safe passage in times of trouble. Though Effie prays to a Christian Lord, tones of magic overlay the narrative because a dog is not what Christians normally associate with angels.

Restated, the Bible usually associates Jesus and human (biblical) figures with guardian angels; all else image magic. The theological implications, therefore, suggest the Christian and non-Christian nature of the Trickster. God uses other savior intermediaries in addition to Jesus in black folk culture. Moreover, the white dog's "I am with you" parallels Jesus' statement to his disciples regarding their missionary calling. (Indeed, Jesus' name, Emmanuel, means "God with you.") Likewise, the dog ascends into the sky. Hence, within the folk's culture, salvific work entails complementary representations of savior. The folk do not pit Jesus' centrality or decisive revelation over against the Way Maker's abundant capacity to choose diverse vessels in which to carry divine liberation.

Fictional Human Characters

In addition to animal characters, folk culture also presents the Trickster's theological aspects in fictional human characters, some of the most prominent being Uncle Wallace, Shine, Stackolee, Karintha, and High John the Conqueror.[38]

"Cry For Me,"[39] a mythical personal narrative, focuses on a Christ-like figure named Uncle Wallace. Wallace comes from down South and the folk mostly know him by his blues album "Big Voice Crying in the Wilderness." Not only is Wallace carrying a lone huge voice calling out in the wilderness, he also wears an extraordinary height, weight, and strength—well over six feet five and surpassing two hundred and fifty pounds, "the size of a black Grant's Tomb" in Manhattan, New York. Coming from the Black Belt South, the foundation for all American black culture, Uncle Wallace's birthplace symbolizes the original basic life of the wilderness. His root beginnings, then, imply primordial African American folk creation where community, family, religious, and educational values—that is, a holistic lifestyle—pervaded black people's essential being. He brings all these cultural values to the self-conscious memory and thus molds black identity toward positive survival and liberation themes.

One day Uncle Wallace comes to New York to visit his family and ends up playing blues on two guitars at a concert in Carnegie Hall.

> Then Uncle Wallace started to play ... and the next thing I knew, everybody was dancing—even me ... and all the rich white folks was on their feet in the aisles and their wives was hugging strangers, black and white, and taking off their jewelry and tossing it in the air and all the poor people was ignoring the jewelry, was dancing instead, and you could see everybody laughing like crazy and having the best old time ever.

Uncle Wallace's very nearness to people coupled with the force and spiritual power of his music causes the rich to renounce their old self of material glitter and the trappings of excess profit and begin to live in harmony through dancing (e.g., the contacts and movement of bodies) and laughter (e.g., a complete state of revelation of one's unguarded self). A voice bellowing out blues in the wilderness of racial and class divisions overcomes human-made hostilities and brings white and black folk, rich and poor to an unbelievable crescendo. Here, people and their body contact in one rhythmic motion have forged a microcosmic society foreshadowing the future Kingdom.

> Then the air changed. ... Everybody in the whole place was sobbing and crying and tears was pouring down their cheeks. ... The people was rushing toward him. They was all crying and smiling too like people busting into a trance in church and it seemed like everybody in the place was on stage, trying to ... touch him, grab his hand and shake it and hug him and kiss him even.

As an intermediary between the Way Maker and a place all people's inner drive longs for, Uncle Wallace induces a spiritual conversion on a mass scale, like a religious camp revival. The air changed because everyone had crossed over a barren desert and reached a mountaintop in their individual and communal reality. They were experiencing ecstatic behavior; cryings of joy replaced tears of sorrow. The entire Carnegie Hall struggled to "touch him" in order to soak in a seemingly divine spiritual power. Perhaps Uncle Wallace ushered in a Holy Ghost power like a mighty wind, thus accounting for the air change.

The story's narrator resumes description of the collective trance: "And the singing stopped. . . . He was dead all right." Uncle Wallace died playing the initial in-breaking that brought the dancers from the old world of capitalism and racism (e.g., "He'd taken all them people . . . and made them forget who they was, and what they come from") to a new horizon of people to people awareness (e.g., "And remember only that they was people"). With his mission accomplished, Uncle Wallace played his life into death so that living dead people could dance their way into a living humanity. From a certain perspective, he took on the collective burden, sacrificed his life, and exorcised evil out of folk trapped in the demonic.

The story "Shine,"[40] concerning the sinking of the Titanic, has the Trickster Shine embodying life at the bottom for black folk. Among African American folk cultural legend, white people did not allow any black people to travel on the Titanic except the servant Shine.[41] Legend also described the Titanic as absolutely unsinkable and thus a supernatural entity. But ocean waters started to flood the great ship on its maiden voyage, and the lone black servant Shine surfaces from the fireroom below to inform the captain. The latter responds: "Shine, Shine, have no doubt. I told you we got ninety-nine pumps to pump the water out." The captain refuses to acknowledge the interpreting ability and common sense of a black worker down in the ship's bottom. Instead of relying on those who work to make machines function and serve to ensure others' comfort, the captain arrogantly dismisses Shine and has a faith commitment in the supremacy of technology.

In contrast, Shine jumps overboard, thereby disobeying and challenging the captain's authority; that is, the act is a dismissal of the accepted economic-employer and social-racial hierarchies. Paramount is Shine's negation of the captain's godlike powers, for on this ship, the captain's decision held the thread between life and death for the passengers and the crew. Instead, Shine's abandoning of the Titanic says his life and identity are *not* in the captain's hands. Likewise, Shine's realization of potential death forces him not to accept the captain's speech. "There was a time when your word might be true," states Shine about the old hierarchical relation. But this is one time "that your word just won't do"; for the man from the bottom of life's boat has seized his independence and moved toward more solid ground.

For the folk listeners of the Shine story, Shine offers liberation with his rhythms of from-the-bottom-to-the-top deliverance. He begins in the ship's bottom, and surfaces to the top to warn the hardened captain. Shine next jumps overboard into the ocean's bottom, only to surface later on dry land with another chance of joy. The Titantic sinks to the sea's bottom, but Shine ends up dry, drunk, and dreaming about living. Shine avoids death's bottom because he outsmarted the all-powerful Titantic and its cultured bourgeois society (e.g., the best of Western science and civilization). Furthermore, he knows better than to give his life totally to sophisticated technology when his God-given knowledge and instinct alert him to pressing flood waters around his victimized life at the bottom.

When Shine plunges into the water, he undergoes at least three temptations or trials. First, the captain finally realizes that his only salvation lies in his former suffering servant, who worked tirelessly below deck. Therefore, as the Titantic is sinking, he desperately screams out across the ocean's surface: "Shine, Shine, save poor me. I'll give you more money than a man want to see." But Shine refuses the water-filled Titantic money and heads toward the authentic currency of solid ground. Now, for Shine, the Titantic money suggests bribery and an undesired definition of success.

Second, the captain's daughter, formerly the epitome of etiquette and womanhood, exposes herself and promises Shine more enjoyment, in her words, "than any black man want to see." The fact that she, as her community's "forbidden fruit," underscores "black man" speaks to her desire to commit the ultimate taboo. Shine refuses the captain's daughter's sexual overtures and conquers another sin. Finally, Shine outswims a deadly shark, king of the ocean, in his own habitat and consequently defeats the evil forces dwelling in nature's bottom.

In sum, this story begins in the second verse with Shine's small stature: "Shine, a little man" in contrast to "the great Titantic" in verse one. He enjoys no authority over people, machines, or money. In fact, Shine does not appear to have control over his own life; he is literally and figuratively a poor working-class black at the bottom of his job and society. But somehow somebody, some force or power, has endowed him with capability to change his stature and station, cross a stormy sea, and defy all human-made laws geared toward his defeat and death. Now, having broken society's established rules, Shine is free to name himself a free person.[42] Likewise the folk see their liberation potential in Shine's victory.

Even more so than Shine, Stackolee[43] typifies the height of the outlaw Trickster figure, taunting every conceivable "civilized" law. Indeed, he possesses the paramount Trickster traits of part of the low-down, common-folk element (as Langston Hughes calls them in this chapter's epigraph). In black culture, some of the folk have lost, and sometimes never have had, absolute respect for American society. This segment defines its true self as not simply a society-imposed condition, but as a voluntary incorrigible force. Its members perceive the extreme effects of American civilization; in turn, they utilize extreme survival techniques and emancipatory goals to cope with, in their view, what are decadent, hypocritical, cutthroat social and cultural norms. More than likely, the majority of folk in black culture are liberated upon hearing Stackolee's boundary-breaking triumphs. But in particular, the real day-to-day outlaws in black life are more easily transported to a new possibility and empowerment sense with the fictional Stackolee character. Theologically, for all the folk Stackolee offers a power of self-independence and self-definition unmatched in the black community or on earth. It seems as if one would have to explain his exploits, charisma, and superhuman machinations as results of some type of spiritual possession.

In brief, Stackolee walks into an eating and drinking "hole-in-the-wall," orders, shoots the bartender, kills anyone who moves too quickly, puts thirteen bullets in the chest of a man who has come to avenge the murder of his bartender brother, and has his way with any woman he pleases. In one version Stackolee accepts a prison sentence as though someone had simply given him the day's time. Thus Stackolee presents the intermediary traits of the folk beyond the law. He is a "bad nigger"; his badness derives from his breaking of and disrespect for all customs and mandates prescribed by most "decent living" Americans. Though condemned as bad by law-and-order America, the ballad teller and listeners hail and, in a sense, worship him. Whereas the normative law accuses and classifies him bad, as an outsider, the folk praise his outside position not as a bad bad but as a superlative good bad.

Furthermore, bad nigger Stackolee is hard on women, surpasses all others in sexual achievements, acts on his short temper with impunity, defies all authority, stands tall and fearless, accepts immediate responsibility for his acts, shoots all targets accurately, and boasts a reputation that precedes him. Truly he is comprehensive mythic desire writ large in folk culture, hence more than human and, at least, a demigod.

But Stackolee's use of women and killings in a raging temper also place him outside of black folk's identity with family and communal culture. Admittedly his intermediary counter-hegemonic lawlessness against the dominating political culture can bring empowerment to poor black people. Still, Stackolee's antifolk culture tendencies can push him into a realm of outlaw even to a healthy African American way of life. The duality of outlawness (outside white and black norms), then, reflects the warring of contradictory spiritualities raging for supremacy inside this Trickster. Consequently, extreme ambiguity can be a Trickster hallmark.

In the category of fictional human characters, different types of women, too, serve the theological office of intermediary. As female Tricksters, they stand between humans limited by their existential constraints and longed-for future possibilities. Jean Toomer's short story "Karintha" substantiates this dimension. At first glance black Karintha appears like all other females. Indeed, Toomer writes, "Karintha is a woman." Yet she has extraordinary qualities not usually possessed by human beings. Her very movements suggest spiritual presence — "her sudden darting past you was a bit of vivid color" and her running "a whir," like spiraling dust. Besides, she signifies perfection and perfected beauty as she carries her immaculate countenance "perfect as dusk when the sun goes down." Completeness and totality usually belong to divinities.

Moreover, Karintha points to the end goal of all those who seek unfulfilled dreams and new lives of perfect happiness.[44] In fact, all people received her unnatural wisdom, for she could tell other folks "just what it was to live." Especially for males, she actualized life. "Men always wanted her," and she fired their spirits on a quest of attainment. Even the preachers found themselves caught in her irresistible web of what could be. Young men literally counted her earlier growing days toward her marrying age. They sought to woo and capture her by giving her money. Some bootlegged whiskey, others went to big cities, and still a third group entered college; all subordinated their personal realities to the one prize of providing finances for Karintha.

Furthermore, Toomer, the author-narrator of this short story, presents a subliminal statement about Karintha's intermediary stature as a parallel with Jesus. Toomer performs a theological image association by linking her with rising smoke and, in the same sentence, having a male character sing out for his soul to be taken to Jesus. The following sentence elaborates on Karintha's own woman-soul. This image grouping positions Karintha as smoke, which the singer wishes to reach and, simultaneously, reach Jesus too. The singer offers up his soul to Jesus (which is linked to smoke and Karintha), followed closely by an explanation of Karintha's (the intermediary) soul. It appears as if the singer's soul finds clarity or direction only in the context of an adequate clarification of Trickster Karintha's soul. Thus word-image connections of Jesus-Karintha-smoke-soul could situate Karintha like Jesus as determiner of men's spirits.

But just as Stackolee Trickster hovers at the crossroads between benevolent theological values and traditions, on the one hand, and retrograde trends, on the other, so too does Karintha. Though she carries beauty and is perfection, she seems to bear a shadowy side to her divine-human nature. She "stoned cows, and beat her dog and fought the other children." And though she promises the ultimate to which all men gear their lives, none of the men ever will possess her; for men do not know that "the soul of her was a growing thing ripened too soon." Bringing her money amounts to nothing because the men will die "not having found" out about her prematurely ripened soul.

Ambiguity in this instance, however, seems to hint at something different from Stackolee's situation. Toomer, the author, develops this story, on balance, more as a critique of men's inability to perceive true beauty and its worth than as an attack on the Trickster Karintha. For example, her seemingly antisocial behavior toward her dog, cows, and friends actually occurred at the age of twelve, a time when such activities do not necessarily typify negative or shadowy behavior. Indeed, such childlike characteristics highlight the human, fallible dimension of intermediary Trickster figures who by definition, occupy the positions of human limitations.

But more important, the Trickster Karintha tells males that they cannot meet ultimate beauty, however defined, and concrete perfection, however perceived, through lust and blind passion. Warped addictions obscure insights into the essential soul of the real Karintha (her smoke soul and as mentioned earlier, by imagery association, her Jesus connection). So the Trickster not only connects a pathway from finite humanity to unrestrained possibilities, but also acts this out in a critical fashion against those suffering from harmful habits.

Specifically, the males try to capture Karintha's divine side by way of money. Through monetary accumulation, they hope to achieve perfected beauty and complete happiness. Ultimate beauty and perfection, fortunately, do not result from slavish adherence to finances. Lacking this critical perspective, the men in the short story die never understanding the nature of Karintha's ripened soul. The Trickster teaches that human beings, too, shoulder a self-conscious and self-critical responsibility in their faith, vision, and witness relative to the intermediary.

Finally, of all the fictional human characters in folk culture, High John De Conquer parallels most closely the work of Jesus Christ, the decisive Christian intermediary. The theological figures found in African American cultural literary imagination act like the divine spiritual go-betweens found in African American biblical literary presentation. The folk's own faith interpretations function that way. Both High John and Jesus bridge black folk over from sinful slavery to God's exalted liberation.

In Zora Neale Hurston's version of the High John folk tale,[45] John is an African American's contribution of hope through laughter and song to those facing hardship. John's signs (his signifying presence) are a laugh, a singing-symbol, and a drum-beat. However, signs mean a representation of a fundamental subtextual presentation, and in John's case, "the source and soul of" black laughter and song, the subterranean "inside thing to live by," was the "hopebringer." Theologically, then, one could interpret John's primary role as a passageway from divine certainty in future "conquering" to the lowly "Johns" all over the world (hence his name, High John de Conquer). Indeed, God does not leave God's little ones vulnerable to lethal attacks of dominators. For "Heaven arms with love and laughter those it does not wish to see destroyed"; thus De Conquer was manna, descending from above.

Like Jesus, John "came to be a man"; for, in Hurston's words, "he was not a natural man in the beginning." Similar to Jesus, who in the beginning was the Word who was with God, John commenced as a Whisper that "put on flesh." Also like the Word, the Whisper originated in Africa and came walking on the waves of sound. Once settled on land, the Whisper incarnated among the poor enslaved African Americans. They knew John in the flesh wherever the "work was the hardest, and the lot the most cruel," and thus the Whisper "helped the slaves endure. They knew that something better was coming." Again the essence and soul of the Whisper, displayed through laughter and song, is as hopebringer in specific social locations. When John "came to be a man," he showed special divine intent and choice by acquiring the flesh of poor people knocked down by slavery's bullwhips. (The "slave folks knew him in the flesh," but "Old Massa couldn't know, of course.") John soothed the victims and undergirded their tribulations with hope in a vision for tomorrow.

Besides the hopeful vision, High John De Conquer actually wrung the possible out of the impossible in his Trickster role.

> And all the time, there was High John de Conquer playing his tricks of making a way out of no-way. Hitting a straight lick with a crooked stick. Winning the jack pot with no other stake but a laugh. Fighting a mighty battle without outside-showing force, and winning his war from within. Really winnning in a permanent way, for he was winning with the soul of the black man whole and free.

The Trickster has two faces and practices "appearance and essence." Suggesting a lack of power, John appeared among the slaves. But the essence of his appearance was radical transformation of the slaves' identity and place. No longer were they bounded by Old Massa's plantation. In the mighty battle between oppression and justice, John realized a new kingdom, a new realm where marginalized people could name themselves and determine their own direction. Appearance showed the slaves still ensnared in Massa's satanic trap; in essence, though, John's hope had made them new beings, who, having tasted divine laughter and song, now could struggle on toward the future.

Again like Jesus, High John returned to the origins, specifically "back to Africa," and will come again to serve his oppressed people; "he is not dead" because he conquered the system of evil. The world's have-nots still maintain an empowering hope in the Second Coming of the Whisper. And while living between the first and the second comings, poor people still engage in John's grace offerings, for "he left his power here," dwelling in the "root of a certain plant." Possessing the root summons the Whisper's power.

We see this divine power persisting in a conversation between Hurston and Aunt Shady Anne Sutton. With living faith in the intermediary, Aunt Shady exclaims: "Sho John de Conquer means power. . . . God don't leave nobody ignorant. . . . He don't want folks taken advantage of because they don't know." Sutton actually has faith in John's salvific work from God because of what the Conquer has done for her people. "My mama told me . . . how High John de Conquer helped us out. He had done teached the black folks so they knowed a hundred years ahead of time that freedom was coming."

For sections of African American folk belief, God sent High John de

Conquer from Africa and heaven. Incarnating in the lowest of the exploited, John provides the gift of laughter and song signifying hope. Because God's servant had told the old folks long ago about inevitable freedom, and because that freedom took place, the work and tales of John have passed from generation to generation, each of which still possessed and possesses his liberation power in the root. From her observations of black folk's convictions, Hurston concludes: "John will never forsake the weak and the helpless, nor fail to bring hope to the hopeless."

In addition to fictional human characters, both lesser-known and well-known real human characters have served Trickster roles in African American folk culture — Harriet Tubman, Nancy Vaughn, and others.[46]

TO GET OVER

The Way Maker or Way Made is ultimately realized hope enjoyed by the poor where the latter reach their true selves and occupy their final space. The multidimensionality of the intermediary connects with the Way Maker's power and, simultaneously, experiences the poor's problems, hopes, and aspirations. To move through the Trickster to the Way is the theological effort of the poor to "get over."

To get over is oppressed people's practical faith of survival and their struggle toward liberation. This lifestyle entails a protracted and nuanced process of imitating the Trickster and, fundamentally, a conscious (and subconscious) faith in the Way Maker or Way Made. To get over enables marginalized folk to cope with imposed, painful predicaments that ensnare the poor in dominating systemic evil (externally) and the unseen deterioration of the victim's will (internally). The very daring movement to get over, therefore, sustains one for transformation of both the wounded self and demonic structures. It is the have-nots' yearning expressions through witness to oppose and move out of all the world's turmoil set against them. The process tends toward higher ground. In African American folk culture, the usually voiceless black people fight to initiate their participation in the fruits of the Way Maker or Way Made with the aid of the Trickster's lessons, thereby reclaiming their original God-given humanity. Three examples serve to amplify this get-over mode of the black poor: song, having fun, and the ancestors.

Song

During the antebellum period, a certain peg-leg sailor known as Peg-Leg Joe developed a "secular" song that, in fact, served as a thread to the slaves' faith movement to a stolen freedom. Calling the song "Foller de Drinkin' Gou'd,"[47] Joe told how the Big Dipper (the Drinkin' Gou'd) would help escaping human chattel pursue the northern direction under cover of night. Joe would show slaves the imprints that his natural and peg-leg made so that, after he had departed, bondswomen and bondsmen could track him to emancipation by both the stars and his footprints.

The Trickster Peg-Leg Joe uses the language of nature in the song both to protect and free black chattel. Particularly, the escaping African Americans deploy a double-faced mask while singing. On the one hand, white slaveowners and accommodating blacks (both representing satanic enforcers of bound human flesh) would interpret the lyrics sung as, perhaps, happy darkies idling their time away. Natural metaphors flood the entire song and bring to mind rhythmic servants engrossed in the idyllic or pastoral. This surface interpretation by the enemy greatly aided slave strategy for deliverance, for it deflected any suspicion away from their subtextual intent. A faith song, therefore, serves to sidetrack and befuddle satanic opponents of an emancipatory journey.

On the other hand, "Foller de Drinkin' Gou'd" is saturated with the real subtext of escape. The song contains coded language, which only those of faith hear and perceive. For example, one verse states: "De riva's bank am a very good road/De dead trees show de way/Lef' foot, peg foot goin' on/ Foller de drinkin' gou'd." The slaves' practical implementation of say one thing and mean another signifies an imitation of the Trickster's scheming personality.

In addition to this singing dual discourse, the song exhibits a spiritual potency that not only leads toward freedom by providing natural landmarks, but also grips the singers into another empowering dimension. One can imagine the constant refrain of "Foller de Drinkin' Gou'd" being quietly sung over and over again as black slaves stealthily moved through the woods in the dark. Repetition of a freedom song in the heat of ever-present danger serves to transpose the victims from a state of hesitancy to an ecstasy of daring. As they "foller," they persist in singing; as they sing, they persist in "follering." The faith statement internal to the song—its spirit of deliverance—intermingles with the enslaved's faith in ultimate destination. Thus, "Foller de Drinkin' Gou'd" further fixates the runaways on emancipation, shores up their determination, puts them in a quasi-trance of anticipation, and helps to carry them along. Poor African Americans under slavery literally sang secular faith songs to freedom.

This secular liberation song encouraged enslaved African Americans to risk life and death for their ultimate Way Made—a chance for a peaceful unchained identity and unrestrained mobility. Their precarious non-guaranteed act, hence a step marked by a faith leap, indicates their unwavering conviction to sing their way to a promised land up north.

Poor blacks have also used work songs to survive, defy, and dream of freedom. "Workin' on de Railroad" shows the survival aspect.[48] The song's black singer pinpoints the contradiction between having physically constructed the railroad while, simultaneously, white men don't pay him enough to ride on the fruits of his labor. Relatedly, the black laborer sings about the systemic absurdities of working for slave wages for a white capitalist and then having no other option than to spend this money at the company store of the same bossman. The employer owns both the railroad and the company store. Furthermore, the lyrics of "Workin' on de Railroad" reveal how poor black men are dead tired after working for rich white men. They finish with shoes worn out, burning blisters, hunger, and no money.

In the face of these contradictions, absurdities, lack of resources, and dismissal as human beings, the victims of racist capital can pursue, among others, three options to survive: suicide, irrational violence, or self-conscious control of their language and themselves. Choosing the latter survival option enables the worker to avoid a complete breakdown of his spirit. Indeed, a work song enables the victim to express creativity uncontrolled by white men.

The song, too, allows the victim literally to have the last word on his or her state of poverty. Sometimes the way to make it through, then, is to sing about one's hardships in order to keep from committing suicide. The song itself sustains the life of the marginalized, which is a means of protest if the victim is to ever pursue his or her Way Maker or Way Made.

The survival issue also comes through in the work song "Can't You Line It," another railroad worker's tune.

> Wonder what's the matter with the walking boss/It's done five-thirty and he won't knock off. . . . /I ast my Cap'n what's the time of day/ He got so mad he throwed his watch away. . . . /Cap'n got a pistol and he try to play bad/But I'm gonna take it if he makes me mad. . . . / Cap'n got a burner I'd like to have/A 32:20 with a shiny barrel. . . .[49]

Here the black singer goes beyond survival as mere expression for sanity maintenance and borders on strategized self-defense and freedom action. At least the notion of physical resistance in ideas and words presents itself and uplifts the poor's spirit beyond passive description of externally imposed oppression. This work song not only serves one to get over through self-expressive ventilation, but also shouts defiance and action plans. So "Can't You Line It" allows the black laborer a pause to think and sing out visceral hatred. At the same time, the singer ponders the possibility of resistance and prospects of victory. The singing dynamic of naming one's oppression and contemplating one's ability powers the poor through.

Survival and defiance, in African American work songs, go along with God's name and movement from the old to the new. The rock quarry tune "Dis Ole Rock Mine" shows survival amid bone-twisting labor.[50] "Lord I done got tired of the way I bin fallin' in dis ole rock mine." The word "fallin'" symbolizes the daily intensification of oppression; both the workers' job and exploited lives entail perpetual downward descent, a state of backbreaking, dead-end existence. "Rock mine" further images a brittle, unchanging hardness of life. Yet blurring the so-called secular-sacred distinction, the black singer calls on the Lord's name to help make a way out of no way. His outcry to and summoning of "Oh Lord," then, mark a conscious connection of singing to ultimate liberation. Here, too, his faith is in fleeing to a new way; that is, God offers a way out.

At the same time, the singing worker's tune shows a get-over process from the old to the new. First, the laborer protests the old way: "I done got tired of the way I bin fallin'." Then he sends his work hammer back to bossman and flees from his exploited situation. Returning of the hammer proves key, for "Dis ole hammer that I bin usin'/Is killing me, oh, yes!" The hammer's meaning, broadly speaking, includes the entire system of victimization and personal degradation of being owned and controlled by cap'n. To surrender that hammer implies transformation from death to life.

As get-over methods, chain gang work songs convey the message of solidarity, naming good and bad, and actual freedom flights. In "Hyah Come De Cap'm," the riding boss approaches a group of convict laborers in order to discover what has happened to Jimbo, an escapee.[51] The second stanza states: "Lookin' fer Jimbo/Don' say nothin'/Go 'head Jimbo/Don' say nothin'/Run in de bushes/Don' say nothin'/Cap'm ain't fin' you/Don' say nothin'." Despite Cap'm's interrogation, the remaining convicts maintain a collegial bond of silence. Clearly they all know Jimbo's plan and whereabouts, but they "Don' say nothin'." Solidarity with Jimbo in song thus gives blacks forced into prison labor some self-controlled movement within chains; that is, silence on Jimbo vicariously enables them to feel linked to his new wanderings in "de bushes."

Though quiet on the escapee, the singer proudly and with jubilation redefines Jimbo from the normative titles (assigned to black male prison labor) to the "Good." To be good, the antithesis of African American male as criminal, is an existing bold flight to emancipation. Indeed, Jimbo is good because he renamed his life status and pursued the good way. And to all other black laboring chain gang members as well as to the Lord, the singer offers a faith statement that he also will take advantage of the opportune time to seize the good Way, the Way Made. "Ah'm goin' on," sings the tune's author, "Lawd, Lawd/Dat same good way," "Dat same good way/Lawd, Lawd/Dat Jimbo gone." The renaming of Jimbo from bad to good inspires others to dare to take their freedom.

In addition to secular freedom and work songs, the blues show a certain theological lifestyle of getting over in African American folk culture. One strand within the blues contains, at its core, perpetual contradictions endured by the folk, yet out of which they triumph: joy in the midst of sorrow, hope in the midst of despair, a way out in the midst of insurmountable trials and tribulations, the ability to sew back up one's heart after it has been torn apart by the troubles of this world, and time to think through and philosophize about the seemingly endless obstacles of life. By giving blues singers space to think, they start to get a handle on the adverse forces acting against them. For instance, verifying the blues' preserving and regenerating life process, Jasper Love of Clarksdale, Mississippi, comments:

> I've heard my grandmother say it was a boat they called Choctaw. She say she used to roll a whole barrel of syrup or molasses. She used to roll them barrels right alongside of her husband, and she used to cut sprouts with him when they was cleaning up. Those blues come from way back when they had to study something to try to give them some consolation. The [white] man was doing them so bad, taking all they had and working them to death. They just had to do something, so they sang about what they felt.[52]

In this blues emphasis, song creates another horizon where singers position themselves in their own consolation. Indeed, consolation acts as a free way for soothing feelings through song because sometimes the folk only have one avenue of constructive self-regeneration. "They just had to do something"; the blues, then, is this doing something. It expresses a profound faith in the oppressed person's ability to act, even if in a mere song. This practical faith represents subversive denial of the white man's law and order, which mandates only that the black poor live to create profitable commodities for the rich.

The blues is a faith act because it can only blossom when African American singers feel deep within their souls that the only thing left for them to do on earth, short of death, is to create a blues melody. The blues sound is a wailing, but a wail that is a last defense against encroachments that have decimated all previous armor of the poor. One can always discern another's faith and ability to move beyond despair by observing what that person turns to when confronted with superhuman pain.

Often personified, the blues also represent a perpetual state of claiming one's being, a process of life that stretches beyond the specific incident which births the blues tune. For instance, though a lover may have left and, thereby, inspires a blues lyric, the act of the lover's departure simply symbolizes the accumulated bad luck in life's other areas (job lost, no money, etc.). Like certain work songs, the blues helps the poor black singer and listener jump deep down within their souls, express the depths of universal catastrophic misfortune, and give vent to the pain as well as think about future possibilities. The blues lets the head figure out the troubles of the soul when the heart has been wounded to the bone. Every conviction to survive, every notion of faith about movement from point "a" to point "b," is stripped to its essence in singing, hearing, and seeing the blues performed. In a certain sense, then, the blues not only carries the singer along but also supports the communal listeners and sharers of despair.

In fact, a strong tendency in blues shouts faith in freedom. One singer announces: "I may be down and out today, but I'll be up some day"; and another wails the blues like riding a freight train with "Goin' where I never been beat, I'm goin' where the chilly winds don't blow." And a third knows that despite daily doldrums, trouble doesn't last forever: "Michigan water tastes like sherry wine. Mississippi water tastes like turpentine."[53]

Here the purpose of humanity is continual motion in the face of sorrow and depression, essentially a hope-keeping and confidence-sustaining trek. "I'm got a mind to ramble, a mind fo' to leave dis town/Got a mind my baby is goin' to turn me down," plays one blues bard as he, apparently, prepares to ramble on to heal his heartbreak. Looking for liberation in his head and an oasis for his body, another sings: "Did you evah ride on de Mobile Central Line?/It's de road to ride to ease yo' troublin' mind."[54]

Sometimes the blues will make a woman and a man turn on each other and shoot each other. Therefore, as a message of getting over, the blues has its negativity and downside. The weight of the blues can break one's heart and dim the vision of freedom, joy, laughter, and communalism. That is the reality of certain parts of folk culture. Human purpose turns into a dog-eat-dog survivalist confrontation. Personhood is violated and folk seek deadly revenge.[55]

Also, the blues entails certain proverbs that (a) help the community establish and maintain order ("You gotta reap jus' what you sow"); (b) aid the individual in navigating through life ("My momma tole me, my daddy tole me too/Everybody grins in yo' face, son, ain't no friend to you"); and (c) set boundaries in the relations between men and women ("Brownskin momma make a rabbit chase a hound").[56] Here blues singing provides a spiritual glue to negotiate both individuality and human relation in community. Without this, an oppressed African American folk would perish through nihilism, lack of ethical codes, or through anarchy, lack of proper (extended) family connections.

Given the above get-over blues description, we can see how a certain affinity must exist between Christianity and the blues. Indeed, on many levels they match each other in their faith ways of living. Bluesman James Thomas (Mississippi Delta) perceptively comments on Christian and blues music's interchangeability:

> You have to match the right verses. Some of them, you hear a blues start off, "Lord, I ain't seen my baby since she been gone." Well, you can turn that around. Instead of saying, "Lord, I ain't seen my baby since she been gone," you would turn around and say, "Lord, come and see about me." ... Some blues you play, you could turn right around and the same blues that you play, you can play a church song on that same blues music you had over there. That's the way that works.[57]

No doubt then the blues musician (if not also the church preacher) is very aware of the interpenetration of substance and form regarding Christian and blues tunes. Repeatedly, one hears blues folk singers calling on the Lord's name ("I've got the worried blues, Lord. I've got the worried blues") or conducting a conversation with God ("Been down so long, Lawd, down don't worry me").[58] In short, Christianity and the blues, two forms of practical faith in survival and liberation, share similar musical forms and similar theological themes—pain, suffering, hope, love, community, deliverance, faith.

Having Fun

Having fun on one's own designated schedule, exemplifying the next get-over faith mode, has become another survival lifestyle and protest force of habit that some within black folk culture have adopted to accommodate their total life convictions. Because white people and bosses have sought to control African American labor, love, and relaxation rights, some of the folk have fought for free space in their daily lives by pursuing their own definition of fun.

The personal testimony of John Junior, a chimney sweep, bears out this point. Speaking with an authority acquired from administering his own agenda in a racist, hostile world, Junior comments:

> I quit the milk truck, couldn't have my fun like I wanted to. Had to get up too early. I was only ten years old then. What I didn't like about the milk truck was I couldn't be wid that sweet little gal next door long enough. Then, I got me a job ridin' a bike. ... I went to work so I could buy the clothes I wanted. ... I always did like to be dressed up. ... That's all a po' man can do—dress up, and have a good time.[59]

Clearly the ultimate issue for his daily life is to subordinate himself and all around him to having a self-determined fun. Instead of a slave-like attachment to money resulting from work, for him, work provides an avenue for extended time to experience pleasurable activities. In his setting white power structures monopolize most businesses. Therefore, to quit the milk truck for fun living also illustrates fun pursuits as critique of white supremacist economic exploitation. His total immersion in fun, which is obviously quite enjoyable, thus acts to challenge oppression and operate in a liberation method. Junior has fun for freedom.

Basically, what is not fun is the larger society's denial of his life. We see this in the substance of his new liberated existence with a free agenda. Now he arranges life to enable his purchase of clothes, consumption of food and drink, loving a "sweet little gal," and time to think for himself. Apparently these were fundamentals, but not all the things that white social systems had denied him from birth. So in the fight to manage his own plans, Junior also cuts former ropes that tied him to others' plans and thus refused him a full life. Fun vivifies the poor; "that's all a po' man can do."

At least one reason why Junior chooses having fun as practical faith is because his life experiences have shown that Christianity is the white man's religion. Resuming his autobiographical conversion and transformation, he proudly reveals a lack of Christian lineage ("we don't believe in that stuff") in contrast to his conviction that drinking bottles of wine in church would increase its membership:

Have fun, live. You don't live but once. When you die, square up the Devil. No, indeed! There never was a Christian in my family, we don't believe in that stuff. My pa used to say, "Get me a bucket full of wine I'll join the church." Spare time? Man, I ain't had no spare time. . . . In my spare time I have my fun!

Christianity is not his way of life; having fun is. Apparently the Christian religion did not work for or appeal to his family because it did not make sense or had not worked for others. However, in Junior's opinion, Christianity helped whites keep blacks on their knees. He claims:

I strictly haves my fun. No, I ain't tendin' bein' no Christian. That's the trouble with niggers now. They pray too damn much. Everytime you look around you see some nigger on his knees and the white man figurin' at his desk. What in the world is they prayin' fo'? Tryin' to get to heaven? They is gon' to get there anyhow. There ain't no other hell but this one down here.

Christianity could never be the way to get over for blacks, says Junior, because it was hell masquerading as genuine religious faith. Certainly the only beneficiaries in the black-white Christian equation were the white profit-makers figuring their dollars and cents while black folk called on Jesus from their knees. Instead of the folk enjoying life, white religion had fixated poor blacks on an ephemeral, impotent prayer-life, a stratagem to keep African Americans' eyes on a nonexistent heaven while the white man monitored the wealth on his desk. Above all, Christianity pacified blacks and kept them subservient to whites by literally placing them in a stationary spot on their knees. Thus whites gave poor blacks a religiously practiced and theologically justified daily way of pacification and immobilization.

Because white religion and profit-making had created the only living hell that African Americans would ever see, Junior opts for renewed life now — clothes, food, shelter, his "good woman," time, and more. Referencing the various aspects of his fun religion to replace white Christianity, Junior elaborates: "I took [my wife] out the white folks' kitchen." First he claims his family as part of power to determine a liberated agenda. "Man, as long as I can make a dollar sweepin' chimneys I ain't goin' to eat nobody' left-overs." Food too is necessary for enjoyment and pleasure, especially food which one purchases instead of begging for whites' leftovers. "I can buy what I want." Here Junior declares independence from all the cruel and exploitative hoaxes that employers played on employees by forcing them to shop at company stores. Junior screams No! He buys where and what he desires. "I'm my own boss." The heart of the get-over matter lies here. Junior gets over by having fun, controlling his own schedule as his primary way of life. Theologically this represents human witness and purpose because it is, first, a conscious attack on a named demonic hell—a white-induced, earthly turmoil against a knee-bent black subserviency—and, second, an independent assertion that consumes the very being of Junior and all the ultimate questions he poses. Christianity is white religion; having fun is religious life.

Venerating Ancestors

In addition to utilizing song and having fun, faith in and veneration of ancestors (such as Trickster intermediaries) emerges as another get-over lifestyle in African American folk culture. Primarily, ancestral adoration bridges into the sacred realm. Those long-departed or not-so-distant predecessors comprise a ritual practice celebrated in poetry, personal narrative, and folk history, among other expressions. Excavation of ancestral traditions that resurrect values and lessons for living rightly, loving in community, and constructing positivity among black folk sustains a movement for empowering convictions. Both tradition and ritual customs, therefore, unravel contemporary problems for liberation and justice purposes. Ancestral veneration serves as a process in which black people's faith in freedom carries itself toward ultimate emancipation by drawing on a liberating lineage.

For instance, James Weldon Johnson's poem "O Black and Unknown Bards"[60] raises a series of rhetorical questions to draw on the creative ethical lessons of enslaved African Americans. The poet seeks to answer how these past black bards were able "to touch the sacred"; how bonded people felt an ancient prophetic faith; how Christian slaves could remain physically enchained but possess free spirits. And, though deadened and captive, how could they still create love, faith, and hope songs? In fact, inherent in the poet's successive queries lies the response. These black and unknown bards succeeded through faith in a prophetic Christ of liberation. The verse "Have stretched out upward, seeking the divine" instructs the descendants of bondage to likewise pursue that which is greater than and beyond themselves.

More precisely, the line "You sang a race from wood and stone to Christ" exactly describes the nature of this divine. Jesus Christ, from slave bards' interpretations, becomes the endpoint post-emancipation from wood and stone shackles. Just as the ancient bard sang the race to Christ and freedom, so too must contemporary artists assume intentional creativity for divine liberation.

Not only does ancestral veneration instruct contemporary artistic theological purpose, it also, through a matriarchal lineage, suggests a link to combative primordial black values; transformative familial love; a fulfillment of freedom dreams; and, through Africa, potency in identity and memory as other get-over modes toward black folk's free identity and own self-determination (divine conditions and spaces).

Paule Marshall's autobiographical story concerning her childhood encounters with her grandmother, "To Da-duh. In Memoriam,"[61] depicts putting on armor from the best in past values for war against contemporary negative assaults on the folk. Marshall, a nine-year-old from New York, visits her grandmother Da-duh in Barbados. That matriarch brought "a past that was still alive into [Marshall's] bustling present."

Furthermore, Da-duh had reconciled seeming opposites of life so that she moved about the world without antagonistic contradictions. She contained "both child and woman, darkness and light, past and present, life and death." Da-duh was at peace with herself, others, and her natural environment. She freely enjoyed such multiple reconciliations because she had been born in a place where she knew her true self and owned space to grow. In her own way she attempted to share and pass on her sense of emancipatory lifestyle to little Marshall. Daily the grandmother would take the granddaughter on walks in sugarcane, breadfruit, mango, apple, lime, and guava groves. From Marshall's perspective, Da-duh intoned "the names of the trees as though they were those of her gods."

Indeed, they were her gods, pointers to the Way Maker and the Way Made. Marshall perceives this fact clearly after she becomes an adult, long after Da-duh's death. "She died and I lived, but always, to this day even, within the shadow of her death," comments Marshall. She resumes:

> For a brief period after I was grown I went to live alone, like one doing penance, in a loft above a noisy factory in downtown New York and there painted seas of sugarcane and huge swirling Van Gogh suns and palm trees striding like brightly-plumed Watussi across a tropical landscape, while the thunderous tread of the machines downstairs jarred the floor beneath my easel, mocking my efforts.

Da-duh's spirit ("shadow") surrounds Marshall, particularly, it seems, as suggested by ritualistic penance. Penance, here, shows the granddaughter's exorcising the sins of misunderstanding her own roots whereas Da-duh, symbolizing all her historical folk, had a practical faith in survival and struggle toward free self-conception and self-direction among nature's gods.

Marshall especially exorcises the sin of accepting her severance from the land. That is why she paints pictures of Da-duh's landscape. Land for Da-duh represented the spot where poor black folk received their identity by owning their own natural resources—a cultural foundation. The fruit groves, moreover, indicated the folk's independent space—a political condition. In the grandmother's generation people had clear and direct knowledge of their origins, signs that pointed them to where they began and to whom they turned for their strength. The fruit groves—their gods—signaled ultimate goals.

It is this spiritual transformation from Da-duh to Marshall that the machines below attempt to jar and mock. The machines, here, mean severing African American folk from land and all its ramifications. The machine sinisterly and wickedly mocks the land. The machine is not inherently demonic. Its satanic nature derives from oppressors' ownership and abusive use against black folk. Theologically speaking, the land reminds the folk that they began historically in a free creation and not in the exploitative machine. And one way to combat the devilish encroachments of an oppressive machine is to paint pictures of the past, to draw on combative primordial black cultural and political values modified for today's new particularities.

The vivifying spirituality of a dead matriarch likewise appears in Ruby Dee's autobiographical essay.[62] Grasping this spirit's nature enables Dee and her entire family to possess a new understanding of familial love. Particularly, the spiritual love of Dee's dead aunt goes into Dee and brings out the child's own loving nature. In turn, the child expresses her accepted loving disposition to her father who, then, becomes a "gentler man" and begins to relate to his wife in a hugging playful way. Seeing the radical change in her parents affects Dee, the child. Thus the movement from the dead aunt to the child to the parents and back to the child again shows the transformative power of love in strengthening the black family.

However, veneration of the ancestral aunt is not a blind faith act grounded on selfish love. Ruby Dee has strong convictions about her aunt's spirit because the matriarch expressed a love for the younger black generation's future. For instance, the aunt worked hard to save money for Dee's and her siblings' college tuition. Ancestral veneration presents a transformative familial love where each generation looks out for the next and the next becomes self-conscious of its debt and responsibility to spirituality, family, and self.

Similarly, in the poem "The Negro Mother,"[63] Langston Hughes shows how awareness of an ancestral African American mother empowers current and future generations. First, the mother's spirit announces its intent: "Children, I come back today/To tell you a story of the long dark way/That I had to climb, that I had to know/In order that the race might live and grow." Children of the ancestors need to know how ancestors climbed— Got Over—a way of toil and troubles so that descendants can also get over. Second, the mother discloses historical perspective: she is "the dark girl who crossed the wide sea"; "the woman who worked in the field"; and "no safety, no love, no respect was" due to her. Third, she renders values of endurance under these hardship cases: "But I kept trudging on through the lonely years"; "I had to keep on!" Fourth, she calls on her African

American offspring to heed a black tradition of suffering and struggle: "Remember my sweat, my pain, my despair. Remember my years, heavy with sorrow"; "But march ever forward, breaking down bars. Look ever upward at the sun and the stars." Fifth, she testifies to maternal spirituality like an ever-present cloud of witnesses: "For I will be with you till no white brother/Dares keep down the children of the Negro mother." Lastly, all the above dimensions of maternal spirituality bear sacredness because they hinge on one point. The mother carries in her body "the seed of the free" from Africa. God gave her this "prayer" and "dream" — that through her descendants, she will enjoy their fullest consummation on earth.

And last, through Africa, ancestral veneration yields potency in identity and memory for free life. We see this in the words of an ex-slave from Georgia who recollects a tale about "flying people," that is, enslaved Africans, brought to the New World, who eventually fly back home.[64] Though chattel on a Georgia plantation, these Africans were proud people ("they fly right back tuh Africa") and not beasts of burden for a bull whip (the overseer "whip um good ... an' dy riz in duh sky") or cogs in a wheel of someone else's economic machinery ("dey didn't know how tuh wuk right") or servants to a foreign oppressive discourse ("nobody couldn't unduhstan' um") or blank minds waiting for slavemaster enlightenment (the overseer "jis caahn' make um unduhstan' ").

A similar version of "flying people" was told by Caesar Grant, a black resident of John's Island, one of the sea islands off the Georgia and South Carolina coasts.[65] Under slavery, a cruel slave driver and overseer would work and beat their black chattel until the slaves died. But one day an old African among them spoke in an "unknown tongue." The overseer and driver ran after the old man with whips at the ready.

And as [the old African] spoke to them they all remembered what they had forgotten, and recalled the power which once had been theirs. Then all the Negroes, old and new, stood up together; the old man raised his hands; and they all leaped up into the air with a great shout; and in a moment were gone, flying, like a flock of crows ... and behind them flew the old man.

The power of collective memory induces a collective awareness of once-held power. Consequently, all arose as one body; power lifted up a group of oppressed slaves into a communal freedom movement. Unified in their liberation flight, the group showed no fear; instead women sang, men clapped hands, and children laughed. Likewise, remembered power facilitates a faith leap — for the grand leap by these ex-slaves is based on belief in their ability to fly and in hopes for an ultimate distant land. Faith, then, dwells in the power of identity and memory. Continual ancestral recollection can cause black folk to press on and get over to the final liberating mark.

CONCLUSION

In Chapter 1 we heard the voices of Christian slaves cry out to a God of freedom; we saw the imagery of an enslaved people calling on the name of Jesus; and we experienced their sacred worship in the Invisible Institution. In Chapter 2 we met a theological interpretation of poor black women's spiritual funk, a liberation revealed through values and traditions.

Here in Chapter 3 we discovered the manifestations of poor black people's faith in freedom rooted in their own folk culture. What do the stories of African American folk culture (a lifestyle of self-identity, self-expression, self-affirmation, and self-conception) found in different aspects of the black community tell us about poor black people's beliefs? What do these tales say to us about (a) an ultimate power or place, (b) an intermediary being between this ultimate divine potency or space and the human situation, and (c) the human practice of survival and struggle toward deliverance? For a contemporary and constructive black theology of liberation, we must engage a faith in freedom that anchors the seemingly infinite variety of black folk's striving to name themselves with their own language, bodies, and spirits; hence a cultural foundation for black theology.

As mentioned in the introduction, a black theology of liberation develops from all manifestations of a faith in freedom. Methodologically speaking, therefore, this chapter identified theological significance wherever a liberation faith witness occurs in African American folk culture. Poor people show belief in areas of language, space, bodies, music, laughter, lies, and movement, among other liberating cultural outlets. The theologian's constructive task calls for intentional systematizing so the folk will more consistently and self-consciously draw on cultural sources that yield a full humanity. Briefly stated, we must venture to reinterpret and reconceptualize accepted theological definitions out of the poor's identity.

The culture of poor black folk expresses belief in an ultimate divine power or place called the Way Maker or the Way Made. This hoped-for reality, or present reality not entered yet, transcends the present human predicament. It is divine because it is a being, a living force, or a way of existing that resolves the problems of this world and provides the answers to our hopes and the final goal of our aspirations. The Way Maker or the Way Made allows poor blacks to be themselves, for themselves and for no one else's self. Broken and wounded humanity can only achieve a sense of the self as a new being when a renewed humanity has been created by the Way Maker or defined by having the Way Made. Only by attaining a new space, a place for the fulfillment of their ultimate quests, can the folk shed the stultifying skin of an oppressive identity and, thereby, model their re-created self for total humanity.

An intermediary figure, moreover, shares in the power of the Way Maker or Way Made and, at the same time, stands with and is connected to our problems, hopes, and aspirations. It is the Trickster figure, whose abilities contain certain powers of the divine being-place while appearing, at first, to hold only human qualities. As a result, its go-between status invites and draws us toward a foretaste of glory. In the text of folk culture stories, the Trickster possesses special knowledge, abilities, and a closer relation to a supernatural reality than the overwhelming majority of human beings. This intermediary can embody and represent all or a combination of traits— realizing a radical reversal of position or circumstance for the weak; using cunning against the strong; breaking chains of bondage; taking unusual risks; and maintaining a vision and plan.

The Trickster in folk culture stories can also serve as a mediator for those listening to or watching a story being told or performed. The audience identifies with the intermediary as it suffers the weaknesses of the listeners or watchers but then employs the Trickster's special relation to the Way Maker or Way Made to finally defeat the oppressor or transport the folk toward their ultimate yearnings. A first appearance finds the intermediary trapped in the clutches of human limitations. Then it rises up to alter human possibilities with ties to abilities beyond apparent human capabilities. The Trickster empowers the powerless.

Consequently, the human practical faith of survival and struggle toward liberation of the powerless is a protracted process to Get Over. Indeed the purpose of human thought and action is to Get Over by relating ourselves to the Trickster so that we can partake of the power, grace, benefits, or new situation of the Way Maker or Way Made. By way of imitating the Trickster, we shed our old present way of life for a new being connected to the Way Maker and the Way Made.

To get over is not a simple movement from the old to the new. It involves an elaborate way of life, a faith in all that we are, a lifesaving belief that despite all that "the system," the demonic, fate, or bad luck has to offer and has done, a Way Maker will make a way out of no way and poor folk will have a Way Made. The Trickster, too, will intervene on the side of the voiceless in society. Therefore, human purpose strives to Get Over. Ultimately, to Get Over means to express faith by telling one's own story through diverse cultural media. This is true because the saying of one's identity acts to re-create oneself against a foreign, master-dominated language and story of oppressive naming and heretical faith.

We discover that in African American culture (oral and written, vernacular and literary) the folk have the freedom and latitude to state their own normative experiences and indigenous languages against American standardization. When the "low down folk" are in the presence of those who define the accepted American identity, we often find poor African Americans parroting white culture. However, in the secluded chambers of their black hearts and in the private spaces they control, the folk "do not care" about acceptable and non-acceptable criteria for self-expression. Alone, they are just themselves.

In black folk culture questions of authority, order, power, special status, and personalities become explicit. Here the language and ways of life of the folk, while hovering on the margin and periphery of a dominating "standard" culture, radically shift to the center of poor black people's justice convictions. No longer are the folk bordering and languishing on the outskirts of standardized bourgeois and white realities. Now their self-affirmation takes center stage in their own self-conception and representation of black identity. And in the reclaiming of their self-image the folk offer their faith as seeds for a constructive black theology of liberation. By themselves, the folk speak "lies above suspicion."[66]

Our "living" with the folk in their life tales has proven that we can interpret numerous theological notions of the Way Maker or Way Made, the Trickster intermediary, and a Get Over human witness. Black cultural horizons display faith, belief, and ultimate focus on a way of self-affirmation and expression in which one's entire life—one's sanity, physical integrity, spiritual moorings—is at stake. In a sense, one is willing to wager all for the radical transformation from deadly daily constraints to a new way of life and a new human being situated with the Way Maker or in the Way Made. Culture offers signs that describe an oppressed people's predicament and it, moreover, indicates emancipatory convictions for a radical transformation of self-definition and self-reliance.

African American poor people speak lies (for example, folk tales) above suspicion to connect with the Way Maker or Way Made through the Trickster figure so the folk can get over from the present old to the final new. Such lies essentially describe black language, both oral and written, and black lifestyles as liberating self-identity. It is what poor African American workers mean in their lying sessions when they state: "Hurry up so somebody else kin plough up some literary and lay-by some alphabets."[67] In the structure and words of folk culture, a people's faith breaks through to provide an important source for constructive black theological development.

PART TWO

THE FAITH OF BLACK LEADERSHIP

4

W. E. B. Du Bois

Theological Reflections on Democratized Political Power

You are embarked upon a great and holy crusade, the emancipation of mankind, black and white; the upbuilding of democracy; the breaking down . . . of forces of evil represented by race prejudice . . . by lynching . . . by disfranchisement . . . by ignorance . . . and by all these and monopoly of wealth.

W. E. B. Du Bois[1]

While seeking a free space of racial acceptance, economic equality, and the exercise of one's voice through voting, African Americans have felt the brunt of entrenched white power. This resistance—a deadly structure and self-perpetuating system—seems like an evil force with its own independent, demonic soul. The heartbeat of this devilish design is monopolized racial power. Black folk have, nevertheless, persisted in the struggle for their God-given right to determine their lives in the United States. On the one hand, we have narrow political self-interest grounded in racial intolerance to hoard the nation's resources. On the other, we find African American movements fighting to make political power democratic in all parts of the North American society.

For example, ex-slave William Craft underscored these two views of American reality when he referred to the relative mildness of his former master as a mere exception to the inherent domination of blacks in America.[2] As the possession of a liberal white master, Craft acknowledged that his slave status was better than that of most black bondsmen and women. But he points to the more profound presence of a slavery system affecting all African Americans regardless of their conditions. The structural relationship between black and white was not based on the practices of individual liberal or conservative masters. On the contrary, it had a life of its own. It was this larger, ever-present sinful reality that had to be dismantled. Otherwise black people "could not call the bones and sinews that God gave us our own."

Likewise, in the post-slavery late nineteenth century an African American movement persisted against accepted white privileges. During that period Ida B. Wells took a leading role in advocating women's rights, exposing lynching of blacks, teaching the poor, and in general crusading for a sharing of civil rights for those not so far removed from bondage.

The founding of the National Association for the Advancement of Colored People (1910) marked a major organizational development for black equality at the beginning of the twentieth century. The NAACP sought to reverse the increased lynching of "Negroes" as well as overturn the entire legal system of racial oppression. Later the oppositional political stream in black life took a more radical turn with the birth of the African Blood Brotherhood (1917). The ABB comprised African American socialists, who advocated and organized for a new economic and political order with both workers' rule and the right of self-determination for black Americans. The 1940s, 1950s, and 1960s saw massive direct action campaigns to expand democracy and share the nation's prosperity. On the national level the struggle was interpreted as issues of civil and voting rights. In local black areas the fight also unfolded around land rights, anti-lynching, quality education, and African American access to and control of local resources.

The late 1960s and early 1970s heard the Black Panther Party and Stokely Carmichael cry for a revolutionary nationalist change in the American "bourgeois" democratic system. Only with the poor in power and the abolition of a profit political economy could black power flourish and all working people achieve dignity. And today Jesse Jackson's Rainbow Coalition bases its platform on empowering the poor majority, black and white, who have been locked out of power by the privileged few.

Regardless of time periods, personalities, and parties, a stream of political struggle for equality and liberation marks a large part of black America's legacy. What is the nature of African American faith in this dogged fight for liberated space and equal resources on earth? A response to that question discloses the political movement among black folk as another source for black theology today.

W. E. B. Du Bois stands squarely within this black political protest tradition. Together his thought and life present one major example of the political aspirations of African American poor folk. Therefore an investigation and interpretation of his theological insight can help us get at how justice beliefs operate within the have and have-not mechanisms of racial politics.[3] The theology of Du Bois's thought symbolizes a faith in freedom present within the overall black political heritage.

Du Bois's beliefs interpret politics in the broader sense of power relations among individuals, groups, and systems as they affect the realization of democracy. In fact key to Du Bois's thinking is his life-long fight to achieve democracy—that is, full equality—through the alteration of existing monopolistic power dynamics in the United States and the world. He pledged his life to reallocate and redistribute social resources. A new society—a radical democracy—would reign on earth in all spheres of human endeavor for African Americans and the poor. What theological insights can we draw out from Du Bois's understanding of politics and democracy in order to develop a black theology of liberation?

Starting from his early academic pursuits, Du Bois chartered plans for his entire public career around the theme of democracy.

> In the days of my formal education, my interest became concentrated upon the race struggle. My attention from the first was focused on democracy and democratic development; and upon the problem of the admission of my people into the freedom of democracy.[4]

The construction of democracy required struggle by blacks and the world's disadvantaged in the political sphere, generally defined as democratic control of the pivotal power connections in economics, electoral politics, social relations, culture, and religion. Du Bois, moreover, noted the decisive role of elitist wealth operating within these broad political examples. Monopolized affluence greatly controlled how various peoples and countries interacted with one another and among themselves in every aspect of human associations. Therefore he worked to dislodge the narrow concentration of resources by advocating public ownership as well as control of capital, natural riches, and industry. The poor and society's locked-out (the majority in the world) could claim their own space on earth only when a new society included their voices. Emphasizing his plan for equitable redistribution of the world's assets, he wrote:

> We must face the fact that the final distribution of goods—the question of wages and income is an ethical and not a mere mechanical problem and calls for grave public human judgment and not secrecy and closed doors.
>
> The careful, steady increase of public democratic ownership of industry [was needed].[5]

The gifts of the earth belonged not to the few or those trained in obscurely specialized techniques and mechanics. Quite the opposite, the ethics of human relations demanded an opening of "secrecy and closed doors."

Furthermore, if religion meant anything, it specified that practical effort is necessary to equalize all human created and natural abundance. To God, Du Bois prayed: "Let us remember, O God, that our religion in life is expressed in our work."[6] For him, God became manifest in human relations that worked for democracy and just power relations. Similarly, Jesus was the actual revelation of that democratic power among all humanity. The human vocation, consequently, was to labor tirelessly and fearlessly toward an earthly kingdom of equality for disadvantaged African Americans and the poor. In brief, a critical engagement with Du Bois's theological views necessitates a vibrant treatment of democracy and politics.

THEOLOGY OF DEMOCRATIZED POLITICAL POWER

Formative Factors

Born in Great Barrington, Massachusetts (23 February 1868), three years after the end of the Civil War, William Edward Burghardt Du Bois had a uniquely productive scholarly life. Until his death in Accra, Ghana, on 27 August 1963, his intellectual pursuits spanned a host of issues and commentaries on major world events. Indeed, Du Bois is not only the most prolific writer produced by African Americans, but also one of the greatest thinkers of the United States. Estimates of his authored and co-edited texts range from twenty-three to over three dozen books, and from several hundred to thousands of articles, interviews, speeches, and correspondence.[7] But the scope of his scholarly work centered around at least one unifying theme that grew out of his early encounters in the Great Barrington community. These childhood experiences had an immense impact on his life's focus on the relation between human beings and the purpose toward which people should dedicate their work.

At the ripe old age of 92, three years before his death, Du Bois's democracy related comments about his teen days pervade his review of his long life of steadfast work.

> In the little New England town where I was born, we had a high school of about 25 pupils. I entered it in 1880, at the age of 12. As I attended town-meeting, annually in the spring, there used regularly to appear one of the dirtiest old men I ever saw. He was fat and greasy, and every year he made a fierce attack on wasting his taxes on a high school. I was always furious. I wondered why the citizens sat silent and let him rant, but they did, and then quietly they voted money for the high school. There I learned my lesson in democracy. Listen to the other side.[8]

Du Bois's account of his formative days sheds several insights pertinent to his foundational concept of democracy. Democratic participation begins at an early stage and thus becomes a force of habit in life. In fact, Du Bois employs a faith metaphor about mandatory presence at major issue debates during "Town Meeting" when he says, "which I religiously attended."[9]

Using his experiences with this New England model, he linked its participatory lifestyle with nurturing of the young. In Massachusetts children were allowed to involve themselves in the proceedings, if not the discussions, of the major concerns of the town's existence. Systemically the youth were being groomed as successors to a tradition of full deliberation and complete democratic determination. Due to his early training, Du Bois could assert: "I understood the workings of local government when I was thirteen or fourteen years of age. ... It was easy for me to conceive and talk about democracy. I saw it and lived it."[10]

Furthermore, democracy entails open and aboveboard airing of views and full accountability. The citizens and their elected representatives engage one another face to face. No smoke-filled-room deals take place in which an insulated powerful clique agrees on one agenda and then reports back to the citizenry with deceitful disguises. Referring to the need for a knowledgeable populace (aware of the use of resources and who is in charge of these resources), Du Bois confesses his understanding of his town's allocation of wealth: "I knew about the hard won appropriations for the high school; the sums set aside for roads and bridges; the provision for the poor, and the various officials who carried out this work."[11]

Democracy, then, is a way of life for a community where all citizens enter into dialogue and decision-making. "Listen to the other side" proves key in this dynamic process. But what permanently impressed Du Bois's thinking on democracy was who could speak and who had to listen. Given the particularly neat, clean, quiet, orderly, New England scene at that time, the appearance of "one of the dirtiest old men" suggested a voice from an ultimate anti–status quo individual. In another text Du Bois describes this same individual in this manner: "He was nothing and nobody"; "this huge, ragged old man came down from the hills."[12]

Du Bois learned to value the basics about who could speak in power relations among people. The voices of the non–status quo citizens—the nothings, the nobodies, the fats, and the greasies—mark an inclusive, non-elitist, and therefore authentic and democratic resolution of conflict, controversy, and contested claims. "Gradually as I grew up," resumes Du Bois, "I began to see that this was the essence of democracy: listening to the other man's opinion and then voting your own, honestly and intelligently."

Du Bois began to define democracy in the realm of electoral politics, that is, open discussion based on involvement of the poor and the society's non-normative folk. From his early childhood, he also learned the necessity for a radical economic dimension in democracy, which he termed "socialist tendencies." However, as we shall discover below, this simplistic notion of socialism, held by the teenage Du Bois, was transformed as his scope and study broadened into a complex analysis of fundamental redistribution of the ownership of wealth. The pursuit of a politics of democracy and equality moved him into forming the NAACP, into the Communist Party USA, and eventually into exile in Ghana, where he died in 1963.

But the cornerstone of Du Bois's economic democracy instinct formed while he was still a youth in high school. Outlining the impact of childhood experiences on his life's basic beliefs, he explains how "without conscious socialist tendencies" the town of Great Barrington collectively and publicly owned key infrastructure components: the water supply, streets, and the sewers. Though volunteers directed the fire department, no private interest controlled it. Technically there existed no public park; however, the town's square served the same purpose as an open free space for the citizens. Finally, the people's taxes invested in the state "looked after the few paupers who were 'on the town.' "[13] Du Bois's early encounter with economic power relations, therefore, left an indelible mark regarding the equalization of ownership within a community's appropriation of scarce goods and service. Within the limitations of existing natural and human possibilities, economics was the allocation of abundance by the collective people, for the collective people, in the public, equal market of exchange, grounded in a consideration for the poor. In his words, it was an "ethical problem."

Still, Du Bois's "education in democracy" in New England did not end with a disjointed separation between economic and electoral democracies. On the contrary, equality and just power linkages mandated a radical rudimentary relationship between the two. "While wealth spoke and had power," he wrote, "the dirtiest laborers had voice and vote. Democracy modified industry."[14] Du Bois views the world and humans who interact within it from the vantage point of the toiling worker and those at the bottom surviving in dirt. Restated, the power of wealth submits and succumbs to the will of a collective, conscious, common folk.

In addition to the influences of democracy and politics, Du Bois greatly internalized, perhaps more thoroughly than he realized, the permanent effect of the Great Barrington Congregational Church's heavy practical theology of work.

> My religious development has been slow and uncertain. I grew up in a liberal Congregational Sunday School and listened once a week to a sermon on doing good as a reasonable duty. Theology played a minor part and our teachers had to face some searching questions.[15]

Sunday after Sunday, Du Bois heard and learned scriptural teachings instructing men and women to work in order to fulfill God's plan for humanity. Likewise, the Protestant (Calvinistic) work ethic pervaded not only his little Sunday School gatherings, but most of Puritan New England. As Du Bois himself admits: "In general thought and conduct I became quite thoroughly New England."[16] In this theological ethos, idleness and slothfulness were akin to sin and among the most damning evils to avoid. Consequently, in a religious sense, tireless and persistent labor toward doing the good represents a divine calling as part of God's intent in a covenantal relation between humanity and the divine. Indeed, to be human is to work for the good.

Du Bois, however, claims that "theology played a minor part" in his religious sessions at church and, by intimation, in his own religious thinking. His assessment seems to result from an apparent interpretation of "theology" as an abstract discourse on the heavenly world separated from human reality. Since he places an almost absolute accent on human vocational effort, one can understand the definitional conclusions he draws about theology.

Yet, at the same time, he does present us with a profound interpretation of theology because he views God and Jesus deeply entrenched in various human activities laboring for the betterment of society's poor and victims of discrimination. Consequently, the human calling to sacrifice for justice is theological precisely because it connects to the notion of a Force or God greater than humanity. For Du Bois, this Force or God does not mechanically direct or block human practical affairs, but relates to the latter in such a way that humanity strives to utilize fully all human capabilities toward social transformation. Theologically, this God-Force's existence does not make human initiative unnecessary.

From early childhood until his death, Du Bois absorbed and formulated religious teachings and experiences that produced theological statements on God, Jesus, and human purpose. However, before we proceed to elaborate fully on these positions as representative political components in the overall development of a constructive black theology of liberation, we first review Du Bois's attitude toward black and white churches as exemplary or non-exemplary models of a theology of politics and democracy. This approach falls in line with his theological understanding of religion being manifested in human work.

Openness of the Black Church

For Du Bois, the African American church exhibits the best manifestation of the teachings of Jesus Christ. He observes: "The Negro church in America comes nearer to being built along the lines of its Founder."[17] First of all, it is an open religious gathering and Christian institution in which all are welcome to participate. No barriers block the fullest input, membership, and airing of views in the "Negro church." "The Negro church is at least democratic," comments Du Bois. "It welcomes everybody."[18]

Furthermore, he expands the democratic traits of the "colored church of Christ" to entail the sharing of decision-making by the entire membership. Not only must a Christian ecclesial formation encourage active and diverse participation, it also must include structurally all members within the power process of running the church. Describing how "the colored church of Christ has certain things of which it might rightfully boast," Du Bois elaborates the following: "It is a democratic church where the governing power is largely in the hands of the mass of membership." Power bubbles up from below, from the underside, instead of down from a church monarchy or through an intermediary level that filters and, thereby, distorts the wishes of the mass membership. Here Du Bois praises the black church for embodying the most radical democracy in North American religious assemblies.

In addition to open participation and full sharing in decision-making, the black church's policy and practice of non-discrimination mark it as an authentic church of Jesus Christ. Pursuing his reflections on ecclesiology, Du Bois believes that the "colored church of Christ" is a place "where everybody is courteously welcomed even if the application of a white person might cause astonishment."[19] Clearly racial discrimination would prevent universal inclusion and negate the participation of a mass membership in church governance.

Similarly, the black church practices democracy by allowing the poor and ostracized access to resources and their allocation. Du Bois specifically examines his personal knowledge of the African Methodist Episcopal church to substantiate the above point in this revealing 1947 observation:

> [The AME church] has achieved a popular democracy unparalleled in any other Negro organization. . . . Particularly have I seen in this institution a social center of astonishing efficiency where the poor and ostracized met in human sympathy, mutual charity and encouragement.[20]

In order for the poor to work for survival and social change, they need to hold the reins tied to sources that determine the abolition of their poverty. Therefore, the poor's control of this political power in the black church occupies the centerpiece in the notion of popular democracy.

Du Bois also associates the African American church with a democratic acceptance of black women's spirituality as well as their roles in leadership. Indeed, their pioneering though seldom heralded works in the Christian church laid the formative planks for the origin and initial institutionalization of that very same gathering of Christian believers. In a flowery tribute to African American women's essential historical function in the building of the "Negro church," Du Bois writes that they "came first, in earlier days, like foam flashing on dark, silent waters—bits of stern dark womanhood here and there tossed almost carelesssly aloft to the world's notice." Powerful ebony femaleness "laid the foundation of the great Negro church of today," thus symbolizing pioneering leadership in church formation.

This advance position of black Christian women was manifested in a spirituality of hard work for social transformation. From such spiritual ancestry, asserts Du Bois, came two powerful black women—Harriet Tubman and Sojourner Truth. Both stood for the highest ideal of African American womanhood in the church. Both embodied the sacrificial efforts of "the females in the early history of the church," who abounded "in good works and in the acts of true benevolence."

Moreover, the existence of democracy in the black church, displayed by the prominent presence of African American female leadership and spirituality, testified to an even more profound commentary on the decisive role and necessary participation of black Christian women. Du Bois goes further and declares that freedom for the entire African American community hinges on the justice work of black women. "To no modern race does its women mean so much as to the Negro nor come so near to the fulfillment of its meaning," claims Du Bois. Quoting ex-slave and national educator Anna Julia Cooper, he agrees that only the black woman can say "when and where I enter"; only then and there can the entire African American race stride toward liberation.[21]

Yet Du Bois did not spare the black church a veritable tongue-lashing during its lapses. Indeed, he argued for a stringent, self-critical voice whenever the church veered away from its democratic power-sharing tradition. He called for an uncompromising struggle against any retrograde theological trends.

At one point he unleashed a barrage of indictments against such trends when he felt black ministers were wasting too much money on church buildings. Similarly, they apparently expressed more interest "in the mouthing of creeds and the orthodoxy of men's beliefs," thereby suffering "the contempt of mankind" for such "heresy hunting" and the act of "burning witches." Furthermore, certain black colleges during his time merely taught a caricature of Christianity with childish beliefs in biblical fairy tales, which expressed themselves in a hearsay confession of dogma.[22]

Du Bois resumed his critique of the black church by contrasting the fight within its tradition between an alien oppressive faith, practice, and theology, on the one hand, and an indigenous democratic belief, witness, and thought, on the other. This latter emphasis marked the high calling of religion for the disenfranchised. Symbolized by black Christians, it has inspired faith in human beings and not orthodox dogma, peace and not war, unselfishness and not greed, and deeds and not creeds. Therefore, if anything, Du Bois exclaimed, Christianity stood for social uplift. Supporting his argument for the justice-oriented church trend, he writes:

The Negro Church in the past has been sewn with superstition and worldliness, but it has always been able to say in its own defense, We believe in man; and in the lowest of men; We open our doors to the despised and hunted; We extend our charity to all forms and faith.

This faith "in the lowest of men" is the African American Christian community's highest mission.[23] To maintain that valiant legacy and move toward the sought-after vision, the black church has to shed itself of all that is childish in theology. It must exorcise the alien negative religious thought of privileged elites of the white church and white theology.

A Religion of Whiteness

For Du Bois, antithetical to the Christian ideal of working for democracy and equal power relations stood a religion of whiteness, theologically defended and institutionally practiced. Such a white religion set up a hypocritical system of rigid dogma, which Du Bois vehemently opposed. Sophistry and illogic in dogma blocked the full potential of humanity and thus helped to maintain the status quo of discrimination toward African Americans and the poor. For instance, in this anti-rational theological absurdity, white religion placed concern for petty disputes over the Christian fight against larger systemic evils such as color and class lines. Any deliberate, democratic dissent against unjust social structures was, therefore, perceived as anathema by the dominant religion.

More specifically, during his college days at Fisk University in Nashville, Tennessee, Du Bois became sharply critical and deeply resentful of institutional religion and its harmful practice for two reasons. First, "the heresy trials, particularly the one which expelled [Charles A.] Briggs from the Presbyterian Church; and [second,] especially the insistence of the local church at Fisk University that dancing was a sin."[24] Any religious discourse and deliberations hinting at dogmatic fervor and fanatical rigidity of heresy trials served as a red flag for Du Bois. Fundamentalism and the subsequent lack of rational discussion in the white church bred a demonic conservatism that strangled the masses of people; specifically, conservatism engendered racial discrimination against blacks.

Similarly, his argument in favor of dancing did not indicate a pro-dancing stance, in and of itself. What piqued his religious antenna and theological sensibilities was the profound irrational and contradictory posture of white faith and practice. Instead of grasping the larger imperatives of the Christian ideal of practicing justice, white religion prevented work toward a radical realignment of societal interconnections and engaged in a privatistic, guilt-whipping biblical interpretation.

He faced this dilemma while at Fisk. A schoolmate of his approached the faculty and charged Du Bois with the sin of dancing. Although his teachers admitted that his dancing might well be harmless, they felt his example might lead others astray. Biblically and theologically, furthermore, they quoted Paul to defend their opinions: "If meat maketh my brother to offend, I will eat no meat while the world standeth." Confronted with this theological rigidity, Du Bois wrestled with this problematical exegesis for years. But he came to resent and disregard such "sophistry," started to dance again in rebellion, and "never since had much respect for Paul."[25]

From Du Bois's perspective, theological dogma assumes two justifying paths in relation to white folk's inhuman treatment of black folk. It either simply removes Christianity from the realm of race interactions and says, "Religion does not enter here"; for Du Bois, this approach is at least an honest abandonment of the Christian ideal, though it epitomizes a retrenchment into "primitive paganism" and "retrogression toward barbarism." Or it chooses the more usual stance of justifying "Color Caste and Christianity." This latter heretical position sees no contradiction between the ethics of religious convictions and the sin of caste discrimination.

Rigid dogma and narrow creedal formulations in white religion covered up the worst instances of injustice and inhumanity against those without resources to sustain themselves or fight back in the United States. Again, Du Bois contrasts the Christian ideal of justice work with the theological and confessional posture of white believers in Jesus Christ. Writing in "The Souls of White Folk," he condemns the dominating religion for crassly polluting its moral and religious proclamations. On the one hand, traditional Christianity professes a respect for truth, despising of personal riches, privileging of personal humbleness, and justice and personal sacrifice for fellow humans. In reality, though, "we have injected into our creed a gospel of human hatred and prejudice, a despising of our less fortunate fellows, not to speak of our reverence for wealth which flatly contradicts the Christian ideal."[26]

Du Bois repeatedly returns to a theological theme of linking the substance of Christianity with nondiscrimination based on race and class. One could not favor white race superiority and monopolization of wealth and remain a proclaimer and practitioner of Jesus' message about the Kingdom coming on earth. On the contrary, a leveling of racial and economic inequalities inaugurates God's will.

But it is around the issue of the nature of God that white theology bares its most blasphemous heretical colors. White North American Christians believed in the whiteness of God in order to claim their divinely ordained ownership of the earth and its riches. Instead of all receiving the earth's natural resources equally, as testament to God's blessing and grace, whites monopolized divine gifts over against all people of color and the poor. God, in this demonic theological equation, "naturally" made whites into a superior race. They, therefore, inherently and automatically receive superiority in the Great Chain of Being in race differences. Revealing the theology of white religion, Du Bois writes:

> This assumption that of all the hues of God whiteness alone is inherently and obviously better than brownness or tan leads to curious acts ... [when whites say to blacks:] "My poor, un-white thing! Weep not nor rage. I know, too well, that the curse of God lies heavy on you. ... Do your work in your lowly sphere, praying the good Lord that into heaven above, where all is love, you may, one day, be born — white! ..." Then always, somehow, some way, silently but clearly, I am given to understand that whiteness is the ownership of the earth forever and ever, Amen![27]

Also Du Bois suggests a biblical basis for white-skinned privileges when he underscores the notion of the curse of God. In Genesis 9, Noah cursed his grandson Canaan (son of Ham) because Noah's son Ham looked at Noah when the latter lay unclothed. Throughout the history of black-white relations in the United States, particularly during slavery, white Christians have used this biblical passage to justify theologically African American "natural" subservience. White Christians believed that just as Canaan was cursed to be a servant so too were African Americans. Like Canaan, the "lowly sphere" of blacks was to be a servant of servants to the rest of humankind.[28]

Since whiteness obviously indicated the preferred hue and inherited the earth's ownership, then whites rightfully claimed the mantle of Son of God. White men survey the world and see its pageantry as an expression of, in Du Bois's words, "white power." Consequently, they crown themselves with praises of royalty: "Surely here is the Son of God and he shall reign forever and forever."[29]

Such theological assertions were not mere words of propagandistic debate; they actually sustained, promoted, and reinforced an institutional practice of the religion of whiteness. Along with his famous and accurate prophecy that the problem of the twentieth century is the problem of the color line, Du Bois likewise predicted the decisive divide in North American Christianity with these words: "The one great moral issue of America upon which the Church of Christ comes nearest being dumb is the question as to the application of the golden rule between White and Black Folk."[30] Despite exceptions of one or two white Christians, as a body the white church in the United States implemented racism, elitist arrogance, monopolization of wealth, and imperialist wars of aggression.

Starting with the bondage of black skins for profit (for example, the Christian slave trade controlled by Europeans and Euro-Americans), the dynamic between the white church and its black chattel left a historical legacy of shame for Du Bois. White institutional followers of Christ actually were the staunchest backers of North American slavery. They used Christianity to aid and abet the black slave trade. Moreover, they joined hands with the richest and the brightest minds to systematize forced breeding, cruel punishment, inhumane treatment, and the dehumanization of enslaved Africans in North America. It was exactly this tradition that produced a white church mission of disunity among the human community, black and white.

Indeed, instead of foreshadowing God's Kingdom of sisterhood and brotherhood on earth, the church had demonstrated the basest tendencies in human nature and the worst attempts at togetherness, more so than almost any other human institution. Demonic deeds of slavery continued to pervade the periods of Reconstruction, post-Reconstruction, and African missions into the twentieth century. Thus his judgment that "the church today is the strongest seat of racial and color prejudice."[31]

Resuming his chronicling of white religious institutions' standing on the wrong side of justice and defending anti-democratic obsessions, Du Bois chastises the anti-working class and anti-labor position of white ecclesiological actions. "I knew what I was looking at," he wrote, "when in New York a Cardinal became a strike-breaker and the Church of Christ fought the Communism of Christianity."[32] At this point, Du Bois reveals his attraction to a form of communism or communalism in which ownership, equally distributed, belongs to those who actually produce. The results of labor, socialized commodities in the human community, belong and revert back to those who toiled in sweat to make these goods and services. Yet instead of humbling themselves before the righteous grievances of workers, church leadership, such as cardinals and clergy, led contingents across laborers' picket lines.

For Du Bois, the role of the Church of Christ was to bring together communalistic and collective ways of life with Christianity. Given his familiarity with the Bible, Du Bois, more than likely, referenced Acts 2:44-45 which reads: "All whose faith had drawn them together held everything in common: they would sell their property and possessions and make a general distribution as anyone might have need." Christian scriptures, then, contained ethical prescriptions for democracy in economic and social relations.

Du Bois argued even stronger for the non-authenticity, hence heretical reality, of "the white church of Christ." Above all, in his opinion, "white Christianity in the twentieth century has been curiously discredited" because it had defended "such evils" as slavery, color caste, the exploitation of labor, poverty, and imperialist wars of aggresssion abroad. Still, Du Bois cautions us to separate radically the heresy of "the White church" from genuine Christian practice when he declares: "These facts do not impugn Christianity but they do make terrible comment upon the failure of its white followers." Unfortunately, in reality the white institution falls so far short of its professed ethical codes "that some would deny that it is Christian."[33]

Du Bois felt passionately about unmasking a do-nothing, obstructionist, credit-claiming, anti-Christian system among white people of faith. Accordingly, he was compelled to pen his thoughts on the sorry state and vexing nature of the world's color line problems:

> This paper is a frank attempt to express my firm belief that the Christian church will do nothing conclusive or effective; that it will not settle these problems; that on the contrary it will as long as possible and wherever possible avoid them; that in this, as in nearly every great modern moral controversy, it will be found consistently on the wrong side and that when, by the blood and tears of radicals and fanatics, of the despised and rejected largely outside the church, some settlement of these problems is found, the church will be among the first to claim full and original credit for this result.[34]

By implication, the church buttressed the status quo of elitist power-sharing until, outside Christian institutions, democratic forces of the despised and poor rose up and risked radicality and fanaticism to bring justice. The signs of the times, theologically speaking, showed the face of God immersed in the movements of the non-white church community. There revelation flowered. But white followers of Christ planted seeds of racism. For if the treatment of African Americans by the dominating institutional church "is called 'divine,' " asserted Du Bois, "this is an attack on the conception of God more blasphemous than any which the church has always been so ready and eager to punish."[35] If anything, the white church's systemic lineage and practice of racism call forth the Devil and certainly do not reveal a just God. Because of white religion's incorrect theology and practice on the nature of God, "The Negro problem is the test of the church."[36]

Given this review of Du Bois's perception of African American and white Christian practitioners of political democratic theologies, we can now focus the bulk of our evaluation on his views of God, Jesus, and human witness.

GOD: THE NIGHT FORCE BELOW

Du Bois knew God through God's works. His aversion to abstract dogma and creeds found in the religion of whiteness, and in certain instances of black church history, made him avoid any talk about God separate from God's movement among and in relation to humanity. For him, God is manifest in human activity working toward equal power relations.

God instituted democratic political connections among human beings from the dawn of humankind. A creator of *equality*, then, indicates the first moment of divine presence among all people. Du Bois recognized this important theological claim in his description of the 1911 First Universal Races Congress. This momentous event saw a majority of all the world's nations congregate on an equal footing and deliberate over the methods to eliminate hatred among people due to racial differences. Du Bois called this global gathering the greatest event of the twentieth century. Organizers had achieved what the church, the state, and peace and labor movements had only talked about — an open frontal assault on world racism, "the nastiest modern survival of ancient barbarism."

In these assembled, multicolored faces representing the human family internationally, Du Bois perceived evidence of God's creative work of equality. This historic convocation verified the touch of divine equality implanted in the very act of bringing together human beings of all races. Theologically, one could say, a foretaste of God's initial intent for people's togetherness revealed itself in this nondiscriminating, nonracial conference comprised of the world's colored peoples. The Universal Races Congress sowed the seeds for the divine in-breaking of God's Kingdom on earth. Underscoring the extraordinary importance of the congress, Du Bois observed:

The Universal Races Congress was great because it marked the first time in the history of mankind when a world congress dared openly and explicitly to take its stand on the platform of human equality — the essential divinity of man.[37]

And so the essential nature of divine creative activity fostered the practice of equality needed for democratic human relations. Again, for Du Bois, traits of God's nature and being reflected themselves in organized political movements where diverse peoples shared power to the advantage of all participants present. The congress exemplifed correct theological practice, as opposed to dogmatic creeds of dominating ecclesial formations (for example, the white Christian church's words).

Even in its planned agenda and resulting platform, the congress highlighted this essential human divineness by publicly and boldly addressing the naturalness of diversity in the midst of the human family's unity. In addition, the world gathering structurally constituted an equal sharing among conferees by allowing all present time to voice their own agendas while all others listened to and engaged issues on the floor. This gathering symbolized different colors of the rainbow — one body with all shades shining brightly and equally.

That God was the creator of human equality further implied inherent divine *freedom* for all humanity. Since God made all in freedom, then God meant for all to be free. One could not have a divinity forging humankind democratically and not simultaneously providing the gift of liberty. We find this theological aspect in the goals of the Niagara Movement, whose "Declaration of Principles," crafted primarily by Du Bois, etches out this freedom detail in its inaugural conference. Written in 1905, the "Principles" included this statement:

> We note with alarm the evident retrogression in this land of sound public opinion on the subject of manhood rights, republican government and human brotherhood, and we pray God that this nation will not degenerate into a mob of boasters and oppressors, but rather will return to the faith of the fathers, that all men were created free and equal, with certain unalienable rights.[38]

Thus the sacredness of ingrained human tendencies to work for emancipation mirrored one's knowledge of God. God sojourns amid oppressed peoples struggling to bring about their divine right to choose how to live their lives. To find God, one has to go where communities engage in independent movements toward real control of the space around them.

If divine self-revelation expressed itself in human equality and freedom, then God's practical nature meant that all of humanity deserved justice and just interactions with fellow races on earth. Du Bois strongly believed in the absolute obligation of each race to provide and afford just treatment to others, especially when one race suffered at the expense of other races. His adamant stand on this point emerged from his associating justice as part of original divine intent. Elaborating on his New Year's resolutions during the early part of the twentieth century, Du Bois offers this conviction:

> I am resolved to defend and assert the absolute equality of the Negro race with any and all other human races and its divine right to equal and just treatment.[39]

God would not be the realization of ultimate creator if the consecrated inborn prerogative of equality and liberty did not also provide for and advocate the defense and maintenance of freedom for the created. God is a God of *justice* for society's victims.

Finally, awareness of God as the creator of equality showed itself in the ideal work of *brotherhood* and *sisterhood*. Herein lies the dynamic unifying principle of the diversified human order. One overarching human race existed because a holy being placed the same blood flowing in the veins of all peoples regardless of color or ethnicity, accenting therefore the universality of men and women. At the same time, each race had its own uniqueness which reached its full meaning and potential only when all races achieved equality, freedom, and justice. Du Bois paints a picture of unity in distinction when he states:

> I believe in God who made of one blood all nations that on earth do dwell. I believe that all men, black and brown and white, are brothers ... differing in no essential particular.[40]

Thus Du Bois perceived God through the divinity's self-disclosure in various creative activities—equality, freedom, justice, and brotherhood and sisterhood.

Furthermore, he maintained a firm belief in a God of *love* (as we shall see below), whose revelation expressed itself specifically in relentless, comprehensive *work* for other human beings. To encounter and know the sacred, one needed to perform acts of ongoing and consistent practical activity and organization in respect to society's oppressed peoples. Accordingly, the ultimate concern of all humanity (the object to which one struggled in life) was laboring for the betterment of the least in the community. Attaining this fundamental goal connected one with a divinity of love.

Expressing his faith in this God in contrast to dominating Christian creeds, Du Bois wrote: "I believed too little in Christian dogma to become a minister. I was not without faith." Then, underlining the nature of the divine goal in which he believed, he resumes, "I above all believed in work, systematic and tireless."[41] Here too, Du Bois does not situate one's encounter with God in the realm of dogma and, consequently, abstracted from the Holy's loving involvement with human affairs.

Even in his prayers we detect this strong belief in the sacredness of work. To be one with the Creator meant total immersion in toil for the other. Indeed, life becomes worth living all the more with daily rigorous effort. Du Bois, in one instance, meditated in prayer over the book of James 2:4-17. This New Testament passage depicts the faith of God as granting the Kingdom to those who are poor and opposing "the rich who oppress." At the same time, it condemns the sterility of dogmatic belief: "What does it profit, my brethren, if a man says he has faith but has not works?" (verse 14). Therefore, the straining of the body and the mind for the poor's interest allowed one to meet and be with the sacred realm. And so Du Bois beseeched God:

> God teach us to work. Herein alone do we approach our Creator when we stretch our arms with toil, and strain our eye and ear and brain to catch the thought and do the deed and create the things that make life worth living.[42]

Using the book of James as a primary source for his faith in work clarifies the type of hard effort Du Bois advocated. The creative energy of God did not imply a mindless, undirected movement without a clear object or plan. Rather, God's revelation in work pinpointed a practice in favor of the poor and against the rich oppressor. It located itself with suffering humanity, the "brother or sister" who was "ill-clad and in lack of daily food" (verse 15).

Surveying his life's accomplishments, Du Bois sums up the characteristics of his protracted strivings in these words: "I have loved a fight and I have realized that Love is God and Work is His Prophet."[43] He pursues a similar theological claim in another of his prayers in which he confesses the nature of God:

> There is no God but Love and Work is His prophet—help us to realize this truth, O Father, which Thou so often in word and deed has taught us. . . . God is Love and Work is His Revelation. Amen.[44]

Consistently Du Bois sought strength to be one with God's nature. To connect to divine love, one had to enter the place of revelation, that is, God's Kingdom was work. Here Du Bois also relates revelation to the prophetic dimension of God. The revealing event itself remains a prophetic task wherein humanity calls communities of faith back to the divine purpose and the sacred realm of serving the poor in society. In sum, in a self-giving movement amid the oppressed, one encounters God's love for, prophetic call to, and work in the interests of those without adequate food, shelter, or clothing. Therefore, tireless and persistent toil provides the true prism for the full disclosure of God's unadulterated appearance.

To be a God who creates equality and the one who loves-in-work for the oppressed suggest that the Holy One gives to those who suffer racial oppression in society the privilege of bearing the grace of democracy. In his article titled "Democracy,"[45] Du Bois offers this insight with his biblical interpretation of Exodus chapter 18.

Here we find Jethro, an Ethiopian priest and father-in-law of Moses, instructing Moses to set up a democratic government for the people of Israel. At this juncture of the Old Testament story, Moses, Yahweh's instrument who led the oppressed Israelites out of slavery, borders on burn-out and possible confusion about the next step in the movement to the Promised Land. Du Bois's reading of the text has, in his words, "Jethro . . . an 'Ethiopian' " entering at this critical moment to resolve Moses' dilemma. Unraveling this passage further, Du Bois describes Jethro as the one to "proclaim Liberty throughout the Land and to the inhabitants thereof." In order to reach Yahweh's freedom for humanity, Jethro tells Moses to assemble around him honest people who will help him govern in the interests of the majority of the Israelites. Thus Du Bois depicts Moses as the recipient of "the excellent plan of democratic government laid down by Jethro." Here, a black African possessed God's gift of and instructions for the implementation of democracy for humankind. Having received this divine knowledge, Moses carries out the Exodus journey, the main liberation story for all slaves.

Furthermore, Du Bois positions Yahweh on the side of the Ethiopians against those who practiced racial discrimination toward them, particularly in the case of Zipporah, the Ethiopian wife of Moses. The Bible, recounts Du Bois, "brings out the anger of the Lord against those who dared speak against the dark wife of Moses." Yahweh's nature includes a partiality toward *oppressed races* (signified by Zipporah) and grants them the authority to give liberating *democracy* to the world (signified by Jethro's relation to Moses).

This Ethiopian connection to Yahweh indicates the divinity's close identification with Africa and, thereby, surfaces the issue of God's color. Through poetry and prayer, metaphor and contrast, Du Bois strongly implies that God is *black* and hell is white. His poem "The Song of the Smoke" expresses the dark shades of the divinity.

> I will be black as blackness can —
> The blacker the mantle, the mightier the man!
> For blackness was ancient ere whiteness began.
> I am daubing God in night,
> I am swabbing Hell in white:
> I am the Smoke King
> I am black.[46]

Du Bois paints God in "night," the image of darkness and blackness. He therefore turns the metaphor of white or light on its head, because dominating theologians usually oppose the goodness of white to the evil of darkness. "Good whiteness" has the everlasting strength to overcome the inevitable weakness of darkness in the end, in orthodox faith in God. Yet Du Bois makes God a powerful night with absolute might, whose origins long precede white. The mightiness of the divinity results from its having been in the absolute beginning of all ancient time. Since whiteness began after black, it has less and only limited power. Ultimately the night will triumph over light. Indeed, the colorful struggle for power between God and hell can only climax with good prevailing over evil. White is hell, a weakness born after and in the shadow of black.

However, the immediate and apparent might of white can cause even the most faithful to hesitate and waver during periods of profound suffering. Du Bois experienced a moment of questioning the God of night. This happened in Atlanta in September 1906 when white people whipped themselves into a racist frenzy and commenced a process of massacring black folk and destroying their property. Whites began to attack any black person they saw. They demonically looted, burned, and destroyed black possessions in their pathway.

Du Bois, who lived in Atlanta, was out of town during this barbaric display of white civilization. However, he returned home when he heard the news that white people had gone mad and had carried out their race riot. On the train back he wrote "A Litany at Atlanta," in which he shows his deep, disturbing wrestling with the nature and color of God. The litany is actually a prayer. It reveals how Du Bois turned to a divine Force in one of the more severe crises in his life. Pressing the God of night to the boundaries, seeking the color of God through contrasting images, he wrote:

Keep not Thou silent, O God!
   Sit not longer blind, Lord God, deaf to our prayer and dumb to our dumb suffering. Surely Thou, too, art not white, O Lord, a pale, bloodless, heartless thing!

If God were white and not of the night, then equality, freedom, justice, sisterhood and brotherhood, love-in-work for society's oppressed races, and democracy for the poor — all traits of divinity — would be prisoners of light. Shaken about whether or not the Smoke King erred when he "daubed God in night," Du Bois passionately questions and answers simultaneously. Surely God cannot be light, "a pale, bloodless, heartless thing!" In fact, Du Bois recovers from his momentary confused rage of blasphemy and reaffirms the mighty night divinity.

Forgive the thought! Forgive these wild, blasphemous words! Thou art still the God of our black fathers and in Thy Soul's Soul sit some soft darkenings of the evening, some shadowings of the velvet night.[47]

God is associated with the velvet night and with Ethiopian fathers and mothers in the Bible because God is black.

God Is the Force

Though Du Bois spoke about the characteristics of God, he nonetheless had a very specific understanding of what the divine meant in his life. First of all, he opposed orthodox and dogmatic notions about God. He felt they were fairy tales and sophistry, which served to befuddle the rational mind. But primarily he argued against the existence of any such divinity claimed by the dominating institutional church because this "god" of white religion and certain trends within the African American church acted as an external being that paralyzed and debilitated human collective struggle. This prevented people from working toward political democracy. "Most educated modern men no longer believe in religious dogma," wrote Du Bois in his ninety-second year. Resuming with a description and critique of the "classic" definition of God, he states:

> If questioned they will usually resort to double-talk before admitting the fact. But who today actually believes that this world is ruled and directed by a benevolent person of great power who, on humble appeal, will change the course of events at our request? . . . One can hardly exaggerate the moral disaster of this custom.[48]

It seems as if Du Bois could not conceive of any independent being who was a foreign element, no matter how benevolently described, distant from the actual activities of human movement toward justice. Such a being was a fictitious alien who maintained a manipulative power, like the director of a puppet show. Such a directing being meant that humanity remained passively trapped in a do-nothing reactive status in the face of painful suffering. Such a being proved to be a theological fallacy precisely because it tied the hands of oppressed people. Furthermore, Du Bois's theological description suggests, the only role remaining for victims in society was to send up humble appeals and wait for the foreign potency of an absentee lord to intervene. Orthodox portrayals of God at first seemed appealing, especially when they pictured the divinity as benevolent and implicitly on the side of those in trouble. But here lay the sinister nature of "classical" dogmatic assertions about God. Though the being appears benevolent, in fact it removed people's power to "change the course of events" themselves.

Theologically speaking, it seems as if Du Bois opposed a two-history view. In this religious belief God has a sacred history separate from human history. The value of human historical effort is worthless and full of sin.

People can do nothing about their situations unless God arrives; even if they move to act, all their motion is inevitably ineffectual and sinful. In other words, God remains absent after creating humanity to suffer in systemic sinful power relations. This is why Du Bois argued so vehemently, "One can hardly exaggerate the moral disaster of this custom." This theological tradition estranged God and men and women from collective dynamic participation in ethical action on earth. Any lack of humanity's prominent role in social transformation equalled a moral disaster.

The heavy emphasis on human action could suggest that Du Bois had no belief whatsoever in an existence greater than people. For example, at one point he stated the following:

> I assumed that human beings could alter and re-direct the course of events so as to better human conditions. I knew that this power was limited by environment, inheritance and natural law, and that from the point of view of science these occurrences must be a matter of Chance and not of Law. I did not rule out the possibility of some God also influencing and directing human action and natural law. However I saw no evidence of such divine guidance. I did see evidence of the decisive action of human beings.

Du Bois experienced and witnessed the power of people changing social relations. Therefore, for him, whatever God existed had to be with and dwell in the realm of human affairs. Otherwise, people simply became robots at the pull and push of "some God" somewhere. If an external "some God" could lift up burdens and change exploitative interactions, then one would have to present Du Bois with substantive evidence. Without any proof, the ultimate power to alter racist and oppressive situations resided among people. When others heard Du Bois's viewpoints, they departed from him. Resuming, he states:

> Here most persons who understood what I was saying left me quite alone and reverted to firm belief in unalterable Law, thus to my mind changing Man to an automaton and making Ethics unmeaning and Reform a contradiction in terms.[49]

Specifically in this writing Du Bois explains his position in the context of seeking the way to black Americans' "betterment through human action." He implies that anyone or anything placing aid to the "Negro" outside of the hands and community of these people actually tied their hands. Thus the ultimate power against racism and for realizing democratic power for black folk has to be intertwined inseparably with the African American movement toward liberation. What exactly is this entity greater than but saturated with black folk's work for social change in Du Bois's faith?

When a priest from Cuba wrote a letter to Du Bois in 1948 questioning where Du Bois placed his belief, Du Bois responded:

> If by being "a believer in God," you mean a belief in a *person* of vast power who consciously rules the universe for the good of mankind, I answer No; I cannot disprove this assumption, but I certainly see no proof to sustain such a belief, neither in History nor in my personal experience [italics added].

Du Bois began his response by refuting or discounting orthodox dogma about an external "person." No outside individual, from his personal encounters and historical studies, ruled over (as opposed to intimately with) people. He knew of no person who held in his or her hands the all-embracing potency to realize (alone) or impose (by themselves) goodness on human beings. For Du Bois to speak of a "person" indicated a living organism with rational abilities; a person indicated an individual who, like other persons, could be seen and verified by other individuals. Not only had he not seen or read about this person, neither had he encountered such an entity with power to bring about conscious good for people while people waited to be acted on. Du Bois offered this concluding response to the letter:

> If on the other hand you mean by "God" a vague Force which, in some uncomprehensible way, dominates all life and change, then I answer, Yes; I recognize such Force, and if you wish to call it God, I do not object.[50]

Why did he believe in a Force greater than humanity? A Force would allow for human initiative unlike a person (no matter how good) who, like any individual, stood outside other people and thereby acted on them. Furthermore, if this person were equipped with omnipotency, then people were left with nothing to do for themselves. Thus, a Force could be both greater than humanity (it "dominates all life and change"), but it (unlike a person) dominates human life and transformation *inside of* and *with* people.

Moreover, Du Bois granted the mysterious nature of this Force. It dominated in "some uncomprehensible way." His belief could feel comfortable with such a description because it did not block humanity's ability to struggle. Though he was a rationalist and social scientist, Du Bois's faith nevertheless embraced things not completely understandable. Thus, the Force was God, an incomprehensible holiness grounded in human affairs and empowering humanity to take initiative in social transformation.

In a similar exchange of letters, this time started by a Jesuit priest in Texas in 1944, Du Bois was asked to join the Roman Catholic church. Du Bois declined the invitation because of the orthodoxy represented by the

Roman church: "I cannot assent to any creed which demands that I accept on faith the elaborate doctrine and dogma of the Catholic Church." And though he opposed abstract theology and hypocritical blind belief, he still confessed the incomprehensible dimension of the faith reality. But this relation to an ultimate concern in one's life had to be tested in practice. He thus combined theological belief with a scientific methodology: "As a scientist I am perfectly aware that there are some things in this world we must accept on faith so long as we rigorously test them by the data of experience. Beyond that I cannot go."[51] Du Bois had faith in a Force or God that labored alongside of and empowered humanity to work for a new democracy and politics. This was his ultimate concern in life; the concept of God as Force let him maintain his faith. For Du Bois, God revealed divinity among people who gave their lives for the subjugated of this world. Thus knowledge and embracing of God's presence takes place in a struggle for equal power relations for blacks and the earth's disenfranchised.

JESUS: BLACK AND LOWLY

For Du Bois, Jesus Christ brought the actual revelation of God achieving democratic power among black people and the lowly. He highlighted this reality by directly critiquing the institutional religion of whites in North America:

The number of white individuals who are practising with even reasonable approximation the democracy and unselfishness of Jesus Christ is so small and unimportant as to be fit subject for jest.[52]

Jesus founded his earthly ministry on the cornerstone of democracy. From that rock he built a way for all followers to share in God's presence with humanity. In contrast, realized democracy did not exist in the United States, particularly in reference to white North Americans. If Christians had involved themselves in that which Jesus was offering, all areas and levels of society would have opened up to include the lowly at the bottom of the nation.

More specifically, the essence of Jesus' ministry expressed service toward those who suffered persecution. He worked to provide space in society for the locked-out voices of the meek and merciful. Du Bois pictured the work of Jesus in the following poem:

> There comes a priest of the meek and lowly
> Jesus—a Servant of the Servant who said:
> Blessed are the Meek,
> Blessed are the Poor,
> Blessed are the Merciful,

Blessed are the Peace-makers,
Blessed are the Persecuted.[53]

Above all, one should see Jesus as the ultimate Servant of the poor. The revelation of Christ takes place in society's communities where the folk endure pain from not having means to determine for themselves the space to be themselves on earth. The muted cries of the meek join with the cry of the Servant; Jesus' fellowship with the persecuted amplifies their screams. And those who have ears to hear and eyes to see will discover that these sounds come from the same place and belong to the same voice.

Du Bois joins the mixed voices of the lowly, expanded by divine revelation, with Jesus' call for peace. One has to stand for peace too because the plight of the persecuted results from the ravages of war. "I believe in the Prince of Peace," exclaims Du Bois. "I believe that war is Murder." In the final analysis, the primary victims of organized violence and murder (the domestic and international taking of life) are those who become non-decision-making objects of belligerent conflicts. For instance, "we cannot forget that under the aegis and protection of the religion of the Prince of Peace — of a religion which was meant for the lowly and unfortunate — there arose in America one of the most stupendous institutions of human slavery that the world has seen."[54] The North American slave system (sustained, programmatic, white American violence) typified all that contradicted Jesus and his religious legacy — peace and righteousness for the lowly.

Peace provided favorable conditions for the implementation of Jesus' plan for equality in power sharing. Nevertheless, to benefit completely from these favorable conditions, one had to rearrange fundamentally domestic political economies. For instance, the North American economic sector remained monopolized and dominated by wealthy billionaires, in contradiction to the prophetic life and work of Jesus.

Still the United States economy, for Du Bois, inherently contained the means and resources to distribute capital in such a way as to level any exploitative social relations. To imitate Jesus Christ, his followers should set their will toward equality over their base instincts toward personal profit and accumulation. Sharing the fruits of work — an agenda focused on shortening the gap between white and black, rich and poor — would mark the presence of Jesus Christ's divine revelatory intent. Chastising those who separate themselves from Jesus in the economic sphere, Du Bois wrote:

Big Business fights and schemes and drafts the 18-year-old youth. Profit is thicker than blood.

This has led many a social thinker to point out that capital for all real human want and improvement could easily be taken from production and leave sufficient income for all consumers, provided, of course, that individual consumption was so limited that no man had cake if any man lacked bread; that mink coats for the rich were not allowed if the poor had no shoes.

The huge profits from industry come from the work and savings of laborers. But big business lacks the will of Jesus to invest in socially responsible projects to prioritize the basic necessities for survival of the majority of the populace. In fact, the centralized monopolizers of capital would rather invest in war machinery, with black and working-class youth doing the capitalists' killing, and use their wealth to speculate on foreign trade and nonproductive projects. Such nonproductive investments accompany a narrow concentration of wealth and an elitist pyramidal chain of command in entrepreneurial hierarchy.

At the bottom, in Du Bois's view, were African Americans and workers who gave their labor and value to the production of commodities. Yet, ownership of both capital and machinery used in product development, as well as the commodities themselves, all belonged to a handful of white men at the pyramid top. In brief, ownership and distribution resided in a few private white hands while blacks and the poor, in socialized production, had no say. A tight control of capital investment decision-making at the top complemented and caused non-democratic social relations in the economic sphere for the triangular bottom.

Concluding his comments on the economic democracy aspect of Jesus, Du Bois states: "What church of the lowly Jesus, who railed against the rich, would for a moment admit or preach such doctrine?"[55] Jesus Christ opposed capitalist political economy because it blocked all mass participation in and ownership of capital formations. Basically, Du Bois links christology with a radical political economy.

To reach a more democratic economy, according to Du Bois, required sustained sacrifice on earth and not a frenzied dash for heaven. "If [self-sacrifice] wouldn't be religion," claimed Du Bois, "then I don't know what religion is." Jesus incarnates sacrifice; those of his faith should do likewise. A person's verbal love of Jesus Christ stands for nothing if she or he does not "forget himself" and carry out persistent work and honest effort.

Orthodox dogma about Jesus incorrectly kept black Christians' minds in the clouds while vineyards of life remained untilled. Straying away from Christ, black folk too often advocated more for their rights and not enough for their duties. They put too much emphasis on talk and not enough on work; too much on religion and not enough on doing right. For Du Bois, the Christianity "which Jesus of Nazareth taught the world means manliness, courage and self-sacrifice or it means nothing." But the activities of some black "prayer meetings seem to teach that it means a rough and tumble scramble for heaven."[56]

Moreover, sacrifice did not demand a blind giving of oneself without sharp focus. Self-sacrifice, like Jesus, called for a clear partiality to the underdog ("Jesus Christ gave his life as a sacrifice for the lowly").[57]

Related to economic democracy and self-sacrifice for the powerless, Du Bois added Jesus' characteristic of unselfishness. Linked to this divine trait was honesty and sympathy, which "in plain English" meant Christianity. Honesty suggested a just handling of funds: an end to cheating, waste, and carelessness. Sympathy suggested realizing the necessary resources for a decent standard of living and actually recognizing other human beings who suffer, strive, and fail. Most of all, Jesus stood for unselfishness.

> Above all, Christianity means unselfishness; the willingness to forego in part one's personal advantage and give up some personal desires for the sake of a larger end which will be for the advantage of a greater number of people.[58]

In other words, a key part of understanding Jesus Christ's empowering political democracy was the individual giving of oneself in and for the commnual betterment. To partake of Christ's revelation, then, one worked and sacrificed hard for the other—the vast majority, not for the elite and powerful privileged.

Similarly, and perhaps most importantly for Du Bois, Jesus and African Americans *together* suffered and survived in this huge conflict between the masses and the elite. Restated, white racism against African Americans also destroyed Jesus' work with the earth's have-nots. Du Bois dedicated his entire life to the long-term task of achieving democracy for black folk. And so his starting point in describing Jesus would have to include Jesus' negative attitude and action toward white-skinned privileges and inequality. The slow genocide against black folk—a destruction of Jesus' work by white racism—meant the slow crucifixion of Christ. Certainly Du Bois's historical survey of race interactions in the United States confirmed a glaring inherent contradiction between the person Jesus, on the one hand, and the unmerited racial advancements of white folk, on the other. Consequently, he observed:

> All through this history of subterfuge and evasion [in black-white race relations] has run the great and dominating fact of a racial prejudice which denies the application of the ethics of Jesus Christ in the relations of men if these men happen to be of a different race.[59]

Yet Du Bois still held out a helping hand with the hope of Jesus. Racial prejudice did not have to remain insurmountable if white and black Americans centered their focus on Christ. "Men may be brothers in Christ, even though they be not brothers-in-law."[60] Though whites suffered from a rabid anti-interracial marriage phobia, nevertheless, different races could be siblings in a black Christ.

Indeed the color of Christ tinted a significant amount of Du Bois's prose, fiction, and poetry. By theologically naming Christ black, he stands as a major predecessor of the 1960s black christological movement.[61] Like this latter theological development, Du Bois expressed convictions on the Black Christ's birth, life, death, crucifixion, resurrection, and second coming in their relation to a tormented black humanity and a despised poor.

The birth of Jesus establishes both his racial identity as well as his poverty status. Tracing Jesus' lineage in his short story "Magnificat," Du Bois starts with "Mary Black," an impoverished African American woman. An angel of the Lord approaches her and declares, "Blessed art thou among women and blessed is the fruit of thy womb." But Mary Black complains and resists the divine will expressed by the messenger angel. She wants to know why is "Another baby coming and none of us with a job." Like Old Testament prophets, Mary resists her calling and raises strong objections to God's commissioning. Not only does she complain about lack of employment, she challenges God's grace of blessing her by comparing it to how white folks on earth have never called her or her people blessed. How can she now be blessed after all the years her people have "slaved and worked and kept decent and gone to church" and no one ever affirmed their existence, reverence, or work? Despite hesitation by the chosen birther and deliverer of the Messiah, the angel persists with prophecy: "The Holy Ghost shall come upon thee ... that holy thing which shall be born of thee shall be called the Son of God."[62]

Significant for developing a black christology is Du Bois's decision to start with Mary. Mary Black's conversation with the angel of the Lord falls partly within the prophetic mode of Yahweh-Deliverer dynamics in the Old Testament. Just as Yahweh chooses Moses to aid the liberation of an oppressed Hebrew people, so too does God's angel call Mary to deliver the Liberator of all humanity. In this sense the prophetic nature of the person Jesus goes back to Moses through a black woman. No mention of Joseph appears in the story.

The power of God is granted to Mary: "the power of the Highest shall overshadow thee." Divine power of and in the divine seed becomes one with her and, therefore, Mary will have part of the omnipotence ingrained in her identity. She is not simply a tunnel for the passage of God through incarnation to earth. No, Mary will possess divineness and help facilitate this characteristic in her son. Mary foreshadows the coming of Jesus biologically (she is his potent mother). And, in the Old Testament prophetic mode, she also symbolizes the prophetic role of the anointed mission on earth. God chooses a black woman, through verbal commission and intimate relation with the Holy Spirit, to birth (and thereby deliver to this world) the Son of God.

In addition, the color and station in life of the Son's mother determine where the Christ will be born. For instance, Du Bois's editorial on "Christmas" exposes those who would search for the divine baby in the "frilled and dainty" places of the affluent sections of town. These places are dead ends because "black men are not welcome there." Consequently, to pay homage to "the low-lying Savior of the World," one has to go to the ghetto and other areas of squalor, to the lives of "the low, the despised."[63] Jesus Christ springs forth from the ground-down sectors of society on the edge.

Similarly, the location of birth radically shifts the social relations between wealth and poverty. Ghettoes lie on the margin both in terms of geographic location and power politics; the center of the city usually contains the positions of privileged white life—financiers, politicians, and priests. But Du Bois's revolutionary reversal forces "the Kings of the Earth" to bow in the black ghetto birthplace of Jesus. The appearance of this baby and where this appearance occurs, then, equalize political relations for the Mary Blacks of this world.

The birth of the black Christ heralds a new earth because it signals the close of Satan's reign at the hands of a black babe. Though the color of Christ is ebony, his birth's implications cover a universal humankind. In this instance God chooses the apparently unimportant in society and the heel of humanity to bring good news for all. Specifically, Du Bois's poem "The Riddle of the Sphinx" depicts and castigates all historical crimes of white folk as the devil's work. And the "devil's strength be shorn" only until "married maiden, mother of God, Bid the black Christ be born." Only with the absence of Satan's activities, and only then, will all of creation gain full maturity and achieve complete potential regardless of color. Du Bois calls this new time the "burden be manhood."[64] The moment the lowly divine-filled African American woman delivers forth the ghetto child, a historic shift redefines the distorted landscape of society. From then on all can reach the peaks of holistic humanity.

Du Bois further shows the power and compassion of the black Christ by correlating Jesus' adult life with black suffering life:

> Yet Jesus Christ was a laborer and black men are laborers; He was poor and we are poor; He was despised of his fellow men and we are despised; He was persecuted and crucified, and we are mobbed and lynched.[65]

Jesus arose from the ghetto and endured the same hardships as African Americans living in such places. Mary Black delivered him into a world of lowliness and persecution; the destiny of African Americans provided the rich soil for him to fertilize his divine manna of life for humanity. Thus the mission and message of Jesus the Christ could only bear fruit within the midst of the black experience. The human person Jesus, son of an earthly mother Mary, revealed his divine self, of a heavenly parent, in the conditions of black suffering.

The African American reality of apparent darkness and despair provided the conditions and catalyst for the brillance of divineness, the living testimony of the Messiah, to shine forth. Only in a depressed state of black life could the world discover and recognize God's gift of salvation. To attain liberation, then, we look toward the hills whence cometh our help, and those are the hills of the shadowy ghetto. Thus, by way of a parallel predicament with the black community, did the black Jesus also become the black Christ.

Not only did Du Bois's theological beliefs find Jesus' blackness in the movement of divine birth and life, Du Bois also painted Jesus black in the cross and resurrection *kairos* (that is, divine possibilities given to humanity). The crucifixion and risen significance of Jesus provided a fundamental and unique invitation and opportunity for humanity to cross over from a world of sin to God's time of liberation—hence the moment of *kairos*. Here, for Du Bois, the lynching-death of black folk (like death on a wooden cross), led to the possibility of victorious freedom and creativity toward full humanity (like the invitation of the resurrection).

Writing about "Easter," Du Bois retells the well-known story of pain at Calvary and resuscitation to life from a tomb. However, the old narrative itself receives new life when Du Bois puts Jesus' death-life account within the context of a bruised black body that is risen. With a new understanding of Easter, Du Bois describes how the white South kills and buries the corporate black people and calls on its brother, the white North, to come view the grave. "But suddenly the World was wings and the voice of the Angel of the Resurrection beat like a mighty wind athwart their ears." "Suddenly" indicates the exact moment of the in-breaking of God's Kingdom, the radical shift in power relations with a gracious gift of the new free existence. The grave contains no body and, therefore, tells the white brothers from North and South that the jaws of death claim no final victory over what God wills for a battered black people. As the Angel of Resurrection exclaims with divine authority:

"He is not here—He is risen."

Risen above half his ignorance; risen to more than six hundred millions of property; risen to a new literature and the faint glimmering of a new Art; risen to a dawning determination to be free; risen to a newer and greater ideal of Humanity than the world has known. RISEN![66]

The act of lynching on a cross contains within itself a wrestling of the old and new world supremacies. In that encounter the realized hope for humanity triumphs when Christ ultimately tears asunder the grip of Satan's kingdom. The fullness of good news (He is RISEN!) emerges from the clutches of the white brothers of death and dawns into the blackness of a new day of life. The cross symbolizes both beaten blackness in pain and also the vertical and horizontal intersection of God's love for a rainbow-colored humanity; divine love consummates in its absoluteness from a barren grave. Consequently, the resurrection of oppressed African American life paves the way for all people to feast on the "Lord's supper" of freedom, culture, and a unique civilization of equality, "a new and greater ideal of Humanity than the world has known."

Finally, Jesus is black due to the second coming of a black Messiah. In "The Second Coming," a short story, Du Bois describes how three religious leaders (a white bishop from New York, a black bishop from New Orleans, and a Japanese priest) converge on an "old, black, rickety stable," which was a hut in Georgia. But, prior to reaching this lowly home, the white bishop first visits the state's white governor, who agitatedly confesses: "I am sorely troubled! I never saw niggers act so. They're leaving by the hundreds and those who stay are getting impudent! They seem to be expecting something." After this meeting the white bishop is drawn to the poor, dilapidated hut far off in someone's backyard. The hut housed a mother cradling a baby, the black bishop, and the Japanese priest, who had arrived ahead of the New York clergyman. The latter heard the black man exclaim:

> "But he was to come the second time in clouds of glory, with the nations gathered around Him and angels—" at the word a shaft of glorious light fell full upon the child, while without came the tramping of unnumbered feet and the whirring of wings.
> The bishop of New York bent quickly over the baby. It was black.

Through story Du Bois maintains a consistent thematic description of the nature of Jesus the Christ. He uses "The Second Coming" tale to underscore the radical contrast between the expectation of official church leadership (bishops and priests) and the reality of extreme impoverished dwellings of the black Christ's second arrival on earth. Church leadership and those in politically powerful high places assume that their interpretation of the biblical prophecy about the Messiah's second coming will ensure Jesus' advent in royal garments, like people with money. Instead, priestly leadership and powerful governors are bewildered and befuddled by an old, black rickety stable and a backyard hut. There the angels of the Lord flutter their messianic wings to announce fulfillment of the written word. There the world's multitudes gather to pay homage to the return of hope and deliverance. But all the white bishop of New York can do is stand aghast. "He stepped back with a gesture of disgust."[67] Despite evidence of the Messiah's arrival, the white bishop refuses to see that the day of the Lord is at hand.

This blindness on the part of powerful, elite wealth becomes more clear in Du Bois's fictional essay, "Jesus Christ in Georgia." In this story a stranger enters a Georgia town and speaks to the rich and powerful. Yet they (the white judge, colonel, naval officer, and rector) either take the traveler, Jesus, for a black servant or look into his eyes and talk directly without seeing Jesus' true self or understanding his real message.

But the outcast and powerless in the story instantaneously recognize the divinity of this "foreigner." A black convict laboring over a pile of stones immediately acknowledges the stranger by dropping his rock hammer in awe. A black butler catches one glimpse of him and falls on his knees and simply whispers, "My Lord! . . . and my God!" A black nursemaid of a little white girl "caught his cloak, trembled, hesitated, and then kneeled in the dust." At another point in the narrative, an escaped convict looks into the stranger's face and comments, "Why, you'se a nigger, too."[68]

This "niggerness" in Jesus Christ touches on the central nature of divine revelation's scandal for the rectors, colonels, judges, and governors of the dominant white church, military establishment, court system, and political leaders. Those with elite monopolized power and resources, in other words, have hardened hearts and have blinded themselves to the saving grace found in the black ghettoes and poor communities of this earth. They cannot understand the reality that the all-powerful God would come to humanity in the form of blackness and lowliness in order to live with and breathe where marginalized folk struggle to maintain daily life.

Yet all who would confess faith in and witness to the Christ have to situate themselves with and base their very beings on serving the poor by systemically rooting out the causes of poverty. Ultimately the calling of all humanity is to change the conditions that give rise to poverty so that wealth and an abundant life become a reality only when the least in society first have as much as the richest. In that sense, Du Bois suggests a radical reinterpretation of the biblical saying to "do unto others as you would have them to do unto you." This is the Christian priority of working for the kingdom of the black and poor, a holy calling for all humanity.

WORKING FOR GLOBAL FREEDOM: A SACRED VOCATION

Du Bois felt that the purpose of humanity was a divine vocation to combat racial privilege and serve the unfortunate in the United States and the world. Commenting on how "color discrimination is . . . an inhuman and damnable shame," he wrote: "Believing this with my utmost soul, I shall fight race prejudice continually. . . . This contribution to the greatest of causes shall be my most sacred obligation."[69] We cannot simply use the intellect or reason to detest racism. Nor can we merely express a noncommital liberal abhorrence. On the contrary, we eliminate racism by feeling a gut-level despising for the oppression of one racial group over another. Accordingly, Du Bois experienced hatred for the act of discrimination in his bones because his very soul was engulfed by divine mission. He could not escape God's calling to devote his entire life to those without means to fight their own battles, especially black folk.

For African Americans, then, the first step along the path of freedom was to get some power. They could not wait for what Du Bois mockingly called God's "vice-regent the White Man." He believed that relying on whites to steer blacks in the direction of liberation was notorious nonsense. Black folk had to achieve the lofty aim of full humanity by self-realization and self-direction. They had to fight and take initiative to create themselves in the process of struggle. They had to decide when, how, and where they were going if their sacred goals were not to remain unfulfilled dreams.

> Conscious self-realization and self-direction is the watchword of modern man, and the first article in the program of any group that will survive must be the great aim, equality and power among men.[70]

The ultimate aim and ultimate concern of black people, he believed, centered on democracy and politics, a yearning for the same status of others and the resources to get there. Without equal power, African Americans would become extinct.

This need for power did not remain a vague idea in Du Bois's head. He specifically targeted the control over and direction of the government in the United States. With intense commitment he believed that poor and working-class folk (where most blacks found themselves) should guide and rule all levels of government for the best interests of the majority population. Similarly, he argued that a country would discover in the downtrodden masses people with sufficient character and ability to perform service for the whole's benefit.

> I had been brought up with the democratic idea that this general welfare was the object of democratic action in the state, of allowing the governed a voice in government.

If the poor took their rightful democratic place of guiding the affairs of state, then black people would also enjoy the benefits of the poor's power. Blacks were poor and on the bottom, a place reserved for objects of the elite, wealthy minority of America. Placing the majority in positions where they could deliberate on and act for the majority would immediately deliver African Americans from the chains of discrimination; they too constituted the crushed-down mass that would finally realize its full potential and decision-making capabilities. With the fiery passion and unyielding resolve of Old Testament prophets, Du Bois linked this democratic irruption from below and freedom for black people to the essence of his being. He continues: "I believe this dictum passionately. It was, in fact, the foundation stone of my fight for black folk; it explained me."[71]

Du Bois believed that the power to control all levels of public government would enable blacks and the poor to regulate modern industry in the interest of industrial democracy. Power over the state went hand-in-hand with the majority of citizens taking over and owning monopolized property. How could it be otherwise? Because the products of industry and industry itself were both created by working people in a collective system, the invested time, energy, and sweat of working people granted them the collective title deed to the monopoly corporations they had built. Du Bois fought for practical ethics in the area of industrial dictatorship when he argued that:

> the control of industry is largely in the hands of a powerful few, who decide for their own good and regardless of the good of others. . . . Just here it is that modern men demand that Democracy supplant skilfully concealed, but all too evident, Monarchy.[72]

The Christian ideal of doing justice for fellow humanity demanded that the welfare, sanity, and health of all should replace the common capitalist assumption that a little group of rich, white families could monopolize all resources needed for human life. Only when the segregated group of industrial monarchs gave their wealth back to the society that rightfully produced it would the sanctity of human beings become a reality.

Unfortunately, the love and worship of profit had replaced the sacredness of human life. Du Bois sought to reverse this heretical cowering before the temples of money. Divinity resides in human well-being, not in the accumulation of capital. For Du Bois, there is "nothing sacred about property; everything depends on the social welfare involved in its accumulation and use." And social welfare (allowing the vast bottom of society to claim rightful ownership and control of capital and its just distribution) replaces the holiness of property with the holiness of humanity. He concludes: "This means that property and its use are proper subjects of political consideration and of democratic decision." Hammering away at the link between socialization of production, the need for communal ownership, and the theme of justice, Du Bois writes: "The product of modern industry is a social product and belongs to society. It should be distributed in accord with the highest standard of social justice."[73] Political democracy includes the eradication of an industrial monarchy for equalization of power relations in political economy.

Patience and confusion on this point, for Du Bois, would only delay the fight to place blacks (as well as the poor) in the commanding heights of industry and state control. Indeed, it proved a harmful stalling tactic to urge black folk to first struggle against a vaguely defined color discrimination and later move toward group economic and political power. To heed such a deceptive call would prove a starvation death for the African American poor. Instead, Du Bois urged blacks to organize immediately for "the power to work out our destiny." For him, "everything else is subordinate."[74] Du Bois relegated all other concerns to correcting the imbalanced and unequal power relations between blacks and whites.

Basically, in the divine vocation to liberation, black Americans required more than freedom to react negatively to "the political tyranny of white folk." Blacks needed to take initiative in electoral politics, control of economics, and social relations. For example, they must have the right to vote and its actual implementation, as well as have their voice proportionally present in government. With fair and unhindered representation, they could then rule with justice over white and black citizens.

Likewise, blacks wanted jobs for the unemployed and sought a hand in deciding the affairs at their workplaces, which placed them at the jugular vein of economic planning. And finally, blacks fought for freedom to move about in society: to breathe the air, live in any neighborhood, travel on all means of transportation, attend whatever educational institutions and associate with whomever they pleased. Briefly, the "Negro must have power"; black folk need to be able to work out their destiny toward freedom.[75]

Du Bois did not limit his sacred obligation to the plight of blacks and the poor within the shores of North America. The fulfillment of black liberation could never succeed without all oppressed racial groups on the planet entering an equal partnership. African Americans and the world's peoples of color suffered from the same system of global white supremacy. This structural privileging of white interests over the rest of humanity's majority disguised itself under the cloak of democracy. But Du Bois knew quite well that the democracy rich, white families advocated did not exist for the overwhelming masses of black, brown, yellow, and red peoples throughout the world. Without these latter groups included in a genuine democracy, then white North American democracy was only a mockery headed for its own destruction.

For example, white democracy callously treated peoples of color as inhuman and legitimate objects of religious persecution, commercial exploitation, and social ostracism. The longer this state of affairs existed, the longer democracy would be impossible on a global scale.

In international relationships, for Du Bois, oppressed people had to struggle for equality by first attacking industrial imperialism. Developing nations of the Third World could reach self-determination and self-integrity when they had access to and control over their own natural and human-made wealth. This effort necessitated an organized movement by the voiceless peoples all over the earth to break the strangle-hold of foreign financiers, credit agencies, and consumer-oriented companies, all originating from North American white monopolies. "Thus industrial imperialism must lose its reason for being," writes Du Bois, "and in that way alone can the great racial groups of the world come into normal and helpful relation to each other." And so, if the death grip of United States imperialism could be broken, then the sun's rays of global cooperation could shine through.

At the same time, Du Bois was no naive student of international problems. He understood the hard, complex, and treacherous nature of world politics. Resuming his exposure of industrial imperialism, he makes this related point:

> It will not be easy to accomplish all this, but the quickest way to bring the reason of the world face to face with this major problem of human progress is to listen to the complaint of those human beings today

who are suffering most from white attitudes, from white habits, from the conscious and unconscious wrongs which white folk are today inflicting on their victims.

The peoples of color in all hemispheres, he stated, held the keys to a better world community, and this required the conquering of economic imperialism propagated by white American monopoly capitalists. The "colored world" had to be seen not just for its own existence, but as a prophetic voice that cried a warning to the soul and well-being of all. Du Bois believed that such a strident signal, once heeded, could awaken the entire world to its true self and wider destiny.[76]

Justice Work—A Sacred Task

For Du Bois "work" and "sacrifice" are sacred. They are the specific paths humanity must follow to reach equal power relations, both domestically and internationally. He relates this purpose for human activity within a Christian mandate when he writes: "If religion and Christianity mean anything, they mean deeds and not the mere words."[77] The followers of Jesus Christ cannot interpret their vocation otherwise because the gift of God's grace for human efforts toward deliverance is precisely the call for all to work.

Emphasizing this theological insight, Du Bois describes and contrasts the inheritance from both our earthly parents and heavenly parent. Mothers may grant us "love" and fathers may offer "wealth"; "but the gift of God is work."[78] Therefore, with reverence and persistence, Du Bois prayed to God to help him base all of his activities, even his recreational moments, on work.

> We would learn, Our Father, to choose our recreations as thoughtfully as our duties—to bring them in and mingle them with our work—to make our life a oneness of work and rest-in-work, of rest and work-in-rest and of Joy in both.[79]

Du Bois experienced joy in relating recreation with work because God mysteriously used the work and sacrifice of human beings to do away with the old order and bring about a structurally new creation. If God sanctioned such a sacrifice, then even rest needed a close connection with work. Rest periods did not grant time for mindless and aimless commotion. Just the opposite, recreation was joy with work, both blessed by divine intent. Thus people had to be ever-mindful of their activities (including recreation) and themselves as divine instruments for social justice on earth. Du Bois stated:

> We make the world better by the gift of our service and our selves, and it is a better world that we ourselves need. So in some mystic way does God bring realization through sacrifice.[80]

God reveals God's plan for creation by using human exertion and sacrifice to forge a new reality of just social relations. In the process, God continually constructs creation. Therefore the only reward or fame worth the struggle is, in Du Bois's words, "the 'Well done' of that master who knows the sweat of the toil and the worth of the service."[81]

Longing for the "master's" approval of the quality of our efforts should cause us to fight against all odds for ultimate freedom, even when the struggles bring death. Here Du Bois correlates human efforts with the literal physical giving of oneself. He expands on this position with the biblical story of Esther (Esther 4:9-16) and her heroic qualities of endurance and daring. "Mighty causes," prays Du Bois, "call with voices that mean work and sacrifice and death." With Esther as a supreme example of how we should respond to the divine call to better the world, he concludes, "Mercifully grant us, O God, the spirit of Esther, that we say: I will go unto the King and if I perish, I perish — Amen."[82] To open ourselves up to God's liberation plan for the world compels us never to remain content with mere plans, ambitions, and resolves; we must fulfill the promise, complete the instructions, and endure to the end. Only then will our salvation be ensured, a result of work, sacrifice, and a well-earned death.

Du Bois, furthermore, equates work and sacrifice with heaven; in this sense, justice and freedom come from heavenly attainment. The road to political democracy travels through heaven. "I believe in Service," confesses Du Bois, "for Work is Heaven, Idleness Hell."[83] Well-engaged toil and sweat (human purpose) create a state of living in which all our purposes in life — that is, service to others — are focused, self-affirming, and self-rewarding.

Through giving ourselves to the other, we become one with ourselves in such a way that we enter a realm of "bliss" for justice. Even money no longer defines the quality of our living. Indeed, Du Bois confirms the priceless nature of work/heaven: "I insist that regardless of income, work worth while which one wants to do as compared with highly paid drudgery is exactly the difference between heaven and hell."[84] Consequently, the heavenly glory of humanity is found in the avoidance of idleness (hell on earth) and in the presentation of our weary, sweating bodies at death's doorstep after living to enhance the poor's "infinite possibility and endless development" for all humanity.[85]

In the final analysis, we participate actively in the dynamic relation among God, Jesus, and human purpose through the spirituality of work for freedom.

CONCLUSION

W. E. B. Du Bois's belief in democratized political power adds further to a constructive black theology. Fundamentally, theology has to come to terms with assisting the majority — blacks, poor, and working people at the bottom—in controlling and directing the space around them, that is, the earth and the concrete materials on earth, and their social relations (how humans relate to one another) and representative connections (how humans govern themselves and each other).

For Du Bois, the issue focused on "an ethical and not a mere mechanical problem." This was true because God had shown the divine self working within human relations struggling for democracy and power based on justice. Jesus was the actual revelation of this democratic power among human beings. And so, human purpose and witness must labor tirelessly toward an earthly realm where African Americans and the marginalized enjoy ownership of complete equalized capital and electoral representation.

A constructive black theology, consequently, has to take seriously a democracy that corrects hierarchical differences, eliminating marginalization and economic monopolization in all of society. The mere appearance of electoral democracy is insufficient. Instead, Christian democracy entails communal ownership of a country's total wealth and economic resources by the majority at the bottom's edge. This is opposed to the heretical conviction that "whiteness is the ownership of the earth forever and ever," in Du Bois's terms. If God, as Du Bois states, created all reality for equality in electoral representation and wealth's control, then black theology must deepen further the relationship between white supremacist evil and a theological political economy. To agree to such equal power, therefore, is to maintain and aid God's sovereignty over each created order on earth.

The democratic reality of the poor's presence in the political economic area indicates the presence of sacred ground. God is the Holy One of total popular democracy.

Knowledge of God and divine love come when the faithful involve themselves in God's work among humanity. Again, God reveals a holy democratized politics through the divine act of equal creation. God breathes free life; every thing, person, and being shares accordingly in life and ownership of life. The divinity's nature also demands justice for African Americans and universal sisterhood and brotherhood for all peoples. In fact, achieving equality for one race brings the fullest community of justice for all races.

In addition, God is love and work is God's prophet. Persistent, comprehensive work for the other shows the Holy's nearness. God is a Force greater than humanity. And God mysteriously works with us in such a way that human initiative reaches a maximum potentiality—a creativity free from all external material or spiritual stumbling blocks. Thus, to know God's love and be fully human, we must work for the poor and working people.

Jesus brought us to the ultimate practical implementation of God's knowledge. In Jesus we meet a sacred power on earth who represents a complete democracy and equality. The "lowly Jesus," commented Du Bois, "rallied against the rich." And this advocate and comforter of the poor was painted in ebony. The blackness of Christ further anchors contemporary black theological discussion to a tradition based on a black Messiah. Thus Du Bois's correct linking of Christ's dark color with economic location and the plight and propects of poor black folk serves to root constructive theological efforts in the ground of history.

At the same time, Du Bois's perceptive theological insights on a black Mary as the prophetic embodiment and power bearer of Christ the Liberator indicates black theology's lack of adequate attention to African American women, mothers, and Holy Spirit power. Knowledge of God moves through Jesus Christ and Mary.

Pursuing further his theology of political democracy, Du Bois called on the church to maintain openness to all who gathered seeking Christ. Based on society's voiceless, the church should be open in decision-making, membership, leadership, and governance. Additional witness for the church included the healthy status of black women (particularly for the African American Christian church); the need for ruthless efficiency in applying self-criticism; a knife-sharp removal of pompous, irrational dogma; and, above all, the social uplifting of the poor.

We have seen how Du Bois knew God as the mysterious but real Force manifesting divine purpose internal to human relations that worked for democracy and just power relations. The event and movement of Jesus Christ were the actual revelation of political democracy. Therefore Du Bois experienced a sacred obligation of tireless and enduring work and sacrifice, which brought his life's efforts into a heavenly realm in sympathy with the suffering of fellow humanity. Commenting on periods of great pain and calamity, when people often relapse into orthodox, formal religious creeds (examples of "ignorance and discouragement"), Du Bois cites the spirituality of work as the indication of social reconstruction out of human crisis.

> Among some people, there comes in time of stress and depression, an increase of determination to plan and work for better conditions. This is not usually called a "spiritual" awakening, but it is apt to be condemned by the ignorant as "radicalism" and an "attack" upon the established order. It is, however, a manifestation of the spirit in the highest sense.[86]

The awakening of God's spirit as given through Jesus Christ discloses itself when we persist in times of crisis. The challenges of hardship offer the possibilities of a new created order. Essentially, then, human work toward the divine vocation of political democracy is one of the highest spiritual regenerations for black folk and all of society's marginalized people.

Our divine vocation calls us to work for democracy, equality, and against racial privilege (both liberal and conservative modes). Work is not just a syndrome in which one accomplishes a task or performs a job before the day's end. Work, for Du Bois, positions us on holy ground. It holds profound theological importance because God calls us with purpose. Divine intent requires both a workstyle and a lifestyle that pursue sacred goals. The first step in such a holy crusade, Du Bois demands, is the attaining of governmental, economic, and decision-making power by African Americans along with the world's disadvantaged.

Only by upholding a practical sacred vow of tireless and fearless labor will Christians and those of faith ever see God's face on earth. And this holy appearance will meet us in democratized politics and equalized economics.

5

Malcolm and Martin

To Change the World

Any religion that professes to be concerned about the souls of men, and is not concerned about the slums that cripple the souls, the economic conditions that stagnate the soul and the city governments that may damn the soul is a dry dead do nothing religion, in need of new blood.
                                                        Martin Luther King, Jr.

The system in this country cannot produce freedom for an Afro-American. It is impossible for this system, this economic system, this political system, this social system, this system, period. It's impossible for this system, as it stands, to produce freedom right now for the black man in this country.
                                                        Malcolm X[1]

A constructive and contemporary black theology of liberation needs a prophetic social analysis and social vision. It requires a look into the racial, poverty, and gender connections existing in today's human relations and also a visionary forecast of the earthly make-up of humanity in the coming Kingdom. To claim the mantle of liberation (that is, to be accountable to the heart of the Christian gospel as well as the liberation motif of African American faith overall), black theology must speak to unraveling demonic and inhibiting systems that strangle the full realization of black humanity and of all the poor.

The previous chapters began to challenge black theology to name more clearly the evils of this world and to chart the type of future Kingdom on earth for the poor. We saw how African American chattel labeled the totalitarianism of slavery as the work of earthly white devils. Even more, women's spirituality offered a theological examination of the demonic Thing and the hope of the Funk. Yet the precise characteristics of the Thing and white devils remain a task unfulfilled for a constructive black theological agenda. Likewise, the Funk of the folk requires more exploration. Therefore, we now turn to social analysis and social vision as fundamental sources for black theology. For an oppressed people to discern the signs of the times, they require insightful theological tools in order to dissect sinful and favorable factors that block and enhance their God-given humanity.

In this chapter we draw lessons from the lives and theologies of Minister Malcolm X and Rev. Dr. Martin Luther King, Jr., in order to detect social analyses and social visions for today's black theology. Both Malcolm and King "stood on the shoulders of a giant"—the masses of black folk in and out of the church. Their life experiences and theological articulations reflected the crystallized dynamic development of an oppressed African American community, which was affected by but also created the leadership of Minister Malcolm and Rev. King. So we study the penetrating social analyses and visions of King and Malcolm as refined propagations of the voiceless black community.

Obviously, Malcolm and Martin offered opinions on a wide range of issues. However, for black theology to develop critical interpretations of society today, part 1 of this chapter will draw on the following aspects of their *social analyses*: race relations, poverty, the international situation, and black women. Part 2 will touch on the following dimensions of their *social visions*: political economy, social relations, and the church or religion. Malcolm and Martin, toward the end of their lives, shared similarities in their prophetic social analyses and visions.

But to unfold such an analytical and visionary discussion, we first need to establish the ground rules for our investigation of King's and Malcolm's lessons for a constructive black theology. To have "shoes that fit our feet" (that is, a justice-oriented analysis and vision accountable to the black poor and thus the world's poor) necessitates a new liberated interpretation, a new prophetic methodology, and a new world outlook. In this new identity and space the black oppressed define a new set of rules for dealing with a white, male, monopoly capitalist power structure. The correct "shoes" require a logic that wicked powers would term illogical, unorthodox, heretical, and even subversive (to their status quo). Malcolm X sets the tone for our discussion and consequently our conclusions when he teaches us the following:

> What is logical to the oppressor isn't logical to the oppressed. And what is reason to the oppressor isn't reason to the oppressed. The black people in this country are beginning to realize that what sounds reasonable to those who exploit us doesn't sound reasonable to us. There just has to be a new system of reason and logic devised by us who are at the bottom.[2]

The language of Martin's and Malcolm's analyses and visions comes from the bottom, from those suffering from race, poverty, and gender pains in

America and, indeed, the world. To miss their radical shift from the status quo of the privileged to the viewpoint and voices from below is to bastardize the life and thought of Malcolm and Martin and assassinate them all over again.

The prophetic analytical and visionary components in today's black theology mean a new logic and a new set of rules. To initiate the theological implications of such an emphasis from the bottom, we turn to their social analyses. Beginning with their positions on "race relations," we will review various points in both men's analyses of existing society.

I: SOCIAL ANALYSIS

RACE RELATIONS

The Crimes of White Theology

For a contemporary black theology the historical theological encounter between white colonizers and Africans provides the starting point and framework for today's race relations. Malcolm's analysis perceptively deepens this encounter. Malcolm knew that a sincere and truthful account of black-white race relations in the United States would take us automatically back to the history of white racism and white Christianity. To speak the truth about the painful legacy between blacks and whites in North America means that we cannot separate the connection between racism and Christianity. More specifically, when white folk dealt with Africans, they equated their white Christian god and their Christian religion with the privileges of white skin. The substance, form, and smell of white Christianity was white racism. Malcolm instructs us that

> one of the first slave ships to come here [to the United States] was piloted by an Englishman named John Hawkins, and John Hawkins' ship was called Jesus, the good ship Jesus. This was the boat that was used ... they used Jesus to bring [African slaves] here. And then [whites] used [Jesus] to keep you here, too.[3]

Since European colonialists had aided the creation of African Americans in slavery, white Christianity forced upon the black religious experience a theology of white superiority and black inferiority. With this initial introduction and definition of Christianity denoting "whiteness," white theology then proceeded to propagate its racist religious interpretation as the gospel message for African Americans.

Malcolm spoke the truth about white theology and white Christianity. He indicted white Christians for brainwashing black Americans into believing in a white Jesus. Malcolm surmised that all the dirty-looking, scrawny-built, stringy-haired white male pictures of Jesus found in thousands of black homes and churches throughout the United States were only the reflections of white male models who had posed for European artists during the European Renaissance and Middle Ages. A white portrait of Jesus had nothing to do with God. On the contrary, a white divinity served further to enslave black folks with psychological and self-denigrating chains. Again, Malcolm chastised his black listeners:

> All other peoples have their own religion and believe in a God whom they can associate themselves with, a God who looks like one of their own kind. But we picture God with the same blond hair and blue eyes as our murderous Slavemaster. The Christian religion teaches us that black is a curse, thus we love everything except black, and can picture God as being anything else but black. We'd rather say God is Invisible, before we'll say He is black.[4]

In addition to serving to enslave blacks mentally, Malcolm asserted, white Christian theology intended to prevent the black church and black community from using religion to struggle for survival and justice here on earth. In other words, Malcolm correctly perceived how white people had interpreted Christianity to mean heaven on earth for whites and a hell on earth for blacks. God, in white theology, had preordained white supremacy on earth and had likewise intended for black Christians to suffer patiently and wait for the latter's reward in their heaven after death. Malcolm attacked this otherworldly, spookism theology found in the majority of black Christian churches. Such a theology of accommodation and paralysis promised African Americans that they "would sprout wings after death and fly up into the sky where God would have a place especially prepared for" them.

Malcolm perceptively claimed that instead of worshiping a black God with a black theology,

> The white man has taught us to shout and sing and pray until we die, to wait until death, for some dreamy heaven-in-the-hereafter, when we're dead, while this white man has his milk and honey in the streets paved with golden dollars right here on this earth![5]

But white Christians did not work alone in their poisoning of black minds with white theology. The crimes of white theology and racism had created willing junior partners within the oppressed group. For Malcolm, the centuries of spiritual sickness and groveling paralysis of African American Christians also resulted from black preachers and certain other handpicked black middle-class elements who collaborated with white theology.

Malcolm persistently exposed those who benefited from the white Christian power structure in the black community. Here he dissects the class relations internal to the African American community and describes the educated black middle class's negative tendency to prostitute itself for white folks.

The black middle class used its gifts and crumbs from the white power structure to symbolize improvements for the entire black community. Not so, said Malcolm. The privileges of the black elite did not reflect the status of the African American masses. Just the opposite, such black middle-class claims that things were getting better only showed how well they had served their white masters. Their action as mouthpieces for the oppressor within the camp of the victims was nothing new. "Since slavery," in Malcolm's insightful reading of history, "the American white man has always kept some handpicked Negroes who fared much better than the black masses suffering and slaving out in the hot fields."[6]

Malcolm called these black middle-class elements, who did the bidding of the white Christian power structure, "house Negroes." Under slavery, white people created two types of Negroes, the house Negroes who lived in the house with the master ("in the attic or the basement") and the field Negroes. The latter group represented the overwhelming majority of African Americans who toiled in the fields and caught hell on earth. Applying the same class analysis to his time, Malcolm pictured the contemporary, somewhat modified, "Uncle Tom" house Negro:

> Today's Uncle Tom doesn't wear a handkerchief on his head. This modern, twentieth-century Uncle Thomas now often wears a top hat. He's usually well-dressed and well-educated. He's often the personification of culture and refinement. . . . This twentieth-century Uncle Thomas is a professional Negro . . . by that I mean his profession is being a Negro for the white man.[7]

Likewise, Martin Luther King, Jr., connected the crimes of white theology to the African American community by identifying black propagators of white Christianity. Originating out of the traditional black church, King also spoke correctly from experience when he critiqued those black preachers who had bought into white theology's accent on otherworldly spookism in order to accumulate riches at the expense of the black masses. These black clergy substituted a gospel of crass materialism for the true way of struggle for social change. They preferred big luxury cars and glittering trappings of capitalist success, while their congregations and communities languished in poverty. Just as white Christians preached a pie-in-the-sky-by-and-by Christianity to blacks, while those same whites had their milk and honey on earth now, certain black preachers aped white religious thought in order to rip off the black community. King felt compelled to expose certain "Negro clergymen who are more concerned about the size of the wheel base on their automobiles than about the quality of their service to the Negro community."[8]

Thus Malcolm and Martin both sought to lay bare a false Christian belief in a non-struggling religion, a belief created by the crimes of white theology. For African Americans, such an incorrect theological practice freezes the black church and community within the clutches of white Christian power and oppression. To break the prison walls of subservience, a black theology for the African American folk needs a social analysis of race relations, encompassing the use of power, both political and cultural.

The Need for Political and Cultural Black Power

The crimes of white theology propagated by the white church externally and certain black preachers and middle-class persons within the black community had left black people without political power. Both Malcolm and Martin spoke to this issue—the ability of blacks to control, own, and self-direct their destiny. King directly confronted the power issue:

> Another basic challenge is to discover how to organize our strength in terms of economic and political power. . . . Indeed, one of the great problems that the Negro confronts is his lack of power. . . . Stripped of the right to make decisions concerning his life and destiny, he has been subject to the authoritarian and sometimes whimsical decisions of this white power structure.[9]

King began to realize, particularly toward the end of his life, that the Civil Rights Movement faced a far broader evil than a stubborn, but lethal, southern terrorist bloc. In time he began to appreciate the sinister nature of the national white power structure, symbolized not only in a regional Dixiecrat section of the United States, but also lodged in the federal government in Washington, D.C. To deal with this broader dimension of white politics—a systemic power structure of white privilege—blacks needed to organize political (and economic) power. A basic problem in black life was the "lack of power," which made them "subject to the . . . white power structure."

Having introduced the issue of power in his civil rights vocabulary, King also developed further his previous analysis of love. Formerly he overemphasized the pricking of white racists' moral conscience through self-sacrificing love. Though he would not throw out "redemptive suffering," that phrase assumed a much more radical and mature meaning for King eleven years after Montgomery. He summed up the previous understanding of love permeating the Civil Rights Movement and noticed a harmful interpretation of "agape." In 1967 King wrote:

> There is nothing essentially wrong with power. The problem is that in America power is unequally distributed. This has led Negro Americans in the past to seek their goals through love and moral suasion

devoid of power and white Americans to seek their goals through power devoid of love and conscience.[10]

From his reading of American history and his own experience in the Civil Rights movement, King concluded that black people had sought goals incorrectly by only using an appeal to morality but not using power. And white Americans had gained their goals through the use of power but without love or morality. Because power in the United States was unequally distributed (between whites who had power and African Americans who had none), black people in the Civil Rights Movement had been fooling themselves by seeking to redeem the white opponent through a love that lacked black power. Put differently, King began to see that integration based on appeals of love and morality was without substance, hypocritical and immoral. Now he saw love linked to the redistribution and equal sharing of political (and economic) power between whites and blacks.

Furthermore, King had learned that if there was to be a genuine reconciliation of the races in the United States, then there needed to be authentic democracy in race relations. King continued to imbue old thought forms with the idea of political power. Not only did "love" undergo a prophetic redefinition with the new starting point of power, but "democracy" likewise rang a new sound once based on power. Hammering away at the redistribution of power theme, and blacks fighting for an equal sharing based on that redistribution, King wrote: "Negroes can never be content without participation in power. America must be a nation in which its multiracial people are partners in power." He then resumes with his radicalized restatement of American democracy. "This is the essence of democracy toward which all Negro struggles have been directed since the distant past when he was transplanted here in chains."[11]

The earlier phases of the Civil Rights Movement had resulted in some legislative victories, which in the eyes of some were indicators of the democratic ideal. But King surmised that when blacks "looked for the second phase [of the Civil Rights Movement], the realization of equality, they found that many of their white allies had quietly disappeared."[12] King concluded that the previous definition of democracy, the first phase, proved incomplete because it failed to stress the realization of equality in power. Though he did not reject the Constitution as a fundamental document in black people's struggle for justice, he did place earlier appeals to the Constitution's guaranteed democracy within the framework of black power. Now the *essence* of democracy was black participation in power.

When King had seen democracy mainly as blacks achieving the right to sit on a toilet or in a chair next to whites, white "allies" flooded to his cause. But a year before his assassination, when he changed the "essence of democracy" to obtaining black power by whites surrendering the privileges of a national white power structure, King stated: "White Americans left the Negro on the ground and in devastating numbers walked off with the [southern segregationist] aggressor."[13]

In addition to the political sphere, black folk needed power in the cultural area. Just as King redefined race relations through a democratization of political (and economic) power, he also eventually saw the shallowness of black and white unity based on the negation of black culture. Speaking at a 1967 Southern Christian Leadership Conference staff retreat, he asserted:

> Where do we go from here? First, we must massively assert our dignity and worth. We must stand up amidst a system that still oppresses us and develop an unassailable and majestic sense of values. We must no longer be ashamed of being black.[14]

Despite his years of leading an integrated Civil Rights Movement with whites, King correctly concluded that blacks were still oppressed based on their culture. Therefore, in assessing the next phase in the struggle for justice, the very first task necessitated a massive assertion of black dignity and worth—aggressively pushing black culture. King further claimed that the progress of black freedom and substantive race relations in America would die if black people did not free their minds from the racist restrictions of white culture. King stated: "Any movement for the Negro's freedom that overlooks this necessity is only waiting to be buried. As long as the mind is enslaved, the body can never be free."[15]

Given the stubborn presence of white power, King eventually perceived a form of cultural genocide engulfing blacks in the Civil Rights Movement. Whites had participated in the movement with the assumption that their culture, language, values, and lifestyle stood as the norm. Even more tragically, blacks had internalized white culture at the expense of their own and had refused to affirm their own self-worth and self-identity. Whites historically, King believed, had attempted to commit cultural homicide against African Americans; this expression of white dominance over blacks represented one of the greatest crimes of white racism in America.

Agreeing partially with the late 1960s' Black Power movement, King exclaimed: "You must not condemn the call for black consciousness today. ... That is a positive power in the call for black power. It's a black consciousness that we need that we've been deprived of."[16] In another context King echoes verbatim a standard Black Power battlecry with his words: "Yes, we must stand up and say, 'I'm black and I'm beautiful,' and this self-affirmation is the black man's need, made compelling by the white man's crimes against him."[17]

The crimes of white culture compelled black folk in the Civil Rights Movement to ignore no longer their contributions to America, to negate no longer their personhood, and to hold back no longer an affirmation of their "Olympian" peoplehood. With a persuasive, passionate plea, King argued for the appreciation of "our great heritage. We must be proud of our race. We must not be ashamed of being black." Speaking to the guts and soul of black America, he also stated: "Now we are saying something else: that there is nothing wrong with black because black is beautiful; we have a rich and noble heritage."[18]

Malcolm X offered an even more caustic critique of white quasi-genocide of African American culture. "The black man in North America," Malcolm shouted, "was mentally sick in his cooperative, sheeplike acceptance of the white man's culture."[19] Black North Americans suffered from ignorance, that is, lack of true knowledge of the black self, history, tradition, language, and culture, and from self-hatred. Obviously, from Malcolm's cultural perspective, to lack knowledge of one's black self and to be enslaved by the wicked knowledge of the white slavemaster's culture automatically and inevitably led to African Americans' hatred of the black self. No greater crime had the white man committed than to teach blacks to hate their African selves. This was a supreme atrocity against black theology—God's grace of blackness.

> We hated the African characteristics. . . . We hated our hair. We hated our nose, the shape of our nose, and the shape of our lips, the color of our skin.
>   When you teach a man to hate his lips, the lips that God gave him, the shape of the nose that God gave him, the texture of the hair that God gave him, the color of the skin that God gave him, you've committed the worst crime that a race of people can commit.[20]

When the foreparents of white Americans savagely stole the black Americans' ancestors from Africa, contended Malcolm, the former attempted to destroy African or black culture, both its practice and memory. Why? Because a people without a cultural consciousness is the easiest group to contain, enslave, and oppress. In fact, blacks loved white culture and hated themselves, reasoned Malcolm, because they hated the root that gave birth to them. You can't hate the root—Africa—without also hating the tree—African Americans.[21] A people without historical and cultural roots become a dead people; for Malcolm, the "so-called Negroes" were the shuffling dead.

Throughout his public career Malcolm debated and analyzed many topics. But it is his calling to arouse the black race from the "dead" that, among other things, marks his contribution to the life and death significance of culture in race relations and black theology. To attain a positive black or African self-image in the black community, Malcolm utilized a dialectic. First, he unleashed a blanket and documented negative critique of white identity and culture. This included blacks' acceptance of white superiority and white cultural normalcy. In this critique he unyieldingly and unflinchingly pressed the reality of black self-hatred and the consequences.

And we hated ourselves. Our color became to us a chain—we felt that it was holding us back; our color became to us like a prison which we felt was keeping us confined. . . . We felt all these restrictions were based solely upon our color. . . . And it became hateful to us.

It made us feel inferior.[22]

Malcolm shook up his black audience by making its self-hatred plain; he pricked the depths of the African American psyche, discovered a deeply entrenched and internalized white cultural monster, and made his listeners accept their addiction and subservience to this white beast. Any honest black person who heard Malcolm's comprehensive critique of the drugging effect of white values on black values felt like a junkie who for the first time began earnestly to pursue detoxification.

Indeed, by first pursuing the radical negative critique of the dialectic—getting African Americans to recognize their dependence on the poison of white values and the resulting black self-hatred—Malcolm attempted to show that the real cultural chains strangling black minds and the real prison bars incarcerating blacks' sense of values were the white culture and not an inherent evil in blackness itself. Malcolm mainly emphasized the positive side of the dialectic—fostering a deep sense of black self-knowledge and love of African American culture and identity.

We have to teach our people something about our cultural roots. We have to teach them something of their glorious civilizations before they were kidnapped . . . and brought over to this country. Once our people are taught about the glorious civilization that existed on the African continent, they won't any longer be ashamed of who they are.[23]

Malcolm believed that it would prove impossible to love someone else without first having a correct and healthy love of the "African" side of the "African American" cultural reality.

Both Martin and Malcolm eventually agreed on stressing the importance of political and cultural power for African Americans. Inequality in black-white race relations necessitated black folk's right to determine their destiny politically and to define the positiveness of their black identity culturally.

The Role of the Black Church

So far we have examined Malcolm's and Martin's analyses of race relations from the perspective of the crimes of white theology and, consequently, the ethical and theological need for political and cultural black power. Now, beginning with Rev. King, we conclude this race relations section with a look at their perspectives on the ethical imperative for black religion and the black church to engage in social justice.

Perhaps Martin Luther King, Jr., is the greatest theologian the United States of North America has ever produced. Never before has a religious leader or theologian in the United States riveted so tightly the justice issue into the very marrow of Christian and non-Christian thought. King could not perceive of Christianity in a do-nothing fashion. For him, theologically, this was apostasy. King interpreted the Bible from the perspective of holistic life, which made him see a healthy spirituality grounded on human struggle in the material world against visible manifestations of real evil. Again, King did not subscribe to a truncated, otherworldly theology. Nor did he pre-scribe such a false worldview for the black church. For him, the laws of the universe inevitably moved toward justice and the God of the Old and New Testaments reigned as a God of love and justice. As a result, a Christian ethical imperative required the black church to follow suit, to participate in a steadfast universal law and in God's divine intention for humanity.

The theological greatness of King lies in his closely connecting justice and the gospel as well as practically organizing thousands in a massive sign of Christian witness for justice. No other theologian or church leader in the United States has both influenced theological discussion and put into practice the implications of that theology to such a degree as Martin Luther King, Jr.

King challenged the theology and the witness of the black church to view Christianity in its completeness, both spiritual and material, both the heal-ing of the soul and sustenance for the body. Speaking about the wholeness of religion, King stated: "The gospel at its best deals with the whole man, not only his soul but his body, not only his spiritual well-being, but his material well-being." Here King attempts to explain two things. First, he tries to pull the black church's gaze out of the skies down to earth in order to appreciate those things which are truly "heavenly" or Christian ("the gospel at its best"). Unfortunately, the black church had capitulated to a pervasive spookism theology that preached "you can have the world, just give me Jesus." King shouted No! Jesus Christ of heaven, though he ascended to the right hand of God, was still concerned about and present in the affairs of the world, "the body."

Second, King sought to broaden the understanding of "the body." In reality, "the body" had to include the systemic body on earth. King resumes:

> Any religion that professes to be concerned about the souls of men and is not concerned about the slums that damn them, the economic conditions that strangle them and the social conditions that cripple them is a spiritually moribund religion awaiting burial.[24]

The black church had to reflect Christian spirituality in an analysis and interpretation of systemic oppression on earth. What were the intercon-necting forces that gave rise to the social evil of racism and the economic evil of poverty? The church had to detect the manifestations of sinful spirits that damned and stifled a healthy spirituality in the lives of the black community and all the poor. Otherwise, the black church existed in the state of the shuffling dead.

King persisted in pushing the African American church toward a theology and ethics of struggle while still accepting the black church's metaphors about the afterlife. "It's alright to talk about 'long white robes over yonder,' in all of its symbolism," King preached. He realized that for sermonic effect as well as theological importance, the black preacher needed to say something about the hope engendered by the longing for inevitable rest in heaven, on the other side of Jordan. But the power of the heavenly symbolism, for Martin, became effective only when this talk of heaven turned the black church's eyes down to the poverty on earth. King resumes:

> But ultimately people want some suits and dresses and shoes to wear down here. It's alright to talk about "streets flowing with milk and honey," but God has commanded us to be concerned about the slums down here, and his children who can't eat three square meals a day.[25]

Note what King defined as the ultimate concern for the black church. The ultimate concern was not proclamations about long white robes and lands flowing with milk and honey. Rather, King perceived the most important theology and Christian witness for the black church to be taking care of the material needs of the poor, the least of these. Only in the struggle for justice for the poor would the spiritualized talk about heaven have any ultimate meaning. As a black prophet amid his people, King proclaimed: "It's alright to talk about the new Jerusalem, but one day, God's preacher must talk about the new New York . . . the new Philadelphia . . . the new Memphis, Tennessee. This is what we have to do."[26]

Similar to Martin, Malcolm linked the heart of his religion to freedom for black people and, ultimately, for all humanity. Malcolm was a Muslim and did not preach primarily to black Christian church congregations. Nonetheless, his attitude toward religion and what a community of faith should do aids our discussion concerning justice, an ethical imperative for black theology and the African American church. To be religious, for Malcolm, meant one should fight for the liberation of poor black people. He could not conceive of a black religion and a black religious community that did not have a religion as a tool of struggle for justice. Malcolm preached: "I believe in a religion that believes in freedom. Any time I have to accept a religion that won't let me fight a battle for my people, I say to hell with that religion."[27] Thus for the black community, hell was not a far away, metaphysical place beneath the earth. Hell existed whenever a religion did not allow, indeed facilitate, black religious groups and the overall black community to organize for freedom. So the ethical imperative for black people was clear: struggle to achieve their God-ordained humanity.

Thus Malcolm and Martin instruct today's black theology and the black church about the religious and theological importance of fighting for black freedom, particularly in the areas of race relations. Racial discrimination is not simply a political or sociological issue. At its heart, it is theological. As Martin King surmised: "What is racism but the notion that one group represents inferiority and another group represents superiority ... and what is it but the notion that God made a creative error?"[28] Therefore black theology must begin with the issue of race in social analysis because the primary identity of and a fundamental divine gift to the black community is blackness.

But we cannot remain at a superficial "black" level. In fact, black theology has to open up the complex nature of African American religion and community relationships. A genuine black theology of liberation will note the external theological and violent attacks forced on black people by white Christians. These crimes from the outside take root because a stratum within the black experience has sold its divine birthright of freedom for crumbs from the white power structure's table.

Black theology, then, must use an adequate social analysis of race that asserts black political and cultural power based on the interests of the poor, the majority of the African American experience. God moves within the positive self-identity (culture) of blackness and the natural right of self-determination (politics) for blacks. To accept what God has granted, black theology demands an ethics of black affirmation and assertion for African American religion and the community. We must claim who we are through self-definition and move in the world through self-direction to share in the resources God provides for all, especially the poor.

POVERTY

The analyses and visions of Malcolm and Martin did not end with only a prophetic interpretation of race relations. Their world outlooks also entailed a sober review of poverty and class inequality in America. In addition to race relations, today's black theological analysis has to include a clear critique of monopoly capitalism, a dog-eat-dog political economy that reaps profit for the rich white minority in the United States by exploiting the humanity of the poor majority of all colors. The faiths of Minister Malcolm X and Rev. King moved more toward a definite anti-monopoly, anti-capitalist position at the end of their lives.

Malcolm developed his systemic analysis because his commitment to black people's freedom led him to fight all impediments and roadblocks in the path to black liberation. He sought truth no matter where it led him, and he believed that truth could set an oppressed people free. He tied race relations to poverty and capitalist exploitation, because he grew to see how the resolution of white racial oppression against blacks was inextricably interwoven with the system of capitalist economic exploitation. "The system in this country cannot produce freedom for an Afro-American," Malcolm asserted. "It is impossible for this system, this economic system, this political system, this social system, this system, period."

Black liberation called for more than a struggle against an individual or group of white racists, for the racial issue now included a structural component. With that connection, Malcolm broadened his exposure of the evil forces constricting black America. Malcolm continued, "It's impossible for this system as it stands to produce freedom right now for the black man in this country."[29] Again, Malcolm's faith and social analysis viewed race relations through the lens of freedom for poor blacks "now." Anything contrary to his justice mission stood as an enemy and he never tired of naming forces of evil.

Due to his faith in the inevitable triumph of poor blacks and the dispossessed in all of humanity, Malcolm predicted the eventual fall of capitalism. In fact, after breaking from the restrictions of the Nation of Islam's theology and traveling abroad to Africa, he began to see the freedom movements on the African continent reclaiming their own destiny and thus threatening Western capitalism. Malcolm observed, "It is impossible for capitalism to survive, primarily because the system of capitalism needs some blood to suck."

But oppressed people's movements in Africa, Asia, Latin America, and the slowly awakening "black revolution" in the United States were altering the spheres of capitalist influence and therefore preventing the blood transfusion necessary for capitalist survival. Without sufficient "blood" (natural resources, markets, human labor), though the capitalist system "used to be like an eagle," "now it's more like a vulture." And based on his social analysis of the third-world poor's struggle against the rich and the black revolution's beginning growth, he concluded, "It's only a matter of time in my opinion before [capitalism] will collapse completely."[30]

Like Malcolm X, though from a different background of practical and theological experiences, Martin Luther King, Jr., eventually groped toward a similar political economic positon. Dr. King had felt that he had set the stage for new race relations in the United States with the passage of the 1964 Civil Rights Act and the 1965 Voting Rights Act. Encouraged by these apparent successes, he attempted to take the old civil rights coalition from the South into the ghettoes of the North. But his northern journey, particularly his encounters with northern urban rebellions and the entrenched and crafty racism of northern white liberals, forced him to dig deeper into his faith and social analysis. There he discovered, more than ever before, his calling to link the race issue with capitalist class relations. Consequently, he began to build a new coalition of conscience and a new movement explicitly focused on poor people.

King began to advocate advancing the Civil Rights Movement to a higher level, where the nation's poor, black and white, would take center stage in a powerful, new, united front. A year before his death, he wrote:

From issues of personal dignity [blacks] are now advancing to programs that impinge upon the basic system of social and economic
control. At this level Negro programs go beyond race and deal with
economic inequality. ... In pursuit of these goals, the white poor
become involved, and the potentiality emerges for a powerful alli-
ance.[31]

More and more King felt compelled to zero in on the poor, the voiceless,
those at the bottom of society. He became increasingly sure that his calling
and his ministry started with the plight of the poor. Even if it cost him his
funding, his liberal white and black allies, and his life, Dr. King consciously
focused his preaching, speaking, and practice on American poverty and the
consequential need for empowering all the poor. Speaking two months
before his murder, he declared:

And when I say poor people, I'm not only talking about black people.
... There are poor people ... in the Puerto Rican community ...
Mexican American community ... the Indian community ... the
Appalachian white community. I'm talking about poor people's power,
that is what is needed.[32]

King believed that he had to bear the cross of the poor and, by example,
others of privilege should bear this cross as well. Now the starting point
for his entire faith and his life was the liberation of the very least in America.

I choose to identify with the underprivileged. I choose to identify with
the poor. I choose to give my life for those who have been left out of
the sunlight of opportunity. ... This is the way I'm going. ... If it
means dying for them, I'm going that way. ....[33]

By the end of his life, King interpreted his calling as a minister of the
gospel of Jesus Christ in such a radical and prophetic way that he felt
anointed to launch a new campaign against the federal government in
Washington, D.C. — the center of systemic oppression. He termed this major
and final movement the Poor People's Campaign. This great moral effort
targeted the national governmental power structure because the issue of
poverty was not local but national. Those who decided on the fate of the
nation's poor had to be forced to provide relief for those who lacked adequate resources to be human.

To grasp King's embracing a radical systemic analysis regarding poverty,
one only has to compare the 1963 March on Washington with the plans for
the 1968 Poor People's Campaign (PPC) in D.C. The PPC, in King's opinion, would be in radical contrast to the 1963 March on Washington, when
people came to D.C., heard speeches, waded in a reflecting pool, and then

left town the same day. The PPC would differ from the 1963 event, when aides to President John F. Kennedy stood near the sound system prepared to pull the plug on any speakers who criticized the Kennedy administration.

In sharp distinction, King planned for the 1968 PPC to "dramatize the whole economic problem of the poor." He was now "trying to deal with the economic problems . . . through massive protest." This new March on Washington would have thousands upon thousands of poor of all colors descend upon D.C. and stay there for months—until the federal government passed meaningful legislation for the poor. Anything short of this fundamental change would force poor people to take over governmental buildings and sit-in in the congressional offices. Thus the PPC would usher in a new form of nonviolent militancy. King commented: "This action may take on disruptive dimensions."[34] The federal government would no longer function in its normal way unless it first addressed the needs of the poor. King continued to hammer this point home:

> We got to go to Washington. . . . We've got to camp in. Put our tents in front of the White House. . . . [The federal government] will have to come to terms with us, because the nation will not move. . . . There will be no rest, there will be no tranquility in this country until the nation comes to terms with our problem.[35]

Given King's conclusion about the essence of the Christian gospel, it is no accident that at his assassination his two major projects included support for the black working class in Memphis and organizing an integrated movement of the poor class to dislocate the normal functioning of the United States government.

The Poor People's Campaign flowed from Martin's maturing analysis of class relations in the United States—the discrepancy between the rich and the poor. Earlier in his public career he sought to aid "the discouraged beggars in life's market place." But a year before his death he saw the need to not only help the beggar, but also reconstruct the causes forcing people to beg.

> We are called upon to help the discouraged beggars in life's market place. But one day we must come to see that an edifice which produces beggars needs restructuring. . . . When you deal with this, you begin to ask the question, "Who owns the oil?" . . . "Who owns the iron ore?" . . . "Why is it that people have to pay water bills in a world that is two-thirds water?"[36]

When King questioned who owned the major resources and the production and distribution of those resources, he questioned and condemned the monopoly capitalist system in the United States. And, likewise, he drew his observations of race relations into a systemic analysis of poverty and class formations. Interpreting society through the eyes of the racially oppressed and the economically exploited, King called on society's voiceless, the least of these, to rise up and claim their God-given humanity by waging a revolution against the system of capitalism.

> The dispossessed of this nation—the poor, both white and Negro—live in a cruelly unjust society. They must organize a revolution against that injustice, not against the lives of the persons who are their fellow citizens, but against the structures through which the society is refusing to take means which have been called for, and which are at hand, to lift the load of poverty.[37]

Here King offers a clear systemic analysis: the need for the poor in the United States to change radically the structures of capitalism in order to abolish poverty by means of a revolution against the system of profit-oriented exploitation.

If today's black theology takes Malcolm's and Martin's social analyses of poverty seriously, it will have to name more concretely the systemic cause of the poor's wretched condition. Roughly a quarter of a century ago, King and Malcolm informed us that the political economy of capitalism in the United States stood against a religion for the oppressed. And for King, the politics and economics of monopoly capitalism were the opposite of everything Jesus Christ represented. To be a Christian means, at least, not being pro-capitalism. Indeed, monopoly capitalism is another manifestation of the Anti-Christ.

Of course, black theology runs a grave risk by placing capitalism in league with the Devil, especially given the fanatical and rabid anti-communism in both white and black churches. But if black theology is honestly to serve the black church and community by continually raising the nature of our faith and what that faith calls us to do, black theology has no option other than to pursue God's liberation of the poor wherever God leads.

Black theology runs the grave danger of fooling itself under the name of "liberation," when most black theologians and preachers do not apply a liberation analysis to the sinister dimensions of the monopoly capitalist system. How can we continue to raise such a ruckus about white racism without realizing that American monopoly capitalism engenders white supremacy? If black theology hopes to remain true to a faith in justice, it will have to move beyond incomplete anti-white attacks and reckon with a reality where a few billionaire families own the wealth of the United States and mold both Republican and Democratic political parties. Through direct and indirect influences, this small minority operates on one principle: how to make more profit. There cannot be an adequate black theology of liberation or any other kind of liberation unless the brutality of poverty is constantly drawn back to the structure of monopoly capitalism, as Minister Malcolm and Rev. King seem to suggest.

Unfortunately, the majority of black religious scholars and preachers have bought into the sheer fantasy that the democracy of monopoly capitalism is true democracy. Capitalist formal democracy lacks majority rule. The majority of North Americans, who are either poor, fighting off poverty, or fortunate enough to have money to pay off their next two bills, do not have their long-term interests represented in the national government. The federal government (the presidential, judicial, and legislative branches) often appears to be a competing system of objective checks and balances. But if the national politics and economics were threatened with a reversal, that is, if the pyramidal monopoly capitalist structure in the United States began to move bottom to top, then the so-called checks and balances system would rally to prevent such a movement. The present system would immediately stop the realization of genuine democracy in which the majority of the citizens—the people at the bottom in the United States—would own all the economic resources as well as the military industrial complex, and would, therefore, control the federal government.

Put differently, the national government is not consistently democratic; it serves as an intermediary body to maintain the rich at the top and the poor at the bottom. Capitalist formal democracy exists to give the *appearance* that the majority vote determines who will run the country. On the contrary, however, elections (formal democracy) mainly act to keep the pyramidal capitalist system running smoothly.

Both Malcolm and Martin died with a committed, non-ambiguous, anti-capitalist social analysis. For them, monopoly capitalism had nothing to do with justice, majority rule, racial equality, political democracy, economic opportunity, or Christianity (for King). Both religious men called for a revolution of the poor against the capitalist system. King maintained that revolution by the poor against capitalism had to be nonviolent. Malcolm, of course, believed that freedom for blacks would result from a revolutionary system, by any means necessary. Despite the differences in "nonviolent" and "by any means necessary," both men agreed that capitalism as a system had to be gotten rid of right away through rudimentary redistribution of power.

Since the 1960s the conditions in the black community and the state of the poor have not improved; they have worsened. Therefore a social analysis for today's black theology can say no less about poverty and capitalism than Malcolm and Martin.

THE INTERNATIONAL SITUATION

Minister Malcolm and Rev. King did not finish their social analyses with race relations and poverty. Their public careers concluded with another plank embedded deeply within the scaffold of their appraisal of North American society. Dr. King, toward his career's end, succinctly described his prophetic analysis:

Now, when I say question the whole society, it means ultimately coming to see that the problem of racism, the problem of economic exploitation, and the problem of war are all tied together. . . .

A nation that will keep people in slavery for 244 years will "thingify" them, make them things. Therefore they will exploit them, and poor people generally, economically. And a nation that will exploit economically will have to have foreign investments and everything else, and will have to use its military might to protect them. All of these problems are tied together.[38]

What does King teach a constructive black theology today about developments in the international situation? From King's perspective, United States imperialism abroad—its aggressive military attacks on the world's underdeveloped countries, its unequal and perfidious foreign investments, and its propagation of a debilitating materialistic culture of consumption—resulted from and was connected to monopoly capitalist self-interest and racism domestically. The political and economic power relations at home spread themselves internationally. By necessity, then, imperialism went hand-in-hand with a structural quasi-genocidal attack on blacks and other minorities—and with an intensified impoverishment of working and poor people of all colors in the United States. Therefore, United States imperialism, monopoly capitalism controlled by the handful of billionaires who decisively influence the United States, simply reflected the domestic system of capitalism and white-skin privileges run wild all over the globe, but particularly in underdeveloped areas. It was the same system.

The United States government's acts of violence through war in the Third World were not simply accidents or aberrations from the normal activities of the federal administration and the monopoly corporations that it served. Employing a systemic social analysis of the international situation, Martin thought it logical that the government was the "greatest purveyor of violence in the world today."[39] For King, imperial war against poor nations of color mirrored domestic capitalist war against minorities of color and the poor. To fight against racial discrimination and poverty at home, then, automatically led into a global struggle. Thus King preached: "I have said that the problem, the crisis we face, is international in scope. In fact, it is inseparable from an international emergency which involves the poor, the dispossessed, and the exploited of the whole world."[40]

Not only was the United States the greatest initiator of violence on the face of the earth, it was also one of the main, if not the primary, economic investors that stole natural resources from and exploited cheap labor in the Third World. A vast unequal exchange existed between the actual value of raw materials and colored peoples' labor in Africa, Asia, and Latin America, on the one hand, and the wages they received and the compensation obtained for wealth stolen from their underdeveloped countries, on the other hand. In the context of calling for a "true revolution of values," King linked the demonic nature of capitalism and its foreign investments:

A true revolution of values will soon look uneasily on the glaring contrast of poverty and wealth. With righteous indignation, it will look across the seas and see individual capitalists of the West investing huge sums of money in Asia, Africa and South America, only to take the profits out with no concern for the social betterment of [these] countries.[41]

Indeed, the countries of the Third World became underdeveloped precisely from a conscious political policy on the part of the United States government, the military-industrial complex, and the elite group of billionaire corporations that sucked third-world countries dry. When King surveyed the international scene, he saw a vast discrepancy between the poverty in third-world countries and the enormous wealth accumulated by Western powers. Monopoly capitalism does not stop at pushing down racial minorities and the poor at home; it needs capital transfusions and consumer markets abroad too.

Furthermore, because Dr. King understood the marriage between United States violence abroad and unjust investments, he stated: "We in the West must bear in mind that the poor countries are poor primarily because we have exploited them through political and economic colonialism. Americans in particular must help their nation repent of her modern economic imperialism."[42] King teaches us that the conscience of an "awakened activist" cannot remain satisfied with a shortsighted focus on local problems, if only because she or he "sees that local problems are all interconnected with world problems."[43] Moreover, if one bears the cross of Christ, one has to assume politically a systemic analysis of international relations because injustice and evil at home will never cease until injustice and evil abroad cease. To limit our vision only to the rough waves of domestic race relations and poverty would be like seeing only Jesus' baptism in the calmness of the river Jordan but not comprehending the Christian mandate that we must walk also with him on the rough seas of Galilee throughout the world.

King accents the political necessity for African Americans to comprehend international power relations. Malcolm X agrees with this position, but deepens it by urging black Americans to understand also the cultural connections they share with others internationally. In particular, he related the conditions of blackness in the United States with the same oppressed conditions in Africa.

You can't understand what is going on in Mississippi if you don't understand what is going on in the Congo. And you can't really be interested in what's going on in Mississippi if you're not also interested in what's going on in the Congo. They're both the same. The same interests are at stake.[44]

Here Malcolm points out "the same interests": whites from Europe had colonized blacks on the African continent and similarly the descendants of European whites had subjugated the descendants of Africans in North America. White racism had created an international connection among Africans in the diaspora; consequently, blacks needed to respond by establishing a Pan Africanist global perspective. It would be futile to restrict blacks' energies to Mississippi without simultaneously stretching forth African American hands to African sisters and brothers on the continent. The black world is one. Not only does Malcolm describe the political parallels, but he draws us deeply into a Pan Africanist cultural unity. Freedom in Mississippi results both from a political recognition of colonial and racial discrimination as well as a cultural solidarity in blackness on both sides of the Atlantic.

Moreover, Malcolm underscored the decisive responsibility of North American blacks maintaining a Pan Africanist analysis. He thought "the single worst mistake of the American black organizations" was their failure "to establish direct brotherhood lines of communication" between themselves and the independent nations of Africa.[45] Why "the single worst mistake"? Such a heavy emphasis on black international solidarity derived from Malcolm's belief that the strength of the branch resulted from the health and vigor of the root. If Africa (the root) attained power and independence, then the offspring from the continent (African Americans) would relish their African culture and heritage and win respect from the rest of humankind. Without a robust Africa, black Americans were doomed to self-shame, and a people lacking a proper appreciation for their cultural lineage and suffering from a weak motherland would inevitably bear the brunt of ridicule and derision from the non-African world. Thus Malcolm warned: "It's only with a strong Africa, an independent Africa and a respected Africa that wherever those of African origin or African heritage or African likeness go, they will be respected."[46] Even in his international analysis, Malcolm continually hammered away at destructive black self-hatred and lifted up the positive cultural identity of the black race.

But Malcolm did not end his world perspective with a Pan Africanist thrust. His emphasis on African American and African unity did not negate his international solidarity with other underdeveloped countries. In fact, the deeper he grasped the importance of Pan Africanism, the more he perceived that the oppressed conditions and justice movements of the African diaspora reflected the same subjugation-resistance struggles of the poor throughout the Third World. The deeper he delved into the international black situation by discovering the same political and cultural unity at home and abroad, the stronger he became and the more he gained self-knowledge as a black person. Therefore, by strengthening and returning to the root

(Africa), the dispersed branches (African Americans) could acquire the self-respect and confidence to move from a position of strength as they linked arms with peoples of color throughout the globe. International black unity led Malcolm to unity with all peoples of color worldwide. Thus the possibility for universal coalitions with the Third World arose out of the particularity of black solidarity.

Yet, despite Malcolm's international rainbow vision, he lamented the reality. The blinders of white miseducation had prevented black Americans from embracing the movements of the Third World. And so Negroes sank deeper into the quicksand of white racism in North America instead of stepping toward liberation by grasping the hands of all peoples of color. Impatiently and with disgust Malcolm commented: "I reflected many, many times to myself upon how the American Negro has been entirely brainwashed from ever seeing or thinking of himself, as he should, as a part of the non-white peoples of the world."[47] A genuine freedom movement of blacks in the United States, therefore, would grow out of African American openness to Africa and all of the world's people of color.

For black theology, the politics and culture of race and class must integrate into the larger picture of the global village. A sharing in God's movement for freedom obligates black theology and the church to link arms with other world races and indigenous peoples experiencing the divine *kairos* breaking into the life of Africa, Asia, and Latin America. A provincial theology merely blurs the lens of African American religious thought.

BLACK WOMEN

Rev. King and Minister Malcolm suffered from the male chauvinist environment that permeated the mid-1950s to the late 1960s, the periods of their public careers. To appreciate the reasons why both men supported the secondary status of black women, however, does not mean we should excuse the weaknesses of their viewpoints. On the contrary, black theology today must avoid the negative lessons of sexism.

For instance, the promotion and recognition of black women in church and society during the Civil Rights era would have given some justice to black women, who also were created in God's image of freedom. Furthermore, black women's equality would have strengthened black men and the entire movement. The suppression of black women meant the suppression of a vital resource that God had provided for an oppressed community in its stride toward freedom. Black men can never be free unless black women attain their freedom too.

Nor can we historically justify black women's suppression by claiming they lacked the ability to play decisive roles in the civil rights era. In fact, an African American church woman, Rosa Parks, initiated the entire civil rights period. Without her, there would not have been a Montgomery bus boycott or Martin Luther King's national and international stature, at least not as we recognize it. Likewise, black women of Montgomery proposed the bus boycott and ran off the first leaflets calling for African American citizens to walk for justice instead of continuing to ride under racism. When King's Southern Christian Leadership Council coordinated regional leadership of the growing southern resistance struggle, Ella Baker served in an executive capacity in the organization. The SCLC's motto called for saving the soul of America, but the black male ministers who led the group failed to see that the spiritual sickness of America, and the SCLC, was also infected by women's oppression.

Oftentimes King quoted from the words of illiterate black women who were maids, cooks, and domestics for white women. One of his favorite sources was Mother Pollard. When asked if she was tired of walking during the Montgomery bus boycott, King recalled, Mother Pollard replied: "My feets is tired, but my soul is rested." Yet King did not share power with black women or point out the specific and unique spirituality that they brought to the justice movement. He waxed eloquent in terms of the demonic nature of segregation and, especially at his life's end, he targeted the evil face of race, capitalism, and imperialism. Though he came to this sharp social analysis because he knew a threat to justice anywhere was a threat to justice everywhere, he was unable to see that the injustice against African American women (particularly those who suffered from the triple sins of racism, sexism, and poverty) also threatened the validity of accomplishments in the entire Civil Rights Movement.

The roll call of African American women in the 1950s and 1960s continues to offer further evidence that King had ample opportunity to work side by side with black women. Yet he was blinded by male chauvinism. Examples abound: Daisy Bates helped organize the movement to desegregate public schools in Little Rock, Arkansas. Septima Clark headed a civil rights training school that prepared movement organizers for the day-to-day struggle. Diane Nash played a leadership role in the Nashville student movement and led students to resume potentially deadly trips on the Freedom Rides. Fannie Lou Hammer was one of the movers behind the Mississippi Freedom Democratic Party. Ms. Hammer, an ex-Mississippi sharecropper, co-headed a poor people's delegation to the 1964 national Democratic Party presidential convention in Atlantic City, New Jersey. On national television she courageously challenged President Lyndon Baines Johnson's party to reject white racism and elitism by seating her poor black people's delegation from Mississippi. Ella Baker suggested the formation of the Student Nonviolent Coordinating Committee. And Marian Wright from Mississippi suggested to Dr. King the idea of a Poor People's Campaign.

Clearly King's patriarchal views placed severe limitations around his social analysis. More important, he fell short of his own theological criteria. He had specifically accepted as his own Jesus' gospel message of liberation found in Luke 4:18-19—to preach good news to the poor and to set free those who were oppressed. Furthermore, he attacked United States imperialist violence abroad and linked it to racism and poverty at home, because he saw himself as a Christian minister whose calling led him to the doors of worldwide evil. Yet, at the same time, he failed to recognize on his own front steps in the Civil Rights Movement one of the most important bearers of black Christian religion and spirituality, African American women.

Consequently, his theological understanding exemplified a profound contradiction. How could his theology of liberation remain true to Christian claims when he did not include black women's religious experience in the development of his theology?

A constructive black theology must learn from the shortcomings of King's social analysis, so that the black church and community today can appreciate the decisive role of black women in any understanding of power relations and self-affirmation that concerns freedom for the African American community and the world's poor.

African American women's experience in King's Civil Rights Movement gives us some insight into the specific contributions of black women to black theology. Black women filled church meetings during the week nights. They also filled the regular church services on Sunday. They brought food to movement gatherings and cooked for their own families when they returned home. Black Christian women served as foot soldiers in demonstrations and marches. And despite the odds against them, they occupied leadership roles in the 1950s and 1960s justice struggle.

Guided and called by God, Jesus, and the Spirit of freedom, the women fought as black people and as women. At a minimum, they added their particular lessons to black theological development. The women endured *triple suffering*: (a) a secondary status as women in the movement; (b) the role of workers on two jobs (laborers for white employers and as homemakers, childbearers, and childrearers in their own homes); and (c) the brutality inflicted upon them by water hoses, dogs, and cattleprods of racist southern law enforcement officers.

More than endurance, African American women exhibited a contagious *perseverance*. For example, Mother Pollard approached King after he gave a somewhat depressed speech and instructed him not to falter because the people and God were with him. The women offered a *holistic spirituality*. They gave their total hearts, minds, bodies, and spirits to the movement. It was reflected in the vigorous way that the Spirit lifted them up through religious spirituals and movement songs. Women took *sacrificial risks*. They jeopardized their jobs as maids and cooks in white homes and were vulnerable as potential rape victims of vengeful white males.

Black women taught us about *grassroots democracy*. Such a genuine democracy took place when poor and working people, the majority women, voted with their hands on major decisions in civil rights church meetings and with their feet when they demonstrated in the streets. The irruption at the grassroots level is an important theological principle for black theology because divine purpose intends to draw those at the bottom into decision-making about their own lives.

African American women displayed *defiance*. We find this not only in relation to the white segregationists, but also relative to the secondary roles black men wished to place them in. They defied both the segregation structures and the patriarchal system of black men who would have preferred them not to assume leadership. Lastly, women showed a *creativity of struggle*. Based on the particularity of their pain and resistance, they created new movement songs and gave new content to old spirituals (e.g., what Alice Walker calls the spirituality or artistic creativity of black women's "mothers' gardens").[48] In sum, the divine Spirit moved among black women and gave them strength to do God's will on earth.

The black women with whom Malcolm X related remained outside the Civil Rights Movement, yet his views toward women did not differ substantively from King's. Malcolm followed the Nation of Islam's theological doctrine on women when he served as this organization's national spokesperson. Theologically, the Nation believed black women naturally maintained a secondary role to black men.

However, once outside of the Nation, Malcolm started to experience a new perspective on African American women's role in the black freedom movement. He traveled to Africa twice in 1964 and saw the power of women in the national liberation and independence struggles. With new insight he asserted:

One thing I noticed in both the Middle East and Africa, in every country that was progressive, the women were progressive. In every country that was underdeveloped and backward, it was to the same degree that the women were undeveloped, or underdeveloped, and backward.[49]

Translating Malcolm's position: the degree to which a black liberation movement or black theology of liberation includes the specific leadership and theological expressions of African American women is the same degree to which it will be successful and accountable to the justice demands of God.

Malcolm's and Martin's positions on women conclude a review of their social analyses on race relations, poverty, the international situation, and black women. Social analysis unravels and defines the existing relations in the present society. But what of King's and Malcolm's beliefs about and projections for a new, transformed social system in the future? To answer this question, we now explore their social visions of a new political economy, social relations, and religion.

II: SOCIAL VISIONS

SOCIALIST POLITICAL ECONOMY

Dr. King presents a direct challenge to black theology with his vision of a new society in North America. He realized that the problem of racism, the problem of economic exploitation, and the problem of war were all tied together by the same thread.[50] So he projected a systemic analysis that called for a new society in which the old capitalist social relations would be radically changed and a new social order of political, cultural, and economic equality would reign.

King unleashed a devastating critique of the economic privileges inherent in a capitalist political economy.

> As we talk about "Where do we go from here," . . . we must honestly face the fact that the Movement must address itself to the question of restructuring the whole of American society. There are 40 million poor people here. And one day we must ask the question, "Why are there 40 million poor people in America?" And when you begin to ask that question, you are raising questions about the economic system, about a broader distribution of wealth. When you ask that question, you begin to question the capitalist economy.[51]

This questioning of the capitalist political economy, this restructuring and redistribution of systemic wealth, for King, compelled the poor, both black and white, to "organize a revolution against that system" of injustice. This would be the only way "to lift the load of poverty."[52]

Because King linked domestic white racism and capitalist economic exploitation with the inevitability of aggressive war perpetrated by United States monopoly capitalists abroad, he likewise wove together his domestic and international social visions. King did not simply offer his vision of a new society for the United States. He moved beyond a mere provincialism to the world stage. For example, he cautioned the "privileged minority of the earth" that there existed no shelter on the planet where they could go and hide from the rising storm of the world's poor. It was impossible to hide as the global poor struggled against unjust systems and attempted to usher in a new moral vision of equal social relations. When King searched for authentic political economic systems in the various countries of the world, he concluded that we in America had much to learn from Scandinavia's democratic socialist tradition.[53]

Clearly, Dr. King was treading on a minefield by raising the possibility of the poor carrying out a revolution against America's capitalistic system and reconstructing a new democratic socialist America. Yet, despite the further loss of financial contributions from white liberals (just as he had experienced after his April 1967 anti-Vietnam War speech), King persisted. He refused to allow anybody to put him in a bind "everytime [he] said there must be a better distribution of wealth, and maybe America must move toward a democratic socialism."[54]

Malcolm X agreed with King's assessment of a socialist vision for a post-revolutionary United States. In addition, Malcolm emphasized a socialist system for North America that would specifically eliminate white racism and enhance the particularity of African American culture. He opened his visionary search to a socialist political economy, because whites who had surrendered the privileges of their white skin inevitably turned out to be socialists. Malcolm commented:

> It is impossible for a white person to believe in capitalism and not believe in racism. You can't have capitalism without racism. And if you find one and you happen to get that person into a conversation and they have a philosophy that makes you sure they don't have this racism in their outlook, usually they're socialists or their political philosophy is socialism.[55]

Malcolm leaned toward socialism because he saw that white supremacy always accompanied capitalism. In his experience no white person who embraced capitalism could reject white supremacy. Conversely, every white person who supported the struggle of African Americans for full humanity was a socialist. Thus Malcolm approached socialist political economy in a post-revolutionary United States from the standpoint of eliminating the evil of racial discrimination. Indeed, he would not have arrived at a socialist vision if not for the abolition of racial oppression inherent in the disappearance of monopoly capitalism. If socialism offered freedom and humanity for black Americans, then he would follow that path.

Dr. King turned toward socialism through his experience with Scandinavian countries. Malcolm, however, turned the corner toward the same social vision from his encounter with third-world countries and African independent nations in particular. From his travels he surmised: "I noticed that most of the countries that had recently emerged into independence have turned away from the so-called capitalistic system in the direction of socialism."[56]

During the last year of his life, Malcolm visited the African continent twice. He had the opportunity to visit black independent African nations as well as have in-depth conversations with third-world socialist representatives and movements for national liberation. He observed how socialism abolished human exploitation while preserving the *cultures* of people of color. That is why Malcolm became excited about examples of socialism displayed in *third-world* models and not examples of socialist experiments of *European* countries. He liked third-world socialist projects because they also promoted the importance of oppressed peoples' culture and racial identities. He summed up his observations in the following way:

> So, when we look at the African continent, when we look at the trouble that's going on between East and West, we find that the nations in Africa are developing socialistic systems to solve their problems.[57]

Here we can see how Malcolm uses his specific Pan African analysis to guide his choice of socialist experiments. He concluded that Africa had avoided both "white" systems from the West and the East. European capitalist and socialist nations, therefore, did not appeal to him. They failed to entice him due to their lack of understanding or concern for the culture of the African diaspora. Consequently, he does not speak highly of non-African political economies. But he does note how African nations distinguish themselves from Western capitalists and Eastern socialists by "developing socialistic systems to solve their [own] problems." What were these problems particular to Africa? Africa had to develop a unique form of socialism because not only did the continent suffer from economic exploitation, it also suffered the pains of white racial attacks against African *humanity* and the desecration of African *culture*.

Since African Americans, the descendants of Africa the Motherland, found themselves in a similar predicament resulting from white racism and cultural arrogance of white Americans (the descendants of Europe), black North Americans had no choice but to seek help from their "roots." That is, Mother Africa's social vision ensured a prominent position for racial pride and cultural creativity within a socialist political economy.

Drawing on Martin's and Malcolm's socialist political economy, a constructive black theology will project a communal politics and economics for North America after monopoly capitalism. Relying more on Malcolm, black theology must learn from the relation between democratic ownership of economic structures and the positive assertion of African and African American value systems. Common ownership of the major United States industries will empower the poor of all colors. However, the dynamics of communal relations in the economic sphere should also serve to enhance the specifics of black culture. Democratic socialism or communalism will correctly foreshadow God's coming kingdom on earth only when the seeds of the new heaven blossom with the simultaneous flowering of African American self-identity.

SOCIAL RELATIONS

A move toward socialism brought a further deepening of Malcolm's and Martin's position on human social relations in their new visions for the United States. King's final understanding of black and white social interactions is most telling. Previously he had waged a civil rights struggle for black Americans who, he felt, had been locked out of the Constitution's "promissory note" of freedom. But a clearer perception of the gospel, the battle scars of the southern movement, the new terrain of northern rebellions and segregation, and the cunning hypocrisy of northern white liberals taught him the impotence of his original "integration" definition. In the following, he modifies his earlier understanding of social relations and contrasts this with his vision for genuine black-white relations in a new United States:

> Integration is more than something to be dealt with in esthetic or romantic terms. I think in the past all too often we did it that way . . . and it ended up as merely adding color to a still predominantly white power structure. What is necessary now is to see integration in political terms where there is a sharing of power.[58]

King confesses his previous subservience to a white liberal's worldview about integration. In such a romantic mindset, one images nice little blond girls and boys playing freely with little black boys and girls in the curvaceous mountains of Georgia. Unfortunately, white liberals presented a fantasy world to the black victims while they (whites) preserved the reins of political and economic power in their own hands. Such a con game, whether conscious or unintentional, upheld capitalism and the related values of cutthroat competition and selfishness — all to the detriment of the black community and the black church.

King strongly denounced a false integration into the capitalist system and called for a new vision in which new values allowed for redistribution of power in new social relations. "Something is wrong with capitalism as it now stands in the United States," preached King during the last year of his life. Black folks "are not interested in being integrated into this value structure." Why? Because "power must be relocated, a radical redistribution of power must take place."[59]

Clearly, King no longer subscribed to an anemic notion of integration. If people were going to relate to one another as people, then they had to permit blacks to enter a socialist society reflecting the redistribution of power. Here King differentiates his view of integration from white segregationists and white liberals. The former opposed integration because they felt that blacks did not deserve to participate in the benefits of capitalism. The latter supported an integration that used a smokescreen to preserve a white capitalist power structure under the guise of an esthetic or romantic definition of integration. For Martin, true integration in social relations called for a political reinterpretation of black-white relationships, one where there was a sharing of power.

Moreover, King also began to refashion a new understanding of black people's right to self-determination (temporary "segregation") in racial social relations in the United States. In the spring of 1968, he advocated the possibility of black separation to facilitate the construction of new social relations:

> There are times when we must see segregation as a temporary way-station to a truly integrated society. There are many Negroes who feel this; they do not see segregation as the ultimate goal. They do not see separation as the ultimate goal. They see it as a temporary way-station to put them into a bargaining position to get to that ultimate goal, which is a truly integrated society where there is shared power.

Agreeing with this position of the right of self-determination by way of temporary separation, he resumes: "There are points at which I see the necessity for temporary segregation in order to get to the integrated society."[60] What moved King to such a position of pro-black (temporary) separation? In his vision it was better for blacks to remain united among themselves if integration (in the white liberal sense) would bring them together with whites who failed to surrender their white power privileges. In fact, the old definition of integration proved that blacks gave up whatever meager power they had, for example, the power over black educational institutions, whenever they "integrated" with white folks. Therefore King cautioned the black community and the black church to struggle for and create new social relations in a new democratic socialist country, "that ultimate goal, which is a truly integrated society where there is shared power."

For King, the primary issue was not the absoluteness of black separation/segregation, because he grew flexible in his tactics as his social vision stretched toward black-white power-sharing. Whatever tactic it took to usher in God's ethical system of non-exploitation of people by people sufficed for King. Nevertheless, this stance did not reflect a whimsical or sinister motive on his part. Quite the contrary, King listened to the voices of many Negroes who felt this. He also perceived the dangerous results of blacks abdicating control of their institutions the more the old style (white) liberal integrationist tentacles strengthened their deadly grip around the black community.

Accordingly, King began to feel no contradiction between the call for black liberation (and *culture*) on the part of certain sectors of the black community and his own emphasis on integration (and *politics*). In fact, black liberation (for example, the black community's control over the ownership and distribution of resources needed for its survival) resulted from his redefining the terms of integration (black and white power-sharing in a new socialist social relation). For King, "liberation must come through integration." And so he paints this picture of a liberation/integration process:

> In our kind of society liberation cannot come without integration and integration cannot come without liberation. I speak here of integra-

tion in both the ethical and political senses. On the one hand, integration is true intergroup, interpersonal living. On the other hand, it is the mutual sharing of power.[61]

For black theology, therefore, a social relation of black-white power-sharing should not obliterate black liberation. African Americans can relate to whites on a genuine interpersonal level without giving up the need for group black liberation. Democratic cultural socialism, then, still requires black communal interests, which liberation expresses. One-on-one interactions between individuals from different races complement the safeguarding of black folks' group interests for liberation. Again, overall power-sharing is the ultimate goal that King pursued. Within that context, all things were possible.

Malcolm X also expressed views on social relations similar to King's. Malcolm saw that all members of the black community who struggled for the betterment of the black community actually had the same ultimate goal. Like King, Malcolm was partial to some form of socialism, though heavily influenced by a unique African culture. Consequently, Malcolm subordinated differences in the black freedom movement to the achievement of his visionary social relations. "All of our people have the same goals," Malcolm claimed and then continued: "That objective is freedom, justice, equality. All of us want recognition and respect as human beings. We don't want to be integrationists. Nor do we want to be separationists. We want to be human beings."

As long as all people in the African American community cherished and fought for the new society in which such ideals would be realized, Malcolm had no problems with which tactics were employed. Supporting certain integrationist sectors of the black community, he continues:

Integration is only a method that is used by some groups to obtain freedom, justice, equality and respect as human beings. Separation is only a method that is used by other groups to obtain freedom, justice, equality or human dignity.[62]

The *politics* of integrationists' struggle complemented the *culture* of separationists' struggle. Both aimed at the same target: freedom.

Like Malcolm and King, black theology should understand that clarity on the nature of social relations in its social visions permits differences in tactics over integration and liberation. Different tactical approaches aid each other on the same path toward true African American humanity. What does it mean to separate if one does not have control over the means of producing and distributing necessities for the survival of the community and thus achieve full humanity? What does it mean to integrate one on one with a white person if one does not share decision-making power and simultaneously realize communal black liberation? True political integration entails cultural liberation and preservation. Thus the politics of culture and the culture of politics interpenetrate in social relations.

THE CHURCH AND RELIGION

We have looked at the political economy and social relations views of Malcolm's and Martin's visions for the future. However, we must not forget the basis of their social visions. Both men grounded their predictions for, faith in, and vision of a new society on the church and religion, in a God who would see them through to the end.

Rev. King saw the African American church having at least four important characteristics that would define its activity from now to the future society. First, the Christian church and the black church in particular must be a beacon of *justice*. If Christians dared to witness as followers of Jesus the Christ, then we would have to practice what Jesus practiced and preached. From King's vantage point, justice stood at the heart of the cross and resurrection; it stood at the heart of Christian suffering, hope, and love. Those persons, black or white, who claimed the name of Jesus deserved that name only if they anchored their Christian faith and identification in justice. "Those of us who call the name of Jesus Christ," preached King, "find something at the center of our faith which forever reminds us that God is on the side of truth and justice."[63]

Accordingly, the church could not be a Christian church if it supported white-skinned privileges or United States military presence abroad. And most definitely, no church could identify itself as Christian if it supported capitalism. Maybe people could call themselves a gathering of like-minded individuals, or a group of people interested in religion. But until blacks and whites placed truth and justice at the center of their faith, then and only then could a people of faith claim themselves believers in and doers of Jesus' words and deeds.

A Christian church of justice, from King's perspective, would emerge once the African American church deemphasized such activities as fundraising for the pastor's anniversary or expanding church physical structures in order to claim bragging rights. Justice would not be found in those black churches where pastors paid more attention to the "size of their wheelbase" than to righting incorrect relations outside church walls. To really have church, he believed, called for centering worship and witness around the fight for justice.

Second, a Christian church distinguished itself through the role of *servant*. Justice manifests itself through active service for those who suffer from physical poverty and need, those who cannot advocate for themselves, and those who lack a full humanity. Toward the end of his life, King summed up all that he had done and asked that his eulogy convey the following message: "I don't want a long funeral. . . . But I hope I can live so well that the preacher can get up and say he was faithful. . . . That's the sermon I'd like to hear." Defining the nature of Christian faith by servanthood, he finishes:

> "Well done thy good and faithful servant. You've been faithful; you've been concerned about others." That's where I want to go from this point on, the rest of my days. "He who is greatest among you shall be your servant." I want to be a servant. I want to be a witness for my Lord, do something for others.[64]

The nature of the Christian church does not define itself by worldly possessions and materialistic acquisitions. In fact, in his list of earthly achievements, King does not detail his Nobel Peace Prize, his many speaking and preaching engagements, his prestigious educational degrees, or his books and articles. In contrast, he hopes the living will remember him for his life-long service to the physical poor and society's powerless victims. Again, the nature of the church is to serve and empower the people, even if (in the case of white capitalist churches) serving implies sharing power equally with the poor.

King bases the servant trait of the Christian church on the Bible. Specifically, he refers to Matthew 25:31ff. Here Jesus uses the parable about the ultimate judgment day, when specific criteria deny or permit passage into heaven. All of humankind face Jesus on the throne and await either permission to enter eternal life or relegation to the fires of hell. On the left, Jesus places the goats—those who pursued an earthly lifestyle of materialistic, profit-oriented activity. In this crowd one discovers all the capitalists of the world, those who placed profit before people, surplus value above human value. Here, too, one meets all those so-called Christians who preached an abstract "spiritual" religion, which primarily encouraged individuals to gaze at the heavens while systems of capitalism, racism, and war enslaved the spirits, souls, and bodies of victims on earth.

On the right hand, Jesus places all the sheep and gives them access to heaven because they had been faithful *servants* to the world's physically poor: people without food to eat or water to drink, people incarcerated or homeless, people sick or without clothes or immigrants to a strange land. King wanted the Christian church to stand with the sheep. As Jesus states in the parable: "Verily I say unto you, Inasmuch as ye have done it unto one of the least of these my brethren, ye have done it unto me" (Matthew 25:40). What the Christian church does to society's poor equals what is done to Jesus Christ.

Third, the church attains its Christian identity when it *organizes* for the God-given rights of the poor. Specifically, what the church organizes for is not the esthetic and romantic notion of integration. For King, the Christian church fights to realize a new definition of equality in which power-sharing would satisfy the new understanding of black-white integration. In other words, racial integration, which King continued to pursue, would arise only when the white power structure surrendered its exclusive monopoly on power.

Clarifying the goal of (black) Christian organizing efforts, Rev. King lectured in 1967: "Now, if we are to recognize that we are in this new era where the struggle is for genuine equality, we must recognize that we can't solve our problems until there is a radical re-distribution of economic and political power." Furthermore, the new power that the poor and the black community would receive in "genuine equality" would reflect the natural rights given by God in God's partiality to the poor. Continuing, he maintained: "We must recognize that if we are to gain our God-given rights now, principalities and powers must be confronted and they must be changed."[65]

Basically King wants to clarify the organizing target of the Christian religion and the church and thus facilitate a full humanity. Christians must sharpen their social tools of analysis and clearly identify and confront the "principalities and powers" on earth that block the achievement of oppressed people's God-given rights. We have seen King define these demonic powers as racism, capitalism, and capitalist war abroad. Thus to enjoy the rights freely given through God's grace—to realize full humanity—entails eradicating systemic evil. To organize toward what it means to be human forces the church to name Satan's activities. Naming evil, then, comprises part of the organizing effort; fully removing that which the church names approaches the restoration of just human relations, a new and equal power-sharing.

Finally, the church has to *heal*, *preach*, and *help deliver*. Here, King uses Luke 4:18-19 as his personal guide and, by implication, instruction for all Christian witness. Not only does the church define itself by justice, servanthood, and organizing, but it also heals those who have broken hearts. At this point King adds a concern for the soul, which encompasses the heart. Just as the physical body needs material sustenance, the soul and the heart likewise require care. Therefore Christians provide relief for the non-material in conjunction with alleviating systemic principalities and powers.

Related to healing is proclamation of the gospel message or Good News for those who are poor. As a fourth generation Baptist preacher, King knew all too well the importance of the proclaimed word in Christian faith in general and the black church Christian tradition especially. The people need to hear a word from the Lord to soothe their souls, direct their vision, gird up their courage to confront and change systems of evil, and assume their God-given rights in the here and now.

In particular, the proclaimed word tells society's poor and afflicted that "the acceptable year of the Lord" is at hand, not tomorrow but now. In fact, the year most acceptable to a God of justice and truth was the year of Jubilee, when all slaves received their deliverance into freedom. Consequently, the church must help in this deliverance by letting society's victims hear that a radical transformation has already occurred with the birth, life, death, and resurrection of Jesus the Christ.

Specifically, the coming of Jesus meant deliverance from evil had taken place. If deliverance into the realm of Jesus' liberation has occurred for the poor, then the church must aid the poor in their own deliverance. Put differently, Jesus shifted the balance of power from the realm of evil to the realm of freedom, thereby making victory of the oppressed assured. Though a historical shift has taken place in terms of guaranteeing Jesus' victory for "the little ones" on earth, the victims must allow this already ultimate deliverance to empower them toward making this liberation concrete. The Christian church has a role in this process; it proclaims and helps organize deliverance.[66]

King spoke about religion and the church through the eyes of a Christian, one who followed Jesus Christ. Malcolm, on the other hand, adhered to the religion of Islam and held a faith in Allah, the Moslem God. Nonetheless, Malcolm, like King, grounded his social vision upon his profound religious faith. Malcolm's religious conviction has often been overlooked because he established two organizations: the Muslim Mosque, Inc., for practicing Moslems and the Organization of Afro-American Unity for any black person interested in the freedom of black folk. Yet Malcolm was a Moslem minister in a faith tradition believing in Allah's presence in all spheres of life, especially the areas of justice and injustice. Hence black theology today has to take seriously the ways in which both Malcolm and Martin based their hopes for a future society in their religions.

Due to his unyielding concern for African Americans' justice and white people's potential role in removing injustice, Malcolm gravitated to Islam's emphasis on the oneness of God. "Perhaps if white Americans could accept the Oneness of God," Minister Malcolm encouraged, "then, perhaps, too, they could accept in reality the Oneness of Man." Embracing God's oneness, then, whites could "cease to measure, and hinder, and harm others in terms of 'differences' in color."[67] For Malcolm, faith in religion guided his projections for a future system of just race relations. Racial discrimination prevented the implementation of God's call for unity among all of humankind. If whites had faith in such a divinity, then all Americans could fulfill themselves as human beings in God's plan for all humanity. Racism impaired God's intent. That is why Malcolm fought so hard for blacks to be human beings in this society by any means necessary.

Malcolm chose the religion of Islam to foster a healthy black-white relationship. Yet he lays out a criterion for all religions in African American life: any religion worthy of black folks' faith must center its beliefs and practice on bettering the sad plight of the black community. "Despite being a Muslim," Malcolm shouted with conviction,

> I can't overlook the fact that I'm an Afro-American in a country which practices racism against black people. There is no religion under the

sun that would make me forget the suffering that Negro people have undergone in this country. Negroes have suffered for no reason other than that their skins happen to be black.[68]

Malcolm followed Islam. Still, his advocating any religion fighting for racial justice opens him up to coalitions with Christians and other religious persuasions in the African American community who likewise follow God's will for black liberation. In a sense, Malcolm's God allows for a variety of expressions as long as those expressions reveal themselves through black empowerment for freedom. Though Islam suited him, he implies a call for unity of all black religions, regardless of labels. Indeed, Malcolm tells black theology to develop its thinking and doing with all religious impulses — Christian and non-Christian, organized and unorganized, institutionalized and non-institutionalized — for an African American full humanity.

In addition to sounding a universal note for all black religions, Malcolm's belief in Islam urged him to speak to the universality of the human condition. Preaching the humanity of all people, Malcolm stated:

I believe in the brotherhood of all men. . . . My religion makes me be against all forms of racism. It keeps me from judging any man by the color of his skin. It teaches me to judge him by his deeds and his conscious behavior. And it teaches me to be for the rights of all human beings.[69]

In fact, his religion taught him to shun all forms of racism. True sisterhood and brotherhood recognized the rights of all regardless of color. Religion avoids forms of racism and inaugurates human togetherness by judging persons' deeds and not the color of their skin, black or white. Malcolm had to conclude such a faith because for him religion was essentially justice. That is why he adhered to Islam; not because black Americans had an inherent attraction to Moslems, but because Islam and Allah were justice. He stood for the rights of all people.

CONCLUSION

As religious leaders, Minister Malcolm X and Rev. King pursued their social analyses and social visions from faith perspectives. Their motivations for justice offer insights for contemporary black theology. Within their social analyses we discovered the importance of race relations, poverty, the international situation, and African American women. Specifically within race relations, we saw the crimes of white theology, the resulting need for black political and cultural power, and the imperative for the black church to fight against these crimes and realize a black and white power-sharing.

Furthermore, Malcolm and Martin linked race relations to poverty and the international situation. A correct social analysis, then, must perceive the interlocking nature of white supremacy and capitalist class exploitation domestically with the inherently violent nature of United States monopoly capitalism on a global scale. Relatedly, an international social analysis instructs African Americans and their churches to link arms with Africa, the Third World, and poor people the world over. No resolution of racial oppression and capitalist dehumanization will be ensured until victims everywhere enjoy and control their full humanity. Unfortunately, Malcolm's and Martin's social analysis of women opens up black theology and the African American church to a persistent contradiction: the continued suppression of black women's God-given humanity as women.

However, Minister Malcolm and Rev. King do not end with comments on what is, that is, social analysis. They go further and offer a new vision, a new free society where God's people reach their created and intended status. Specifically, we learned about the crucial role of political economy in black theology's social vision. With the abolition of capitalism, the new United States will (1) allow the poor to own the major industries and control all dimensions of the economy, and (2) will also enhance African American culture.

Finally, a future vision entailed a fresh look at social relations and the church. No longer will integration mean blacks sitting with white folks while the latter keep power. Instead, true black-white integration will work only when the existing white power structure is abolished and, simultaneously, the African American community secures the right to self-determination (for example, the right of temporary separation).

Of course, the black church has a central role to play in future social relations. In fact, the witness of the church for the new society begins now by serving the poor and bringing in God's justice for the majority of the United States and the world who lack power. The full realization of the Kingdom is to come. But the business of the church is to receive God's grace, which empowers the people of faith to witness as if God's promise of liberation is already fulfilled.

Conclusion

Shoes for Constructing Black Theology

Black theology exists because God's purpose is the liberation and full humanity of the poor. In trying to reach this place on earth — without poverty and with all people enjoying their complete creativity — poor and working communities confront individual and systemic resistance. The schemes of the demonic create complex webs to trap and squeeze the life of society's victims. The African American poor are located at the bottom of the victims' bottom. The work of black theology, therefore, is continually to bring together God's liberation activities with the justice practices found in the black church and community.

God grants us Good News. God works with those who respond to a divine call to give themselves so others may share in and claim this Good News. Living a life for the "least of these" in society is the highest expression of Christian witness, indeed, the highest example of God's presence on earth. We find indications of divine spirit overcoming humanity where segments of our churches and nation struggle with the poor to achieve space for their humanity and identity filled with sacred value.

Black theology works for the life of the African American poor, so the latter can in fact determine their rightful place in a society of equal ownership and voices, a society where they can name themselves based on their own definitions. Lack of clarity on this calling and commission will find black theology serving the interests of the most self-centered and evil forces today. If it takes this route, black theology will suffer both ultimate divine judgment and immediate dismissal by the poor.

Again, the purpose of black theology is to turn its face to the signs of the times in the broader society and to what the church is or is not doing to uplift and empower those without means to enjoy life. More and more these signs indicate fundamental structural shifts, which are propelling the African American folk further into a spiral of societal neglect and disinterest. In today's priorities, to be black and poor carries the same importance and value as prehistoric dinosaurs. The only difference is one class of animals is already extinct while black people experience the slow danger of a living hell. The life-and-death urgency of the situation requires black theology and the church to be even more faithful to the Good News. For in the depths of human evil, God hovers over and among the voiceless, carrying them upon divine wings and nurturing their bodies and spirit to run the race toward full humanity. Black theology has to speak to and occupy those places of pain and hope.

Signs of the Times

Every sign points to a long-term systemic decline from the perspective of people at the lower levels of the United States structure. For the first time in the contemporary era, we have the "structurally unemployed." With an over-representation from the African American community, these people will never find a job, have stopped looking for a job, or have developed their own means of "illegal" survival. Major sectors of wealth and decision-making have decided to value short-term accumulation of profit and capital at the expense of *permanently* writing off many depressed communities. Unlike previous economics, unemployment and employment do not follow a cyclical crisis-recovery scenario. Neither does the boom or bust of opportunities mirror the job possibilities that international wars historically offered. Wars in the past helped to ease recession by putting people back to work. Not anymore.

Further adding to permanent joblessness for black folk is the foundational move in the United States economy from wealth accumulation in industrial smokestack investments to service and computerized technologies. Thousands of African Americans lack the requisite skills for this transformation, and racial discrimination will block any avenues for retooling to meet the new industries' demands.

On the national political level presidential elections signify voters' clear suspicion, disdain, and distrust of bourgeois democracy. Voter registration continues to follow a downward curve on the scale of citizens' hope in and desire to affect the country's leadership. Similarly, from long-term projections, the registered voter rolls find more and more people refusing to exercise this citizenship franchise. Both potential new voters and voter turnout have shrunk. This lack of voter interest is itself a protest vote against the state of elected officials, particularly on the national and state levels. It is as if the nation's disconnected population has been organized by an invisible hand of protest.

Even the reality of African Americans voting disproportionately to their population percentage does not reflect a counter trend of black optimism in the electoral process. Rather, it means that an oppressed community is more inclined to explore all instances that could possibly bring some temporary relief. For communities in pain, voting serves as a quick-fix band-aid to stall the hemorrhaging loss of their quality of life. Moreover, given black folk's minority status, even their unusual turnouts at the polls cannot substantively stop the majority population's turn away from national electoral politics.

The area of national culture fares no better. The country values its patriotic identity and sense of national will when war bombs burn and maim the foreign "enemy." Factually, during the periods of most recent regional wars around the globe, large segments of the American people have purchased more American flags than at any other times. Thus part of the country's identity comes from rallying around the blood of United States military targets abroad.

The cultural identity also revolves around reality-creating "sound bites." The sound-bite trend speaks to the nature of mass communication, particularly in creating pictures of the real and the imagined. The most prominent cases occur in electoral campaigning and nightly news shows on television. The most successful candidate, more than likely, will come from a campaign strategy mastering the art of sound bite. The sound bite, again, signifies the American people's acceptance of false and perverted reality. They prefer a picture of themselves and the events around them not based on what is real but what are distorted facts or projected fantasy.

Similarly, nightly news shows do not report daily events. News programs offer a barrage of snippets and short images, all suggestive of an unreality and all blocking serious analysis with in-depth proposals for corrective measures. For the African American community, the sound-bite trend can only cause further manipulation of black and poor predicaments. The sound bite reflects a way of life and self-identity that leaves the nation callous toward powerless people.

In every major category of the quality of life for African Americans, the overwhelming majority of black people (that is, poor and working poor folk), are worse off than they were before the urban rebellions of the 1960s. This picture becomes even more sobering when one stops measuring the black community by the relatively successful black middle class and focuses on the majority African American population.

Which Way for the Church?

With some exceptions, white and black churches have failed to respond to the conservative consolidation of structural dislocation of African American and poor people in the United States. White religious gatherings on Sunday, in prayer meetings, and other holy occasions refuse to discuss politics on principle. Instead of worship with God being a time of self-examination of service to the poor and the oppressed, too many white churches tend to retreat into the realms of "we're not so bad" and "thank God we have a place to feel good." For them, evangelism often means bringing people out of this world. Likewise, conversion relies on changing an individual without asking for political, social, and worldly commitments to voiceless people. Spirituality entails connecting the individual's spirit to an invisible, hocus pocus force. Consequently, growth of the church translates into showing up on Sundays with one other person and paying dues regularly.

Though victims of systemic racial discrimination, most African American churches fall short in identifying evil and God's presence in larger social analyses and visions. Preaching promises of a better life in the hereafter and fostering the (impossible) possibility of sharing a piece of the American pie miss the Christian mark. The target of God working through Jesus Christ is full empowerment of victims in new social relations on earth. God came and divine spirit continues to appear to religious gatherings that prophetically proclaim "thus saith the Lord" and then witness ways to realize God's justice now.

True, the Christian hope is based on nothing less than Jesus' "blood and righteousness." But the churches have forgotten that it is Christ's "crucifixion" blood and "resurrection" righteousness. The crucifixion symbolizes God in Jesus working the very blood from the divine body so that oppressed people may have life abundantly and have it now. The crucifixion blood gives us hope that today those who have life resources will sacrifice themselves to empower those who, in many instances, are literally losing blood every day.

The resurrection righteousness is God's ultimate gift of hope to keep struggling within the tentacles of social and individual evils. Liberation and full humanity of the poor will eventually triumph. Righteousness will prevail. Most churches have lost sight of this essential vision and have capitulated to either an acceptance of the status quo or a critique that is actually a veiled plea for a piece of the crumbs from the powerful few. Blood and righteousness bring hope and certainty that the United States can be one day a place fostering values and practices based on what maintains and what eliminates poverty and racism.

A Response: Black Religious Scholarship

Black religious scholarship is offering different responses to deal with today's society and church. Present religious thinking attempts to generate clarity amid shifting structural evil. These current writers grow out of and work with the first generation of African American religious scholars, who laid the foundations in the 1960s.

Almost thirty years have passed since the ad hoc National Committee of Negro Churchmen (NCNC) published its 1966 *New York Times* theological statement on the Black Power movement. In 1969 James H. Cone wrote the first and classical text *Black Theology and Black Power.*[1] Both events marked a radical shift in theological studies. NCNC's declaration linked faith in God to urban rebellions and cries of African American cultural freedom; in other words, American Christianity needed to address the imbalance between power and conscience. Furthermore, Cone's book grounded all of Christianity and talk about God on the liberation of the black oppressed and the universal poor. Lacking the essential emphasis on Jesus' liberation mission, the white church, therefore, was the Anti-Christ.

These pioneering trails carved out by the first generation of African American theologians[2] have provided firm footing for further doing of black theology today. Specifically, the earlier emphases of James Cone, Gayraud S. Wilmore, and Charles H. Long offer possibilities for systematically understanding the nature of the black church's faith in the contemporary period. The heart of Cone's work has centered on the political and systemic manifestations of white racism as demonic. If Jesus Christ calls the oppressed African American community to fight for its liberation, then this faith gathering must wage a battle to deconstruct white supremacist power relations. There can be no participation in God's liberation movement on earth if poor black folk do not achieve their liberation from visible and evil skulduggery created and perpetuated by principalities and powers with white faces.

Historically, Wilmore has called attention to the non-institutionalized black church and non-Christian realities of God's justice revelations. God is also manifest on urban street corners and in non-traditional black religious faith groups.

With Long, we confront the challenge to recognize how white people have conquered black religion intellectually. Long's project seeks God's manifestations in the process of creating new black ways of thinking religiously. Language, the expression of thought, is reality. Intellectually, African American religious scholars need to cast aside the theological thought categories of the white oppressors. The black religious scholar should dare to pursue the creativity of black folk faith discourse without the deadly and suicidal baggage of preconceived white theological mind games.[3] An ultimate power appears in black people's own way of talking and thinking.

The decades of the 1980s and 1990s reveal the work of younger African American scholars, who have branched out into a variety of black theological concerns. On the one hand, they seek to pursue further the first generation's trailblazing agenda of liberation theology and its relation to the broader society and church. On the other hand, they claim their own distinct approaches.

We find the clearest development of a younger movement in the novel work of womanists (black religious female scholars). They have boldly asserted their presence and their right to do theology from the particular perspectives of African American women. They deal with any and all disciplines that promote justice in black women's experience. In contrast to the first and second generation male writers, womanists have consistently welded together issues of gender, race, class, and sexual orientation.[4]

Womanists are also a model for doing black theology against evil and for the poor because they share in strong self-critique. If Christ's message is to prevail among the people focused on powerless humanity, then self-critique is healthy and vital for speaking the truth to free victims. Thus black women's unity has not led womanists to a false peaceful coexistence. On the contrary, just as they apply a rigorous analysis to black men, so too do they engage in creative and sharp differences among themselves.[5]

Like the womanists, several second generation male writers have sought to deepen black theology, specifically by taking seriously popular culture, the unlettered poor folk, and Afro-centricity.

First, regarding popular culture, a group of African American religious scholars have launched a journal titled *Black Sacred Music: A Journal of Theomusicology*. It contains scholarly writings in the areas of black sacred and secular music.[6] After popular culture, the religious experiences of unlettered black folk surface in *Cut Loose Your Stammering Tongue: Black Theology in the Slave Narratives*.[7] This text is a collective examination of the religious reflections of illiterate bondswomen and men. A third black theological source draws on a broad 1980s revival in Afro-centricity—a closer look at the African faith heritage of black Americans.[8] Finally, new writers have linked black theology domestically to international religious practices of resistance and creativity. These writers warn black theology in the United States of the dangers of isolation unless it stretches forth its hands in partnership with poor people in Africa and the Caribbean.[9]

The first generation of black thinkers also persists in pacesetting writings from the perspective of the African American poor and victim. James H. Cone's groundbreaking work *Martin and Malcolm and America: A Dream or a Nightmare?* reclaims theology as a weapon of critique, a way of theological reflection from below, and a signpost for new national relations.[10] Continuing his original push for justice for the poor, Cone critically looks at Malcolm X and Martin Luther King, Jr., so that black theology moves out of the academy and into a broad mainstream discussion. Similarly, C. Eric Lincoln's *The Black Church in the African American Experience* has become the most recent starting point for any sober review of the state of African American churches today.[11]

A Method for Our Shoes

A systematic black theology of liberation requires both the inclusion of first and second generation faith reflections and more. In order to have shoes that fit the feet of the black church and the overall African American experience, a constructive black theology of liberation must deal with the method one uses actually to develop such a systematic theology.

The previous five chapters have sorted out theological suggestions, values, and traditions from the religious thought and practices lodged in five sectors of the African American experience—slave religion, black women's spirituality, African American folk culture, W. E. B. Du Bois's political thought, and Martin's and Malcolm's social analyses and social visions. However, none of these five sources presents a systematic theology. On the contrary, these people and communities signify more unrefined faith think-ing and practice about their own convictions in and encounter with the ultimate justice reality to which they submit their lives; as a result, they are gripped by the quest to attain this ultimate freedom.

All people have an ultimate concern and dream to which they dedicate their lives and in which they have faith. (It is faith because that which is sought after is not yet totally realized, thus a faith dimension appears for fulfillment.) The theologian develops a method to make systematic that which is basic. The theologian is called by God to raise critical and self-critical questions about what the church and the community are called by God to preach, say, and do. And the theologian's role is to see if the called church, community, and theologian are practicing their vocations.

This points to theological methodology. How does one go about trans-lating the unrefined and basic faith thoughts and practices of the poor into a systematic theological tradition toward God's liberation? Basically, a con-structive black theology of liberation is a mediation between what poor African Americans of faith believe and do by force of habit, on the one hand, and a systematic tradition where oppressed black folk self-consciously struggle for full humanity in God's divine realm, on the other hand. Sys-tematic theology brings to the surface existing liberating manifestations of God's presence among the African American poor. The above-mentioned five sources illustrate the hidden and partially concealed divine justice rev-elations. Systematic theology, then, attempts to uncover and make powerful the beautiful black crossroads between God's grace of justice and poor people's multiple yearnings to realize a freedom faith.

There are three basic guidelines for constructing a systematic black the-ology of liberation today. First, God has called humanity to empower all the earth's poor as a gateway to a universal freedom and a universal the-ology. The Old Testament story talks about God's involvement with a band of persecuted slaves. In the particularity of these slaves' relation with the Holy lies the general oppressed condition. Thus to reconnect with the divine, to reimmerse ourselves in the former right relationship held prior to humankind's Fall, we must journey through a God-slavery way.

In the New Testament we hear tales of the ultimate Christian revelation of Yahweh. That is, Jesus Christ shows clear, conscious intent that God chose to manifest among specific oppressed groups in the real world. God decided to be born in a manger amid cow manure, dirt, and straw. In Jesus, God publicly proclaims a heavenly mission on earth geared to freeing the poor and those victimized by discrimination. Jesus also lived out criteria for entrance into heaven's halls by separating sheep and goats in relation to justice work with the poor. And God, through Jesus, opted to die as a persecuted outlaw, a perceived threat to ruling powers and dominating church and theological authorities. Jesus Christ's funeral takes place with two thieves and, lacking any resources, the Anointed One had to be buried in someone else's tomb. Then the Holy Spirit resumes the work of the

Liberator, blowing through old barriers and creating new opportunities for a full humanity out of the flesh and bones and talk and work of the oppressed. In a word, God calls us to empower the poor.

Second, a constructive black theology has to rely on its own indigenous sources as foundation, but not exclusively. Black theology has to be based on the faith and religious experiences of the African American poor, thus accenting liberation and justice for today's least in society. Black theology has a wealth of resources and sources in black history and life from Africa until today out of which to study and learn about religious practices and construct theology. God is not an abstract floating God in a nether land; the Holy's justice is always and absolutely incarnational. Thus, throughout black life, historically and today, there exists and has always existed some form of striving for freedom.

The dominant example of such a liberation quest has appeared within the African American church since slavery. However, the thirst for, belief in, and work of freedom have appeared and continue to appear in non-institutional church movements. God's brilliancy goes beyond human restrictions and offers the presence of grace in diverse global ways. Therefore, because God's loving freedom always comes to us concretely, black theology looks for signs of the times wherever and whenever the African American poor are struggling for freedom. Out of this foundation based on "the least of these" (with the black church at the center), a sorely needed dialogue and coalition must be pursued with the rest of society. A justice striving clothed in black is the cornerstone source and resource from which black theology builds itself in conversation with others.

Third, to begin a theological dialogue a constructive black theology should link to Africa and third-world liberation theologies. Specifically, black theology has to deepen its relation to liberation theologies developing in Africa, Asia and the Pacific Rim, the Caribbean, and Latin America.

For example, in Asia and the Pacific Rim, we find such Christian theologies as Minjung (in South Korea), Dalit theology (in India), Jesus Christ is a Coconut Tree (in Tonga), and God is Rice (in Japan). In Africa we perceive instances throughout the Continent of African traditional religions, which are Christian; we also encounter liberation theology in Cameroon, Zimbabwe, and of course in South Africa. In Latin America and the Caribbean there are emerging black consciousness movements that are crafting black theologies in places such as Cuba, Brazil, and Haiti. All of these global regions are posing similar questions: What does it mean to be Christian in the specific context of the developing world? Does the future survival of worldwide Christianity and God's revelation in other forms depend on what is happening in Africa, Asia and the Pacific Rim, the Caribbean, and Latin America? A working coalition of people and nations of color can form the hub for a more universal discussion.

In addition to three guidelines, a constructive and systematic black theology of liberation recognizes the importance of four relationships: political and cultural; women and men; Christian and non-Christian; and church and non-institutional church.

Regarding the politics-culture link, faith expressions among the black poor occur within a contested terrain where systemic power institutions and individuals abound. To ignore this fact would make black theology stick its head in the sand while structural political power reigns over the folk and persists unchallenged. So we need to engage a theology arising out of efforts that find the poor attempting to determine their own space. As we note this political right to self-determination, we also parallel a move toward cultural affirmation. Black culture concerns itself with both identity and lifestyle. Black folk's cultural creativity shines out as self-recognition of God's unique African American creation, equal to all humanity. Likewise culture speaks to a way of life, ingrained as a unique force of habit (of survival and liberation techniques). Culture may arise from power institutions. But it can become relatively independent and, in turn, affect and determine political systems. Structural power and group identity go together and interpenetrate.

Similarly, black theology deals with African American female-male connections because both share equal original creation and both embody resources for liberation. Moreover, black women comprise at least half of the African American community and close to two-thirds of the black church. Both from the perspective of divine justice and mutual interdependent humanity, the faith experiences of women and men must share in and act as sources for constructing theology; both must share in their God-given expressions of political and cultural life. The degree to which poor African American women (those suffering economic hardship, racial stereotypes, and gender abuse) achieve justice will measure the success or failure of faith in and acceptance and realization of God's plan for poor humanity.

Christian and non-Christian along with church and non-institutional church communities round out the four relationships. Because God manifests freedom faith movements holistically, Christians and the church must evangelize non-Christian and non-institutional church realities and be evangelized by them. Of course, cross-fertilization evangelization hinges on all the poor's co-laboring with God toward realization of an ultimate free kingdom on earth. Here we touch on ecumenical and interfaith dialogue and partnership within the African American community as well as without.

Just as God incarnates within the plight of the poor (as we saw in the three guidelines), and the poor find themselves connected in diverse manners (in four relationships), so too does systematic theology find itself involved with the creativity of related disciplines. While interacting with other disciplines, theology seeks to discover how best to get at divine vocation for concrete liberation.

For instance, political economy surfaces the issue of power control of politics, culture, and economics. This discipline demands a social analysis of structural interrelations: who has ownership, control, and decision-making power. Political economy is an unmasking of the surface rhetoric that obscures the bottom line powerbrokers. After all is said and done, in the real world of people, classes, strata, races, and gender, someone or some bodies make decisions about other people's lives. What and who are these power systems and people? Furthermore, political economy paints the constructive practical vision of the new democratic society. The new democracy on earth will include communal ownership of all the major industries in a society, whether those industries are economic, cultural, political, or linguistic. The politics of economics and the economics of politics help to deconstruct as well as reconstruct.

Along with political economy, the discipline of biblical criticism also aids in constructing a black theology. Source, form, redaction, and textual methodologies should be applied to scripture itself. These methodologies must be used with examples of how African American folk understand, use, and appropriate the Bible in their own indigenous lifestyles. Biblical criticism is not an abstract phenomenon. Thus, from the perspective of the Bible's poor and that of the black poor's use of the Bible, we employ biblical criticism.

Literary criticism, a third discipline, allows black theology to have a three-dimensional dialogue. In viewing various African American sources for constructive theology, we seek to question them as texts. One conversation partner is the oral or written text itself, specifically the form and structure of the text within its own cultural and political context. Then the text's implications are put in dialogue with the text's effects on the readers and listeners (the second "talker" in the conversation), who are also questioned in relation to their own cultural and political context. And finally, noting his or her political and cultural context, the author's presuppositions and intentions enter the conversation. Here a method of interpretation (of author-text-reader/listener) primarily helps the unearthing of nuanced theological meanings in poor black folk's literary and vernacular traditions. In addition to fostering a three-way interchange, literary criticism will help to privilege a black English of the poor.

Comparative religion, the fourth and final discipline, lends itself directly to any efforts at constructing a black theology from the entire African American religious experience. Because Christianity, though the dominant form, is not an exclusive faith reflection in black life, we need methods of comparing other expressions of ultimate convictions. Christianity, non-Christian institutional religions, and non-institutional religions pervade black beliefs about survival and liberation. Our review of theological practices in the previous five chapters have shown a tradition within the African American community. This religious tradition is embedded in the cultural and political fabric; it is a religious faith and quest for final justice and freedom. To detect such multifaceted forms, we need an instrument that will sound comparative theological notes from different songs with the same liberation faith riff.

Role of the Theologian

Our methodology of doing black theology with three parts (guidelines, relationships, and disciplines) shows us an approach to constructive work on indigenous sources. Still, a word needs to be said about the path the systematic theologian walks while implementing such a methodology. Black theology and the black theologian both need shoes that fit their feet.

The theologian brings presuppositional intent and vocational obligations to the liberation method of doing black theology. First, the theologian is called to make the church and the community accountable to what God has called the church and community to do as co-agents in the current divine Kingdom inbreaking for the poor on earth. This calling derives from the Bible, Jesus Christ (birth, life, death, and resurrection), and God's spirit of a living justice presence today.

In addition, the theologian places herself or himself in a community of faith. A communal gathering with convictions enables the systematic theologian to discern good and evil. A Christian church or faith group, linked to the theologian, is guided by and serves the interests of the poor.

Moreover, the theologian uses the tools and lifestyle of criticism and self-criticism. Criticism signifies a prophetic role vis-à-vis faith groups and the poor. Self-criticism suggests a servant role dimension. There exists a dynamic, loving, and straightforward examination and self-examination where both parties—faith community and theologian—submit to the norm of freedom for the African American folk and the poor.

Furthermore, the theologian has to work with other African Americans (as a group) and justice-oriented people (in coalition) who labor in other spheres of society and are trained in other professions and jobs. The entire calling of a systematic theologian, we must remember, is not to privilege the theologian's status but to change the world for the better.

Shoes for the Twenty-first Century

Black theology stands at the threshold of the twenty-first century. To walk forward, a liberation faith planted in African American life must be the source for making shoes that fit black theology's feet. Through the door of the year 2000, we hear the painful cries of our unborn demanding to know what type of "shoe" preparations we have made for the children to be. Basically, we need to integrate a gospel of full humanity, a critical acceptance of African American religious history, and an understanding of theological, cultural, and political power in the United States today.

But there exist blatant and subtle forces that attempt to negate formally trained intellectuals, the church, and the community from drawing on a potential radical African American spirituality and thinking. On the one hand, this occurs when persons in mainstream decision-making positions say no to us or try to coopt our strengths. On the other hand, we trip and fall when we fail to balance the basic prophetic and servant roles in black theology's vocation.

In fact, black theology has a calling to organize itself at the service of silenced voices. We must listen to and help empower them, and thereby ourselves. Without a faith context and the interest of the majority, we can often seem like a new form of intellectual minstrels performing before white folk's voyeurism in the academy. However, at the same time, in our servant role we shoulder a prophetic and critical responsibility. Not all black churches are preaching and practicing the Christian gospel of returning all of society's wealth to the poor; to have an African American preacher and congregation can mean the propagation of a demonic theology. Service to, love for, and affirmation of the poor and the entire church and the community mean keeping black churches accountable to what they have been called to say and do. Ultimately, black theology will have the right shoes for the twenty-first century when our faith and works risk a new way of thinking, speaking, and living. We need to get our shoes and walk this road toward freedom.

Notes

INTRODUCTION

1. One could argue that Stokely Carmichael (the founder of the 1960s Black Power movement) was motivated profoundly by spirituality and theology. Toni Morrison states: "Stokely Carmichael was a student of mine [at Howard University]. ... In 1964 when he was graduating, I said, 'Stokely, where are you going now?' and he said, 'I've been accepted at Union Theological Seminary.' He was going to study theology, but first, he was going to Mississippi to work one summer in the field." See Rosemarie K. Lester, "An Interview with Toni Morrison, Hessian Radio Network, Frankfurt, West Germany," in *Critical Essays on Toni Morrison*, ed. Nellie Y. McKay (Boston: G.K. Hall & Co., 1988), p. 51.

2. For an examination of African traditional religious views of God and God's relation to humanity, see John Mbiti, *African Religions and Philosophy* (Garden City, New York: Anchor Books, 1970), pp. 39-43, 53-54; Gwinyai Muzorewa, *The Origins and Development of African Theology* (Maryknoll, New York: Orbis Books, 1985), pp. 9-14; E. Thomas Lawson, *Religions of Africa* (New York: Harper & Row, 1985), pp. 94-95; Albert J. Raboteau, *Slave Religion: The "Invisible Institution" in the Antebellum South* (New York: Oxford University Press, 1978), pp. 8-15; and Mercy Amba Oduyoye, "The Value of African Religious Beliefs and Practices for Christian Theology," in *African Theology En Route*, ed. Kofi Appiah-Kubi and Sergio Torres (Maryknoll, New York: Orbis Books, 1979), pp. 111-12.

3. For example, the theology of the Marcus Garvey movement, the thought of Minister Malcolm X, and various strands within black folk culture. See Randall K. Burkett, *Garveyism as a Religious Movement: The Institutionalization of a Black Civil Religion* (Metuchen, New Jersey: Scarecrow Press, Inc., 1978); James H. Cone, *Martin and Malcolm and America: A Dream or a Nightmare* (Maryknoll, New York: Orbis Books, 1991); and Gayraud S. Wilmore, *Black Religion and Black Radicalism*, 2d ed. (Maryknoll, New York: Orbis Books, 1983).

4. See Wilmore; also see James H. Cone, "Black Religious Thought in American History, Part 1: Origins" and "Black Religious Thought in American History, Part 2: More Recent History" in his *Speaking the Truth* (Grand Rapids, Michigan: Eerdmans, 1986).

5. See Raboteau; John W. Blassingame, ed., *Slave Testimony: Two Centuries of Letters, Speeches, Interviews, and Autobiographies* (Baton Rouge, Louisiana: Louisiana State University Press, 1977); and Norman R. Yetman, *Life Under the "Peculiar Institution": Selections from the Slave Narrative Collection* (New York: Holt, Rinehart and Winston, 1970).

6. A similar version of chapter one was presented in Dwight N. Hopkins and George Cummings, eds., *Cut Loose Your Stammering Tongue: Black Theology in the Slave Narratives* (Maryknoll, New York: Orbis Books, 1991).

7. I know of no writings specifically on Du Bois's theology and only two articles on his religion: see Herbert Aptheker, "W. E. B. Du Bois and Religion: A Brief Reassessment," *The Journal of Religious Thought* 39, number 1 (Spring-Summer 1982): 5-11; and Manning Marable, "The Black Faith of W. E. B. Du Bois: Sociocultural and Political Dimensions of Black Religion," *The Southern Quarterly* 23, number 3 (Spring 1985): 15-33. Arnold Rampersad, *The Art of Imagination of W. E. B. Du Bois* (Cambridge: Harvard University Press, 1976) makes a religious reference to Du Bois on page 86.

1. RELIGIOUS MEETINGS IN DE BUSHES

1. Thomas Wentworth Higginson, *Army Life in a Black Regiment* (New York: W. W. Norton, 1984; originally published 1869), p. 49.

Higginson commanded "the first slave regiment mustered into the service of the United States during the . . . civil war" (ibid., p. 27).

2. Ex-slave John Brown, quoted in *Weevils in the Wheat: Interviews with Virginia Ex-slaves*, ed. Charles L. Perdue, et al. (Bloomington, Indiana: Indiana University Press, 1980), p. 62; hereafter cited as Perdue.

3. For a review of the European trading in Africans and their implantation of Africans in the "New World," see Vincent Harding, *There Is a River: The Black Struggle for Freedom in America* (New York: Harcourt Brace Jovanovich, Inc., 1981), chapters 1-2; and John Hope Franklin, *From Slavery to Freedom: A History of Negro Americans* (New York: Alfred A. Knopf, 1980), chapters 3-5.

4. Ogbu U. Kalu, "Church Presence in Africa: A Historical Analysis of the Evangelization Process," in *African Theology En Route*, ed. Kofi Appiah-Kubi and Sergio Torres (Maryknoll, New York: Orbis Books, 1979), p. 18.

This quote comes from a white missionary at the beginning of the twentieth century. However these theological views were held since the first European contact with Africa.

5. Kofi Asare Opoku, *West African Traditional Religion* (Jurong, Singapore: FEP International Private Limited, 1978), p. 27.

6. John S. Mbiti, *Concepts of God in Africa* (London: SPCK, 1970), p. 6. Also see Gwinyai H. Muzorewa, *The Origins and Development of African Theology* (Maryknoll, New York: Orbis Books, 1985), p. 9.

7. Mbiti, pp. 8-21.

8. Mbiti, pp. 31-76. Also see Muzorewa, p. 10.

9. Mercy Amba Oduyoye, "The Value of African Religious Beliefs and Practices for Christian Theology," in Appiah-Kubi and Torres, p. 111. Also see Muzorewa, p. 17; E. Thomas Lawson, *Religions of Africa* (New York: Harper & Row, 1985), p. 97; and John Mbiti, *African Religions and Philosophy* (Garden City, New York.: Anchor Books, 1970), p. 141.

10. Oduyoye, p. 111. Kofi Asare Opoku concurs when he writes: "A close observation of Africa and its societies will reveal that religion is at the root of African culture and is the determining principle of African life. It is no exaggeration, therefore, to say that in traditional Africa, religion is life and life, religion. Africans are engaged in religion in whatever they do" (p. 1).

11. For treatments of the African influence in slave religion, see Gayraud S. Wilmore, *Black Religion and Black Radicalism*, 2d ed. (Maryknoll, New York: Orbis Books, 1983), chapter 1; and Albert J. Raboteau, *Slave Religion: The "Invisible*

Institution" in the Antebellum South (Oxford: Oxford University Press, 1978), chapters 1-2.

12. Ex-slave Becky Ilsey, quoted in Lawrence Levine, *Black Culture and Black Consciousness: Afro-American Folk Thought From Slavery to Freedom* (New York: Oxford University Press, 1981), p. 41.

13. Ex-slave Archie Booker, quoted in Perdue, pp. 52-53.

14. Ex-slave Charles Grandy, quoted in Perdue, p. 119.

15. Ex-slave Arthur Greene, quoted in Perdue, pp. 124-25.

16. Ex-slave Levi Pollard, quoted in Perdue, p. 230.

17. These ex-slave quotations are excerpted from James Mellon, ed., *Bullwhip Days: The Slaves Remember, An Oral History* (New York: Weidenfeld & Nicolson, 1988), p. 190; and Norman R. Yetman, *Life Under the "Peculiar Institution": Selections from the Slave Narrative Collection* (New York: Holt Rinehart and Winston, 1970), pp. 53, 231, 56.

18. These ex-slave quotations are excerpted from Mellon, pp. 186-87, 195-95.

Other ex-slave references to the cultural dimension of the Invisible Institution can be found in Levine, pp. 41, 42; Perdue, pp. 100, 322; Clifton H. Johnson, ed., *God Struck Me Dead: Religious Conversion Experiences and Autobiographies of Ex-slaves* (Philadelphia: Pilgrim Press, 1969), p. 153; and Eugene D. Genovese, *Roll, Jordan, Roll: The World the Slaves Made* (New York: Pantheon Books, 1974), p. 214. For example,

" 'Cause we wanted to serve God in our own way. You see, 'legion needs a little motion—specially if you gwine feel de spirret" (Perdue, p. 100).

"White folks can't pray right to de black man's God. Can't nobody do it for you. You got to call on God yourself when de spirit tell you" (Genovese, p. 214).

19. Perdue, pp. 93 and 161. Throughout the slave narratives one discovers this reference to the turned over pot. Also see Yetman, p. 229.

20. Ex-slave West Turner, quoted in Perdue, p. 290.

21. Ex-slave Ishrael Massie, quoted in Perdue, p. 208.

22. Perdue, pp. 183, 230, 150, 71.

23. See Yetman, p. 33; and Mellon, pp. 196-97.

24. See John W. Blassingame, ed., *Slave Testimony: Two Centuries of Letters, Speeches, Interviews, and Autobiographies* (Baton Rouge, Louisiana: Louisiana State University Press, 1977), p. 411.

Similarly, ex-slave Frederick Douglass writes: "For of all the slaveholders with whom I have ever met, religious slaveholders are the worst. I have ever found them the meanest and basest, the most cruel and cowardly, of all others" ("Narrative of the Life of Frederick Douglass, An American Slave," in *Black Voices: An Anthology of Afro-American Literature*, ed. Abraham Chapman [New York: The New American Library, 1968], p. 256).

25. Ex-slave Oliver Wendell Jackson, quoted in William C. Emerson, M.D., *Stories and Spirituals of the Negro Slave* (Boston: The Gorham Press, 1930), p. 35.

26. See B. A. Botkin, ed., *Lay My Burden Down: A Folk History of Slavery* (Chicago: University of Chicago Press, 1957), p. 91.

References for quotations on white sermons and catechisms can be found in

Perdue, pp. 241, 183; Harriet A. Jacobs, *Incidents in the Life of a Slave Girl, Written by Herself* (Cambridge: Harvard University Press, 1987), pp. 68-69; and Frederick Douglass, *Life and Times of Frederick Douglass* (New York: Collier Books, 1973; the first condensed version originally published in 1845), p. 157.

27. See Yetman, pp. 231-32. Also review Levine, pp. 41-42, 46; and Perdue, pp. 207, 290.

28. Other ex-slave narratives substantiate white theological hubris. See Botkin, pp. 25, 94; Yetman, pp. 180-81, 262.

29. Charles Davenport, quoted in Yetman, p. 75.

30. Henry Bibb, *Narrative of the Life and Adventures of Henry Bibb, An American Slave, Written by Himself* (Philadelphia: Rhistoric Publications, n.d.), p. 114. Bibb originally published his book in 1849.

31. For only a sampling of slave accounts of praying for freedom, see the following slave stories in Perdue, pp. 94, 115; Mellon, pp. 190, 196; Yetman pp. 177, 308, 312; and Blassingame, pp. 661, 700.

32. Solomon Northup, *Twelve Years a Slave* (New York: Dover Publications, 1970; originally published in 1854), p. 68.

33. Botkin, p. 26.

34. Charles Grandy, quoted in Perdue, p. 115.

35. J. W. Lindsay, quoted in Blassingame, p. 404. Also note Horace Muse's comment, "No res' fer niggers 'till God he step in an' put a stop to de white folks meanness," in Perdue, p. 216.

36. The theological view of "momentary God" comes from a narrative in Botkin, p. 34. The reference to Ole Aunt Sissy comes from Perdue, p. 127.

37. Miles Mark Fisher, *Negro Slave Songs in the United States* (Secaucus, New Jersey: The Citadel Press, 1978), p. 54.

38. Ex-slave James L. Bradley, quoted in Blassingame, p. 690.

39. Blassingame, pp. 125-26.

40. Perdue, pp. 72, 33; Yetman, p. 48; and Botkin, p. 178.

41. Ishrael Massie, quoted in Perdue, p. 206. Also see another ex-bondsman's similar claim on pages 80 and 93-94.

42. Perdue, pp. 274, 1. Other references to the theology of the heaven-hell kingdoms can be found in Mellon, p. 178, and Botkin, p. 121. George White stated: "Dey ask me de other day if I thought any of de slaveholders was in heaven an' I told 'em no 'cause dey was too mean" (Perdue, p. 311).

43. Botkin, p. 163; Perdue, pp. 93-94.

44. Yetman, pp. 113-14. For a description of the slaves' image of Jubilee, see Fisher, p. 121. For the slaves' self-interpretation as the children of God, see Yetman, p. 205.

45. Perdue, p. 184.

46. Levine, p. 28.

47. Fisher, pp. 66ff. and John Lovell, Jr., *Black Song: The Forge and the Flame* (New York: Paragon House Publishers, 1986), pp. 125, 191, 228, 379. For further examination of the theological and religious thought of Rev. Nat Turner, see Stephen B. Oates, *The Fires of Jubilee: Nat Turner's Fierce Rebellion* (New York: The New American Library, 1975). For Harriet Tubman's theology, review Sarah Bradford, *Harriet Tubman: The Moses of Her People* (Secaucus, New Jersey: The Citadel Press, 1961).

48. The slaves considered all aspects of Jesus as prophetic in the sense of sub-

verting white Christianity. Therefore I do not develop a specific section on Jesus' prophetic office.

49. See Levine, p. 43; and William F. Allen, Charles P. Ware, and Lucy M. Garrison, eds., *Slave Songs of the United States* (New York: Books for Libraries Press, 1971; originally published 1867), p. 11.

50. Fisher, pp. 16-17.

51. See Harding; also see Wilmore.

52. Jacobs, p. 70; Fisher, p. 48.

53. Yetman, p. 228.

54. Allen, Ware, and Garrison, pp. 70, 97.

55. Yetman, p. 225.

56. Former slave Phillip Ward recalls, "Marsa bringing his son, Levey . . . down to the cabin. They both took her [a black woman] — the father showing the son what it was all about" (Perdue, p. 301).

57. Rev. Bentley, quoted in Levine, p. 49.

58. Ex-slave Charlie Moses, quoted in Mellon, p. 182.

59. Ex-slave James L. Bradley, quoted in Blassingame, p. 689.

60. Bibb, p. 17.

61. Ex-slave Thomas Likers, quoted in Blassingame, p. 395.

62. Ex-slave Arthur Greene, quoted in Perdue, pp. 125, 153.

63. Fisher, p. 74.

64. Botkin, p. 176. For the reference to the black woman plowing in the field, see Botkin, p. 175.

65. Perdue, pp. 55-56.

66. Perdue, p. 85. For fuller details on the theological significance of the Underground Railroad, see Bradford.

67. Yetman, p. 53. Other quotes can be found in Botkin, p. 26, and Perdue, pp. 245, 226.

68. Perdue, p. 124.

69. Genovese, p. 605.

70. Genovese, p. 602.

71. Blassingame, p. 652.

72. Bibb, p. 17.

73. Ex-slave Lunsford Lane, quoted in Gilbert Osofsky, ed., *Puttin' On Ole Massa* (New York: Harper & Row, 1969), p. 9.

74. Ex-slave Robert Smalls, quoted in Blassingame, p. 377.

75. Ex-slave Ishrael Massie, quoted in Perdue, p. 210.

76. Ex-siave Jennie Patterson, quoted in Perdue, p. 220.

77. Langston Hughes and Arna Bontemps, eds., *The Book of Negro Folklore* (New York: Dodd, Mead, 1958) p. 56.

78. Perdue, p. 128.

2. BLACK WOMEN'S SPIRITUALITY OF FUNK

1. Toni Morrison, quoted in Sandi Russell, " 'It's OK to say OK' " in *Critical Essays on Toni Morrison*, ed. Nellie Y. McKay (Boston: G. K. Hall & Co., 1988), pp. 45, 46.

2. J. Grant, "Black Theology and Black Women," in *Black Theology: A Documentary History, 1966-1979*, ed. Gayraud S. Wilmore and James H. Cone (Maryknoll, New York: Orbis Books, 1979), pp. 418-33.

3. Katie G. Cannon, "Moral Wisdom in the Black Women's Literary Tradition," *The Annual of the Society of Christian Ethics*, ed. L. Rasmussen (1984): 175.

4. Delores S. Williams, "Black Women's Literature and the Task of Feminist Theology," in *Immaculate and Powerful*, ed. C. W. Atkinson, C. H. Buchanan, and M. R. Miles (Boston: Beacon Press, 1985), and "Womanist Theology: Black Women's Voices," *Christianity and Crisis* (March 2, 1987).

5. Toni Morrison, *The Bluest Eye* (New York: Washington Square Press, 1970), p. 62.

6. Ibid., pp. 52-53.

7. Ibid., pp. 109-10.

8. Toni Morrison, *Beloved* (New York: New American Library, 1987), pp. 15-17.

9. Ibid., p. 256.

10. Toni Morrison, *Song of Solomon* (New York: New American Library, 1977), p. 91.

11. *The Bluest Eye*, p. 104.

12. Toni Morrison, *Sula* (New York: New American Library, 1973), p. 50.

13. Ibid., p. 142.

14. This is what Alice Walker means when she defines womanist in *In Search of Our Mothers' Gardens* (New York: Harcourt Brace Jovanovich, 1983, p. xii). "Womanist is to feminist as purple to lavender," writes Walker. Specifically, black and white women both endure male chauvinism and thus overlap in a common spirituality, like purple and lavender. But just as purple is not quite lavender, so too African American women's spirituality differs from white feminism due to white women's potential participation in white supremacy against black women.

15. Toni Morrison, *Beloved*, pp. 31ff. and 78-85.

16. Toni Morrison, *Tar Baby* (New York: New American Library, 1981), p. 208.

17. *Sula*, p. 55.

18. *The Bluest Eye*, p. 19.

19. Ibid., p. 20.

20. Ibid., pp. 159-60.

21. *Beloved*, p. 180.

22. Even Jadine in *Tar Baby* originated from poor working-class origins. As a recent member of the black middle class, she still struggles with the spiritual roots of her African American ancestry and the anemic spiritual aspirations of the white petty bourgeoisie.

23. *The Bluest Eye*, pp. 109-10.

24. Ibid., p. 71.

25. Ibid., p. 75.

26. *Tar Baby*, p. 203.

27. *Beloved*, p. 150.

28. *The Bluest Eye*, p. 68.

29. *Sula*, p. 17.

30. *Beloved*, p. 189.

31. *The Bluest Eye*, p. 62.

32. *Sula*, pp. 28-29.

33. Ibid., pp. 92-93.

34. Ibid., p. 143.

35. *Tar Baby*, p. 207.

36. *Beloved*, p. 142.

37. *Song of Solomon*, p. 149.

38. *Sula*, p. 52.

39. Ibid., pp. 31-35.

40. *Beloved*, p. 162.

41. In *Just a Sister Away* Dr. Renita J. Weems writes: "We are frequently just a sister away from our healing. We need a woman, a sister, who will see in our destitution a jagged image of what one day could be her own story. We need a sister who will respond with mercy" (*Just a Sister Away* [San Diego, California: LuraMedia, 1988], back cover).

42. Woman-to-woman connectedness is not a naive utopian relation. It has intense moments of betrayal and pain as shown by Nel's discovery of adultery between her husband and Sula. Even though a rift occurs between the two women over this affair, in the long term the woman-to-woman spiritual bond proves unbreakable. The story concludes with Nel realizing that loving Sula was really like the left and right arm on the same body. "We was girls together," confesses Nel on the last page of the novel.

43. *Sula*, pp. 84, 95.

44. *Song of Solomon*, p. 311.

45. *Sula*, pp. 127-28.

46. *Song of Solomon*, pp. 288-89.

47. *Beloved*, pp. 248-49.

48. Ibid., p. 247.

49. *Sula*, p. 95.

50. See Pilate, *Song of Solomon*, p. 141; and Denver, *Beloved*, pp. 244-45. Sethe also goes to the Clearing, a place where Denver's grandmother used to preach before she died, to commune with and seek advice from this same grandmother (*Beloved*, p. 89).

51. *The Bluest Eye*, p. 9.

52. *Beloved*, p. 31.

53. See William Mosley, *What Color Was Jesus?* (Chicago: African American Images, 1987).

54. *Tar Baby*, p. 183.

55. *Beloved*, p. 87.

56. In addition to characters mentioned in the text, other examples of healing-saving conjurer women are Ella, "a practical woman who believed there was a root either to chew or avoid for every ailment" (*Beloved*, p. 256); and Circe, the "healer and deliverer" who saves the life of Pilate and Macon Dead the elder (*Song of Solomon*, p. 248).

57. For references to Pilate's abilities and feats, see *Song of Solomon*, pp. 142, 150, 132. Other indications of Pilate's love of community and unique spiritual gifts are found in the following description: Pilate "never bothered anybody, was helpful to everybody, but who also was believed to have the power to step out of her skin, set a bush afire from fifty yards, and turn a man into a ripe rutabaga" (p. 94).

58. *Beloved*, p. 137.

59. Ibid., p. 177.

60. For the quoted descriptions of Baby Suggs's Christian and unorthodox faith, see *Beloved*, pp. 146, 87. For a description of the Christian and non-Christian women who gather to exorcise Beloved, see *Beloved*, p. 257.

61. *The Bluest Eye*, p. 108.

62. Ibid., p. 14.

63. *Song of Solomon*, p. 94.

64. *Tar Baby*, p. 281.

65. *Beloved*, p. 16.

66. *Beloved*, p. 266. The description of Sethe's slow demise to an infantile state is found on page 250.

67. See Pilate in *Song of Solomon*, p. 54; Sethe's talk with Denver, *Beloved*, p. 62; and the yellow-dress African woman in *Tar Baby*, pp. 45, 46, 48.

68. *Beloved*, pp. 87-89.

3. "NOW, YOU GOINTER TO HEAR LIES ABOVE SUSPICION"

1. Langston Hughes, "The Negro Artist and the Racial Mountain," in *On Being Black: Writings by Afro-Americans from Frederick Douglass to the Present*, ed. Charles T. Davis and Daniel Walden (Greenwich, Connecticut: Fawcett Publications, 1970), pp. 159-63.

2. "The Man Makes and the Woman Takes," in *Afro-American Folktales: Stories from Black Traditions in the New World*, ed. Roger D. Abrahams (New York: Pantheon Books, 1985), p. 43.

3. Ibid., p. 42.

4. Zora Neale Hurston, *Mules and Men* (Bloomington, Indiana: Indiana University Press, 1978), p. 151.

5. Abrahams, p. 42.

6. Abrahams, p. 43.

7. Abrahams, pp. 42-44.

8. Abrahams, pp. 65-66.

9. Unless otherwise stated, the following quotations from James Weldon Johnson, "The Creation" are taken from *Black Voices: An Anthology of Afro-American Literature*, ed. Abraham Chapman (New York: New American Library, 1968), pp. 364-66. This sermon/poem is also cited as "The Creation," in *Talk That Talk: An Anthology of African-American Storytelling*, ed. Linda Goss and Marian E. Barnes (New York: Simon and Schuster, 1989), pp. 187-89.

10. The folk culture offers various female images of God, for example, in the creation of humanity. "This Great God,/Like a mammy bending over her baby,/ Kneeled down in the dust/Toiling over a lump of clay/Till He shaped it in His own image" (Chapman, p. 366).

11. "The Preacher and His Farmer Brother," in *American Negro Folklore*, ed. J. Mason Brewer (Chicago: Quadrangle Books, 1968), p. 116.

12. Frederick Douglass, "Letter to His Master, Thomas Auld," in *Dark Symphony: Negro Literature in America*, ed. James A. Emmanuel and Theodore L. Gross (New York: The Free Press, 1968), p. 21.

13. Mrs. E. L. Smith, "The Spirit Defeats the Devil," in *American Negro Folktales*, ed. Richard M. Dorson (Greenwich, Connecticut: Fawcett Publications, 1967), pp. 203-4.

14. "Barney McKay," in Goss and Barnes, pp. 322-25.

15. Rev. A.C.W. Shelton, "Wasn't It a Storming Time?" in *Gumbo Ya-Ya: Folk Tales of Louisiana*, ed. Lyle Saxon, Edward Dreyer, and Robert Tallant (Gretna, Louisiana: Pelican Publishing Co., 1988), pp. 477-78.

16. Owen Dodson, "Black Mother Praying," in Chapman, pp. 451-54.

17. "Why We Come to Church," in Brewer, pp. 119-20.

18. Tommy Carter, "Old Boss and John at the Praying Tree," in Dorson, pp. 153-54.

19. Harrison Stanfill, "A Dime for the Sack," in Dorson, p. 155.

20. Julius Lester, "How the Snake Got His Rattles," in Goss and Barnes, pp. 82-87.

21. C. L. Franklin, "The Prodigal Son," in Goss and Barnes, pp. 190-98.

22. Ruby Dee, "Aunt Zurletha," in Goss and Barnes, pp. 278-83.

23. Langston Hughes, in Davis and Walden, pp. 179-80.

24. Arna Bontemps, in Chapman, pp. 422-24.

25. Langston Hughes, in Davis and Walden, p. 268.

26. See Sterling Brown's poem "Sister Lou," which also presents us with various theological interpretive meanings (*The Book of Negro Folklore*, ed. Langston Hughes and Arna Bontemps [New York: Dodd, Mead & Company, 1983], pp. 549-50).

27. J. California Cooper, "The Life You Live (May Not Be Your Own)," in *Breaking Ice: An Anthology of Contemporary African-American Fiction*, ed. Terry McMillan (New York: Penguin Books, 1990), pp. 146-63.

28. Very often the Trickster is motivated by basic necessities, thereby standing for the fundamental survival needs of society's have-nots. The Trickster's life does not emphasize or prioritize profit and frivolities like those with stomachs full. On the contrary, Rabbit tales are motivated by those who hunger. Rabbit seeks water ("Tar Baby," in Hughes and Bontemps, pp. 1-2.), hogs ("Rabbit Teaches Bear a Song," ibid., p. 3), milk, goobers, and land for his family ("Brer Rabbit and His Cow," ibid., p. 4, "Brer Fox and the Goobers," ibid., p. 10, and "Sheer Crops," ibid., p. 13, respectively), collard greens (John Courtney, "Take My Place," in Dorson, p. 85), and peanuts (Patricia Jones-Jackson, *When Roots Die: Endangered Traditions on the Sea Islands* (Athens, Georgia: University of Georgia Press, 1987), p. 102.

29. In Abrahams, pp. 53-62.

30. For another example of Brer Rabbit's encounters with God, see "Brer Rabbit and the Lord," in Jones-Jackson, pp. 116-18).

31. Silas Altheimer, "The Quail and the Rabbit," in Dorson, p. 109.

32. William J. Faulkner, "Brer Tiger and the Big Wind," in Goss and Barnes, pp. 25-28.

33. "The Tug-of-War Between Elephant and Whale," in Abrahams, pp. 89-91.

34. John Blackamore, "The Elephant, the Lion, and the Monkey," in Dorson, pp. 98-99. Another version appears in Abrahams ("The Signifying Monkey," pp. 101-5). Yet another rendition is told in Roger D. Abrahams, *Deep Down in the Jungle: Negro Narrative Folklore from the Streets of Philadelphia* (New York: Aldine Publishing Co., 1970), pp. 113-19. In this last version Lion kills the Monkey, but Trickster Baboon (Monkey's cousin) finally kills Lion.

35. "Buh Lion an Buh Goat," in Brewer, pp. 16-17. For other examples of the liberating nature of word power, see Hughes and Bontemps, pp. 1-8; John Blackamore, "Who Ate Up the Food?," in Dorson, p. 71ff.; and Jones-Jackson, pp. 120-22.

36. J. D. Suggs, "The Bear in the Mudhole," in Dorson, pp. 80-81. For a similar theological interpretation, see John Blackamore, "Old Boss Wants into Heaven," in Dorson, pp. 157-162.

37. The following stories are found respectively in Brewer, pp. 55-57, pp. 57-59, and pp. 63-64; and in Goss and Barnes, pp. 320-21.

38. Other trickster figures in the tradition include John in the "John versus the Old Massa" cycle (see Dorson, pp. 166, 271; Hurston, pp. 90-91) and Joe Meek in "The Ballad of Joe Meek" (Chapman, pp. 414-18).

39. William Melvin Kelley, "Cry for Me," in Emmanuel and Gross, pp. 456-70.

40. Abrahams, *Deep Down in the Jungle*, pp. 101-2.

41. "Sinking of the Titantic," in Hughes and Bontemps, pp. 366-367.

42. For another folk hero who exhibits some Shine traits, see "The Ballad of John Henry" (Brewer, pp. 201-2).

43. Abrahams, *Deep Down in the Jungle*, pp. 136-42. For two other versions of the Stackolee (or Stackalee) story, see Hughes and Bontemps, pp. 359-61 and pp. 361-62.

44. Jean Toomer, "Karintha," in Chapman, pp. 64-65.

45. Zora Neale Hurston, "High John De Conquer," in Hughes and Bontemps, pp. 93-102.

46. For examples, see the poem on Harriet Tubman (Goss and Barnes, p. 472); the short biography of Nancy Vaughn, the black prophetess (Brewer, pp. 36-38); the play about Otis Redding (Ben Caldwell, "The King of Soul or the Devil and Otis Redding," in *New Plays From the Black Theatre*, ed. Ed Bullins [New York: Bantam Books, 1969], p. 176); the pantheon of Tricksters in poetry (Davis and Walden, p. 260; Chapman, pp. 402-3); poems on Malcolm X, the liberating word (Ted Joans, "My Ace of Spades"; Etheridge Knight, "It Was a Funky Deal"; and Kattie M. Cumbo, "Malcolm," all in *Black Out Loud: An Anthology of Modern Poems by Black Americans*, ed. Arnold Adoff (New York: Dell Publishing Company, 1970), pp. 53, 54, and 56 respectively); and the histories of King Charley (Brewer, pp. 32-34) and the Zulu King of Mardi Gras (Saxon, et al., p. 2ff.), both of whom link Africa, the drum, poor blacks, African American culture, and pageantry to freedom.

47. Brewer, pp. 184-85.

48. Brewer, pp. 190-92.

49. Hughes and Bontemps, pp. 400-401.

50. Brewer, pp. 194-95.

51. Hughes and Bontemps, pp. 405-6.

52. Jasper Love, quoted in William Ferris, *Blues from the Delta: An Illustrated Documentary on the Music and Musicians of the Mississippi Delta* (Garden City, New York: Anchor Books , 1978), pp. 25-26. Also see the Hughes and Bontemps section on the blues.

53. See Brewer, pp. 172, 174, 181, respectively for the above three songs.

54. See Hughes and Bontemps, pp. 379, 380.

55. See Brewer, pp. 179-80.

56. Hughes and Bontemps, p. 375.

57. James Thomas, quoted in Ferris, p. 79.

58. See Brewer, p. 174, and Hughes and Bontemps, p. 385.

59. John Junior, quoted in Brewer, pp. 265-69.

60. In Emmanuel and Gross, pp. 71-72.

61. Chapman, pp. 205-14.

62. Goss and Barnes, pp. 278-83.

63. Langston Hughes, quoted in Emmanuel and Gross, pp. 206-7.

64. Brewer, p. 309.

65. Caesar Grant, in Hughes and Bontemps, pp. 62-65.

66. Hurston, p. 21.

67. Ibid., p. 93.

4. W. E. B. Du BOIS

1. W. E. B. Du Bois, "Behold the Land," *Freedomways*, First Quarter (October 20, 1946): 14.

2. Ex-slave William Craft, *Running a Thousand Miles for Freedom: Or, The Escape of William and Ellen Craft from Slavery* (Salem, New Hampshire: Ayer Company Publishers, 1991), p. 1.

3. Du Bois also spoke to and reflected on the cultural identity and self-affirming aspirations of African Americans. For example, he wrote: "From my childhood, I have been impressed with the beauty of Negro skin-color and astonished at the blindness of whites who cannot see it" (*Dusk of Dawn: An Essay Toward an Auto-biography of a Race Concept* [New York: Harcourt, Brace and Company, 1940], p. 272). Foreshadowing the cultural renaissance of the 1960s Black Power movement, he wrote in 1939: "A racial technique in art and propaganda is inevitable. . . . Our Art can make black beautiful" (see "The Position of the Negro in the American Social Order: Where Do We Go From Here?" in *Writings by W. E. B. Du Bois in Periodicals Edited by Others, Volume 3: 1935-1944*, comp. and ed. Herbert Aptheker [Millwood, New York: Kraus-Thomson Organization Limited, 1982], pp. 79-80. Hereafter cited as *Periodicals* along with the specific volume).

4. W. E. B. Du Bois, *The Autobiography of W. E. B. Du Bois: A Soliloquy of Viewing My Life from the Last Decade of Its First Century* (New York: International Publishers, 1968), p. 156. Hereafter *Autobiography*. Also see his *Dusk of Dawn*, p. 28.

5. W. E. B. Du Bois, *Darkwater: Voices from Within the Veil* (New York: AMS Press, 1969, reprinted from the 1920 edition), p. 159.

6. Herbert Aptheker, ed., *W. E. B. Du Bois: Prayers for Dark People* (Amherst, Massachusetts: University of Massachusetts Press, 1980), p. 33.

7. For notable works on Du Bois's life and writings, see Robert W. McDonnell, *W. E. B. Du Bois: The Papers of W. E. B. Du Bois 1803 (1877-1963) 1979* (Amherst, Massachusetts: Microfilming Corporation of America, A New York Times Company, University of Massachusetts, 1981); Gerald Horne, *Black and Red: W. E. B. Du Bois and the Afro-American Response to the Cold War 1944-1963* (Albany, New York: State University of New York Press, 1986); Manning Marable, *W. E. B. Du Bois: Black Radical Democrat* (Boston: Twayne Publishers, 1986); Herbert Aptheker, *The Literary Legacy of W. E. B. Du Bois* (White Plains, New York: Kraus International Publications, 1989); and Arnold Rampersad, *W. E. B. Du Bois: The Art of Imagination* (New York: Schocken Books, 1990).

8. W. E. B. Du Bois, "Socialism and the American Negro (May 1960)," in *Against Racism: Unpublished Essays, Papers, Addresses, 1887-1961 W. E. B. Du Bois*, ed. Herbert Aptheker (Amherst, Massachusetts: University of Massachusetts Press, 1985), p. 303.

9. *Autobiography*, pp. 91-92.

10. See Du Bois, "Federal Action Programs and Community Action in the South," in *Periodicals, Volume 3*, p. 127.

11. Ibid.

12. *Autobiography*, pp. 91-92.

13. Ibid., p. 92.

14. See Du Bois "Federal Action Programs and Community Action in the South," p. 127.

15. W. E. B. Du Bois, "My Character," in *The Seventh Son: The Thought and Writings of W. E. B. Du Bois, Volume 2*, ed. Julius Lester (New York: Random House, 1971), p. 732.

16. *Autobiography*, p. 93.

17. See W. E. B. Du Bois, "The Church," *The Crisis*, vol. 11, no. 6 (April 1916), p. 302. Also review his "The Negro As a National Asset," in *Periodicals, Volume 2*, p. 206.

18. W. E. B. Du Bois, "Selah!" in *W. E. B. Du Bois: The Crisis Writings*, ed. Daniel Walden (Greenwich, Connecticut: Fawcett Publications, 1972), p. 366. Hereafter cited as *Crisis Writings*.

19. W. E. B. Du Bois, "The New Negro Church," in *Against Racism*, p. 84.

20. See W. E. B. Du Bois "The Winds of Time," *The Chicago Defender*, 4 January 1947, p. 15.

21. W. E. B. Du Bois, "The Damnation of Women," in *The Seventh Son, Volume 1*, pp. 517-19. Anna Julia Cooper was a black woman; born a slave in Raleigh, North Carolina, 10 August 1858, she died in 1964. See "Anna Julia Cooper," in *Black Women in Nineteenth-Century American Life*, ed. and intro. Bert James Loewenberg and Ruth Bogin (University Park, Pennsylvania: Pennsylvania State University Press, 1976), pp. 317-31.

22. The reference to "mouthing of creeds" comes from Du Bois's "Postscript: Darrow," *The Crisis*, vol. 35, no. 6 (June 1928), p. 203; for remarks on "biblical fairy tales," see his "The Future of Wilberforce University," *The Journal of Negro Education*, vol. 9, no. 4 (October 1940), p. 564.

23. W. E. B. Du Bois, "Postscript: Darrow," p. 203.

24. Du Bois, *Dusk of Dawn*, p. 33. Briggs taught at Union Theological Seminary in New York City and was suspended from the Presbyterian ministry in 1893 for opposing the inerrancy dogma of Presbyterian theology. Du Bois sided with Briggs because Du Bois believed that religion was life and not the literal words in a book. Furthermore, he believed that God became manifest in human activities toward the full realization of human potential, which irrational biblical theology fenced in. On Briggs, see H. Shelton Smith, Robert T. Handy, and Lefferts A. Loetscher, eds., *American Christianity, An Historical Interpretation with Representative Documents, Volume II* (New York: Charles Scribner's Sons, 1963), pp. 275-79 and 324-25.

25. *Autobiography*, p. 111.

26. W. E. B. Du Bois, "The Souls of White Folk," in *Periodicals, Volume 2*, p. 29.

27. Du Bois, *Darkwater*, p. 30; "The Souls of White Folk," pp. 25-26.

28. It is quite likely that Du Bois was citing this Genesis passage. As noted earlier, he grew up in the Congregational Church and its Sunday School. He also wrote *Prayers for Dark People*. His writings are filled with Old Testament prophetic imagery; for instance, see his "Niagara Address of 1906," in *A Documentary History of the Negro People in the United States, Volume 2*, ed. Herbert Aptheker (Secaucus, New Jersey: The Citadel Press, 1972), p. 909, and his "Editorial," *The Crisis*, vol. 8, no. 1 (May 1914), p. 26.

29. See W. E. B. Du Bois, "Superior Race," in *Periodicals, Volume 2*, p. 187.

30. See Du Bois, "The Souls of White Folk," p. 29; regarding his "color line" view, see *The Souls of Black Folk* (New York: The New American Library, 1969), p. 54.

31. Examine W. E. B. Du Bois, "The Church and the Negro," in *Crisis Writings*, p. 334; "Postscript: Rose Ward Hunt," *The Crisis*, vol. 34, no. 5 (July 1927) p. 168; *The Christian Century*, 9 December 1931, p. 1554; and "Will the Church Remove the Color Line?" in *Periodicals, Volume 2*, p. 315.

32. *Autobiography*, p. 286.

33. See Du Bois, "The Church," p. 302; *Autobiography*, pp. 285-86; *The Seventh Son, Volume 2*, p. 733; and "The Negro Church," in *Against Racism*, p. 84.

34. Du Bois, "Will the Church Remove the Color Line?" p. 315; and *The Christian Century*, 9 December 1931, p. 1554.

35. Du Bois, *Periodicals, Volume 2*, p. 316; also see *Crisis Writings*, p. 72; and "Declaration of Principles," in *The Seventh Son, Volume 1*, p. 431.

36. Du Bois, "The Church and the Negro," in *The Crisis*, vol. 6, no. 6 (October 1913), p. 291.

37. W. E. B. Du Bois, "The World in Council," in *Crisis Writings*, pp. 234-35.

38. "Declaration of Principles," in *The Seventh Son, Volume 1*, p. 430. Du Bois organized the Niagara Movement in 1905 as a political movement. The first protest organization at the turn of the century, it stands as the historical predecessor of the National Association for the Advancement of Colored People.

39. W. E. B. Du Bois, "I Am Resolved," in *Crisis Writings*, p. 57.

40. See W. E. B. Du Bois, "Credo," in *Darkwater*, p. 3.

41. W. E. B. Du Bois, "My Evolving Program for Negro Freedom," in *What The Negro Wants*, ed. Rayford W. Logan (New York: Agathon Press, 1969), p. 38; also see *Autobiography*, p. 124.

42. Du Bois, *Prayers for Dark People*, p. 62.

43. W. E. B. Du Bois, "On Growing Old," in his *An ABC of Color* (New York: International Publishers, third printing, 1983), p. 185.

44. Du Bois, *Prayers for Dark People*, p. 60.

45. W. E. B. Du Bois, "Democracy," in *The Crisis*, vol. 12, no. 1 (May 1916), p. 29.

46. W. E. B. Du Bois, "The Song of the Smoke," in *The Horizon*, vol. 1, no. 2 (February 1907), p. 5.

47. W. E. B. Du Bois, "A Litany at Atlanta," in *Darkwater*, p. 27.

48. *Autobiography*, p. 43.

49. See Du Bois's 10 January 1956 letter to Herbert Aptheker in *The Correspondence of W. E. B. Du Bois, Volume 3, Selections, 1944-1963*, ed. Herbert Aptheker (Amherst, Massachusetts: University of Massachusetts Press, 1978), pp. 395-96. Hereafter cited as *Correspondence* along with specific volume number.

50. *Correspondence, Volume 3*, p. 223.

51. *Correspondence, Volume 3*, p. 27.

52. Du Bois, "The Souls of White Folk," in *Darkwater*, p. 36.

53. W. E. B. Du Bois, "Satterlee," in *The Horizon*, vol. 1, no. 6 (June 1907), pp. 4-5.

54. Du Bois, "Will the Church Remove the Color Line?" p. 1554; and in *Periodicals, Volume 2*, p. 312. The "War is Murder" reference comes from *Darkwater*, p. 4.

55. Review W. E. B. Du Bois, *In Battle for Peace: The Story of My 83rd Birthday* (New York: Masses & Mainstream, 1952), p. 170.

56. *Periodicals, Volume 1*, p. 17.

57. See W. E. B. Du Bois, "The Over-Look," in *The Horizon*, vol. 5, no. 2 (December 1909), p. 1.

58. See Du Bois, "The Future of Wilberforce University," pp. 564-65; also *Periodicals, Volume 3*, pp. 107-8.

59. Du Bois, in *Periodicals, Volume 2*, p. 67.

60. Du Bois, *An ABC of Color*, p. 18; also found in *Darkwater*, p. 3.

61. For the decisive place of a black Jesus Christ in the nascent black theology movement, see Albert B. Cleage, *The Black Messiah* (New York: Sheed and Ward, 1968) and James H. Cone, *Black Theology and Black Power* (New York: Seabury Press, 1969).

62. Du Bois, *An ABC of Color*, pp. 167-68.

63. W. E. B. Du Bois, "Christmas," *The Crisis*, vol. 3, no. 2 (December 1911), p. 65.

64. Du Bois, *Darkwater*, pp. 54-55.

65. W. E. B. Du Bois, "The Church and the Negro," *The Crisis*, vol. 6, no. 6 (October 1913), p. 291; also in *Crisis Writings*, p. 334.

66. W. E. B. Du Bois, "Easter," in *The Seventh Son, Volume 2*, p. 19.

67. W. E. B. Du Bois, "The Second Coming," in *Darkwater*, p. 107.

68. W. E. B. Du Bois, "Jesus Christ in Georgia," in *The Seventh Son, Volume 2*, pp. 20-29; also see a similar story titled "Jesus Christ in Texas," in *Darkwater*, pp. 123-33.

69. Du Bois, *The Crisis Writings*, p. 60.

70. W. E. B. Du Bois, "The Immediate Program of the American Negro," in *Crisis Writings*, p. 73.

71. Du Bois, *Dusk of Dawn*, p. 285.

72. *Darkwater*, pp. 157-58.

73. *In Battle for Peace* (New York: Masses and Mainstream 1952), pp. 168-69.

74. "Social Planning for the Negro, Past and Present," in *Periodicals, Volume 3*, p. 37.

75. Du Bois, *The Crisis Writings*, p. 72; and *Darkwater*, p. 4. Du Bois specifically defines freedom: "By 'Freedom' for Negroes, I mean and still mean, full economic, political and social equality with American citizens, in thought, expression and action, with no discrimination based on race or color" ("My Evolving Program for Negro Freedom" p. 65).

76. Du Bois, *Dusk of Dawn*, pp. 169-72; also see "What Is Americanism?" in *Periodicals, Volume 2*, p. 95.

77. Du Bois, "Postscript Darrow," p. 208.

78. Du Bois, "Problem of Work," in *Periodicals, Volume 1*, p. 177.

79. Du Bois, *Prayers for Dark Peop'e*, p. 10.

80. Ibid., p. 13.

81. W. E. B. Du Bois, "St. Francis of Assisi" in *The Voice of the Negro*, vol. 3, no. 10 (October 1906), p. 422.

82. W. E. B. Du Bois, *Prayers for Dark People*, p. 21. See also pp. 57, 27.

83. Du Bois, *Darkwater*, p. 3.

84. Du Bois, "On Growing Old," p. 185.

85. Du Bois, "The Joy of Living," in *Periodicals, Volume 1*, p. 219.

86. Du Bois, in *The Correspondence, Volume 1*, pp. 477-78. See also Du Bois, "Jacob and Esau," in *Periodicals, Volume 3*, p. 217.

5. MALCOLM AND MARTIN

1. From King's sermon "Thou Fool," delivered at the Mount Pisgah Baptist Church, Chicago, Illinois, 27 August 1967, p. 2; found in the Martin Luther King, Jr., Papers, Martin Luther King, Jr., Center for Nonviolent Social Change, Atlanta, Georgia. Hereafter the King Center.

From Malcolm's speech at a May 1964 forum "What's Behind the 'Hate-Gang' Scare?" in *Malcolm X Speaks: Selected Speeches and Statements*, ed. George Breitman (New York: Grove Press, 1966), pp. 68-69.

The first comparative study of Malcolm and Martin was written by Louis E. Lomax, *To Kill a Black Man* (Los Angeles, California: Holloway House Publishing Co., 1968). However, the most comprehensive and definitive text examining their lives and thought is James H. Cone, *Martin and Malcolm and America: A Dream or a Nightmare* (Maryknoll, New York: Orbis Books, 1991).

2. Malcolm X, "The Leverett House Forum of March 18, 1964," in *The Speeches of Malcolm X at Harvard*, ed. Archie Epps (New York: William Morrow & Company, 1968), p. 133.

3. Malcolm X, *Malcolm X on Afro-American History* (New York: Pathfinder Press, 1979), p. 32.

4. Malcolm X, "We Arose From the Dead!" *Moslem World & The U.S.A.* (August-September 1956): 25. Also see his, "God's Angry Men," *New York Amsterdam News*, 18 May 1957, p. 2, and *The Autobiography of Malcolm X* (New York: Ballantine Books, 1989), p. 220.

5. See *The Autobiography of Malcolm X*, pp. 220, 313; also see his "God's Angry Men," *New York Amsterdam News*, 25 May 1957, p. 3.

6. See *The Autobiography of Malcolm X*, p. 239; *Malcolm X Speaks*, p. 222; "Not Just an American Problem, But a World Problem, February 16, 1965," in *Malcolm X: The Last Speeches*, ed. Bruce Perry (New York: Pathfinder Press, 1989), p. 172; and "Speech on 'Black Revolution,' New York, April 8, 1964," in *Two Speeches by Malcolm X* (New York: Pathfinder Press, 1981), p. 12.

7. *The Autobiography of Malcolm X*, p. 243; *Malcolm X Speaks*, p. 11.

8. Martin Luther King, Jr., *Where Do We Go From Here: Chaos or Community?* (Boston: Beacon Press, 1968), p. 36.

9. Martin Luther King, Jr., "The President's Address to the Tenth Anniversary Convention of the Southern Christian Leadership Conference, Atlanta, Georgia, August 16, 1967," in *The Rhetoric of Black Power*, ed. Robert L. Scott and Wayne Brockriede (New York: Harper & Row, 1969), p. 156. (Hereafter "August 1967 Speech.")

10. King, *Where Do We Go From Here?*, p. 37.

11. Ibid., p. 54.

12. Ibid., p. 4.

13. Ibid., p. 4. Also see King's speech to "Mississippi Leaders on Washington Campaign," p. 2, at the St. Thomas A.M.E. church, Birmingham, Alabama, February 15, 1968; found at the King Center. Here King juxtaposes the "struggle for genuine equality" with "a radical redistribution of economic power".

14. "August 1967 Speech," p. 155.

15. Ibid., p. 155.

16. Review King's speech, "Sleeping Through a Revolution," at the Chicago Joint Negro Appeal meeting, Chicago, Illinois, 10 December 1967, p. 11; found at the King Center.

17. Ibid., p. 156.

18. Martin Luther King, Jr., in David Garrow, *Bearing the Cross: Martin Luther King, Jr., and the Southern Christian Leadership Conference* (New York: Vintage Books, 1988), p. 492. Also refer to King's 6 January 1968 Chicago, Illinois, speech, p. 4; and his 18 September 1967 speech, p. 5, at Mt. Moriah Baptist Church, Atlanta, Georgia; both speeches found in the King Center. Also see "August 1967 Speech," p. 155.

19. Malcolm X, *The Autobiography of Malcolm X*, pp. 312, 254, 267-68.

20. Malcolm X, "Not just an American Problem," pp. 166-67.

21. See Malcolm X, "After the Bombing," in *Malcolm X Speaks*, p. 168; also see *Malcolm X on Afro-American History*, p. 16.

22. Malcolm X, "After the Bombing," p. 169.

23. Malcolm X, "The Leverett House Forum of March 18, 1964," p. 142.

24. Martin Luther King, Jr., "Pilgrimage to Nonviolence," in *A Testament of Hope: The Essential Writings of Martin Luther King, Jr.*, ed. James M. Washington (New York: Harper & Row, 1986), p. 38. Also see King, "Thou Fool," a sermon given at the Mount Pisgah Baptist Church in Chicago, Illinois, on August 27, 1967, p. 2; located at the King Center.

25. King, "I See the Promised Land," in *A Testament of Hope*, p. 282.

26. Ibid.

27. Malcolm X, "The Homecoming Rally of the OAAU, New York, November 29, 1964," in *Malcolm X: By Any Means Necessary*, ed. George Breitman (New York: Pathfinder Press, 1980), p. 140.

28. See King's sermon "Mastering Our Fears," Ebenezer Baptist Church, Atlanta, Georgia, September 10, 1967, p. 6; found at the King Center.

29. Malcolm X, "Remarks at Militant Labor Forum Symposium on 'Blood Brothers,'" in *Two Speeches by Malcolm X*, p. 17; "The Harlem 'Hate-Gang' Scare," in *Malcolm X Speaks*, pp. 68-69.

30. Malcolm X, "Interview with Malcolm X," in *Malcolm X Talks to Young People* (New York: Pathfinder Press, 1982), p. 21.

31. King, *Where Do We Go From Here?*, p. 17.

32. Martin Luther King, Jr., "A Proper Sense of Priorities," speech to Clergy and Laity Concerned about Vietnam, New York Ave. Church, Washington, D.C., 6 February 1968, p. 4; found at the King Center.

33. Martin Luther King, Jr., quoted in Garrow, p. 524.

34. Martin Luther King, Jr.,"We Still Believe in Black and White Together," in *Black Protest Thought in the Twentieth Century*, ed. August Meier, Elliott Rudwick, and Francis L. Broderick (Indianapolis, Indiana: Bobbs-Merrill Educational Publishing, 1980), pp. 586-90. Also see Garrow, p. 586.

Also review King's "Need to Go to Washington" press conference speech, p. 5, January 16, 1967, Ebenezer Baptist Church, Atlanta, Georgia, where he says: "We aren't going to be run out of Washington. We plan to stay in Washington . . . if it takes months and months to do the job that we are going there to do"; located at the King Center.

35. Martin Luther King, Jr., speech at a rally in Birmingham, Alabama, following

a press conference in that same city, 11 November 1967, p. 3; found at the King Center.

36. King, "August 1967 Speech," p. 162.

37. Martin Luther King, Jr., *The Trumpet of Conscience* (New York: Harper & Row, 1967), pp. 59-60.

38. King, "The August 1967 Speech," pp. 162, 163.

39. King, *The Trumpet of Conscience*, p. 24. King reiterates this point in his "A Proper Sense of Priorities" speech, to Clergy and Laity Concerned about Vietnam, p. 4. New York Ave. Church, Washington, D.C., February 2, 1968; found at the King Center.

40. *The Trumpet of Conscience*, p. 62.

41. Martin Luther King, Jr., "Beyond Vietnam" (New York: Clergy and Laity Concerned, 1982), p. 9.

42. King, *The Trumpet of Conscience*, p. 62.

43. Ibid., pp. 49-50.

44. Malcolm X, "At the Audubon," in *Malcolm X Speaks*, p. 125.

45. Malcolm X, *The Autobiography of Malcolm X*, p. 347.

46. Malcolm X, "The Homecoming Rally of the OAAU," p. 136.

47. Malcolm X, *The Autobiography of Malcolm X*, p. 346.

48. Alice Walker, "In Search of Our Mothers' Gardens," in *Black Theology: A Documentary History, 1966-1979*, ed. Gayraud S. Wilmore and James H. Cone (Maryknoll, New York: Orbis Books, 1979), pp. 434-42.

49. Malcolm X, "Our People Identify with Africa: Interview with Bernice Bass, December 27, 1964," in *Malcolm X: The Last Speeches*, p. 98. Also see *By Any Means Necessary*, p. 179.

50. King, "August 1967 Speech," p. 162.

51. Ibid., p. 161.

52. King, *The Trumpet of Conscience*, pp. 59-60.

53. King, in Garrow, p. 364.

54. Ibid., p. 537.

55. Malcolm X, "The Harlem 'Hate-Gang' Scare," p. 69; also see "Remarks at Militant Labor Forum Symposium on 'Blood Brothers,' " p. 17.

56. King, "The Harlem 'Hate-Gang' Scare," p. 65; and "Remarks at Militant Labor Forum Symposium on 'Blood Brothers,' " p. 15.

57. King, "At the Audubon," p. 121.

58. King, in Garrow, p. 608.

59. King, in Garrow, p. 581.

60. King, "Conversation with Martin Luther King," *Conservative Judaism* 22 (Spring 1968): 8, 9.

61. King, *Where Do We Go From Here?*, p. 62.

62. Malcolm X, "Speech on 'Black Revolution,' New York, April 8, 1964," in *Two Speeches by Malcolm X*, p. 9.

63. Martin Luther King, Jr., "The Current Crisis in Race Relations," in Washington, p. 88.

64. King, in Garrow, p. 555.

65. Martin Luther King, Jr., "Speech at Staff Retreat Penn Center, Frogmore, South Carolina, May 23-31, 1967," p. 7 (author's copy).

66. Ibid., p. 30.

67. Malcolm X, *The Autobiography of Malcolm X*, p. 341.

68. "The Harvard Law School Forum of December 16, 1964," in *The Speeches of Malcolm X at Harvard*, p. 164.

69. "Speech at Militant Labor Forum, Jan. 7, 1965, on 'Prospects for Freedom in 1965,' " in *Two Speeches by Malcolm X*, p. 22.

CONCLUSION

1. The most recent edition of Cone's book is published by Harper & Row, San Francisco, 1989. The NCNC statement is found in *Black Theology: A Documentary History, 1966-1979*, ed. Gayraud S. Wilmore and James H. Cone (Maryknoll, New York: Orbis Books, 1979), pp. 23-30.

2. The published works of the following usually signify the first generation: James H. Cone, Gayraud S. Wilmore, Vincent Harding, J. Deotis Roberts, Charles H. Long, C. Eric Lincoln, Major J. Jones, William R. Jones, Preston Williams, Charles Shelby Rooks, Cecil Cone, Joseph Washington, Carlton L. Lee, Albert Cleage, Charles Copher, and Henry Mitchell. For the historical roles of first generation participants, their similarities and differences, see James H. Cone, *For My People: Black Theology and the Black Church* (Maryknoll, New York: Orbis Books, 1984).

3. For critical interpretations of theological debates among the first generation of African American theologians, see James H. Cone's "Epilogue: An Interpretation of the Debate among Black Theologians," in Wilmore and Cone, pp. 609-23; also see Dwight N. Hopkins, *Black Theology USA and South Africa: Politics, Culture, and Liberation* (Maryknoll, New York: Orbis Books, 1989).

4. Examples of womanist writings are Katie G. Cannon, *Black Womanist Ethics* (Atlanta: Scholars Press, 1988); Renita J. Weems, *Just a Sister Away: A Womanist Vision of Women's Relationships in the Bible* (San Diego, California: LuraMedia, 1988) and *Marriage, Sex and Violence* (Minneapolis: Fortress Press, 1992); and Jacquelyn Grant, *White Women's Christ and Black Women's Jesus* (Atlanta: Scholars Press, 1989).

Other representative, but not exhaustive, womanist voices include Kelly Brown, Jualynne Dodson, Cheryl Townsend Gilkes, Cheryl Sanders, Shawn Copeland, and Delores Williams.

As more womanists complete their Ph.D. degrees, we may note a trend toward broadly affecting mass culture and media regarding African American women's theological issues. See Karen Baker-Fletcher, "Tyson's Defenders and the Church of Silence," in *The New York Times*, Op-Ed, Sunday, 29 March 1992, p. 17.

5. Some of their unities and distinctions over what constitutes "womanist" can be found in "Roundtable Discussion: Christian Ethics and Theology in Womanist Perspectives," *Journal of Feminist Studies in Religion* (Fall 1989). In addition to this journal, womanist viewpoints are presented in the *Journal of Religious Thought*.

6. This journal is published by Duke University Press in Durham, North Carolina. Also see Jon Michael Spencer, *Protest and Praise: Sacred Music of Black Religion* (Minneapolis: Fortress Press, 1990).

7. Dwight N. Hopkins and George Cummings, ed., *Cut Loose Your Stammering Tongue: Black Theology in the Slave Narratives* (Maryknoll, New York: Orbis Books, 1991).

8. Samplings of Afro-centric writings include: in the biblical field, Cain Hope Felder, *Troubling Biblical Waters: Race, Class, and Family* (Maryknoll, New York:

Orbis Books, 1989); in theology, Robert Hood, *Must God Remain Greek? Afro Cultures and God-Talk* (Minneapolis, Fortress Press, 1990), and Josiah Young, *Pan-African Theology: Providence and the Legacies of the Ancestors* (Trenton, New Jersey: Africa World Press, 1992); and in ethics, Theodore Walker, *Empower the People: Social Ethics for the African-American Church* (Maryknoll, New York: Orbis Books, 1991).

9. See Noel Erskine, *Decolonizing Theology: A Caribbean Perspective* (1981); Josiah Young, *Black and African Theologies: Siblings or Distant Cousins?* (1986); Dwight N. Hopkins, *Black Theology USA and South Africa: Politics, Culture, and Liberation* (1989); and Kortright Davis, *Emancipation Still Comin': Explorations in Caribbean Emancipatory Theology* (1990). All are published by Orbis Books. Also see Simon S. Maimela and Dwight N. Hopkins, eds., *We Are One Voice: Essays in Black Theology in South Africa and the USA* (Johannesburg, South Africa: Skotaville Press, 1989).

10. James H. Cone, *Martin and Malcolm and America: A Dream or a Nightmare?* (Maryknoll, New York: Orbis Books, 1991).

11. C. Eric Lincoln and Lawrence H. Mamiya, *The Black Church in the African American Experience* (Durham: Duke University Press, 1990).

Index

ABB, 132
Africa, 72, 78-80, 97-98, 148, 178, 190, 194, 196-97
Africanisms, religious, 15
Afro-American Unity, 204
"Agape," 175
AME Church, 138
Ancestors, 17-18, 124
Baker, Ella, 192
Baptism, 31, 189
Bates, Daisy, 192
Bates, John, 23
Beloved, 52, 54-56, 59, 64, 67-69, 71, 80
Bentley, Rev., 34-35
Bibb, Henry, 23, 37, 38, 44
Bible, 6
Black Panther Party, 132
Black Power Movement, 177
Blues, 117-18; and Christianity, 119-20
Bluest Eye, 51, 53, 55-56, 58, 60, 70, 75, 76
Bontemps, Arna, 97
Booker, Mollie, 40
Bradley, James L., 25, 36
Brer Rabbit, 100-105
Brer Tiger, 101-2
Briggs, Charles A., 140
Broaddus, Susan, 40
Brown, John, 15
Brown, Julia, 25
"Burden be manhood," 158
Cannon, Katie G., 49-50
Capitalism, 182-83, 186, 196, 203
Carmichael, Stokely, 132, 219n1
Carruthers, Richard, 19
Caste discrimination, 141
Chilton, Samuel Walter, 20
Christianity, 143, 201-5; and the

future, 209-10; white man's religion, 121-22, 156
Church, black, 48, 179-82; white, 142-43, 161
Church and future society, 201-5
Civil Rights Movement, 175-77, 183, 192-93
Civil War, 24, 26, 46, 48
Clark, Septima, 192
Communalism, 47, 197
Communist Party, 135
Community, 17
Compromise, Hayes-Tilden, 2
Cone, James H., 210-12
Congregational emphasis on practicality, 136
Conjurer, 73-76
Connectedness: to broader community, 67-69; to immediate community, 63-66; to nation, 70-72; to self, 60-63
Conservatism, 140
Consolation, 118
Conversion, 32, 209
Cooper, Anna Julia, 139
Craft, William, 131
Creation, 167
Criticism, biblical and literary, 216-17
Da-duh, 123-24
Dancing, 140
"Daybreak in Alabama," 98
Dee, Ruby, 96, 124
Democracy, 132-33, 134-36, 148, 153, 156, 162, 164, 167, 176, 187, 193; economic and electoral, 136
Devil, 87-88
Distribution of goods, 133
Dixon, Emily, 19
Dodson, Owen, 92
Dogma, 153